D1319954

ROYAL INSTITUTE OF PHILOSOPHY LECTURES

VOLUME NINE · 1974–1975

IMPRESSIONS OF EMPIRICISM

ROYAL INSTITUTE OF PHILOSOPHY LECTURES
VOLUME NINE · 1974–1975

IMPRESSIONS
OF
EMPIRICISM

Edited by
GODFREY VESEY

ST. MARTIN'S PRESS NEW YORK

146
I34

Copyright © 1976 Royal Institute of Philosophy

All rights reserved. For information, write:
St. Martin's Press, Inc., 175 Fifth Avenue, New York, N.Y. 10010
Printed in Great Britain
Library of Congress Catalog Card Number: 75-29964
First published in the United States of America in 1976

CONTENTS

HUNT LIBRARY
CARNEGIE-MELLON UNIVERSITY
PITTSBURGH, PENNSYLVANIA 15213

FEB 22 '78

FOREWORD

Two senses of 'empiricism' may be distinguished. The term may be used to refer to a *method*: the empirical method of basing theorising on, and testing it by, observation and experiment. Alternatively it may be used to refer to a philosophical *theory*, held in one form or another by, amongst others, John Locke, David Hume, the two Mills, and, more recently, Russell and Ayer. The theory is about knowledge and meaning. It has roots in dualistic theories of perception and communication, and fruits in epistemological problems about how we can possibly know things it does not ordinarily occur to us to question, such as that tables and chairs continue to exist when unperceived, and that other people have minds. The papers in this collection are about empiricism in both senses, and about how they are related. Some of them touch on that most exciting question (exciting to an empiricist *manqué*, that is): whether empiricism, as a theory, is itself empirical. Others, towards the end of the volume, challenge a widely accepted view: the view that science, whatever else it should be, should at least be empirical. The final contribution is an original defence of empiricism — the method, not the theory — in ethics.

To provide a point of reference for my comments on some of the individual lectures I shall say a little about the philosophical theory, in the form it takes in Locke's *Essay*.

Empiricism as a theory has, as I said, roots in dualist theories of perception and communication. The theory of perception is one according to which a person's mind, as well as his body, is acted on when he perceives something. And just as there is something, the 'stimulation' of the sense-organ and nervous system, which is the result of his *body* being acted on, so there is something else, sometimes called a 'sense-impression' or 'sensation', which is the result of his *mind* being acted on.[1] It is on these sense-impressions — and on the inner awareness of the operations of the mind (remembering, discerning, reasoning, etc.), the ideas of which could not be had from sense-perception — that all our knowledge is founded.

The theory of communication is that to be found in Hobbes' *Leviathan* and in numerous other writings up to the present day (including George Steiner's *After Babel*), the theory that language is needed only because one person cannot get at another person's thoughts directly. I translate my thoughts into sentences, which you hear or see, and then translate back into thoughts.

To this 'translation' theory of communication has to be added the notion that thinking is a matter of being employed about things called 'ideas': ideas are the objects of the understanding in thinking. In the everyday use of the term 'idea' this may seem a fairly innocuous thing to say. It may seem to be not more than a rather pompous way of saying what is implicit in our use of expressions like 'I've got a good idea: let's go and call on Aunt May', 'He had an idea she was hiding something', and 'The same idea had obviously occurred to both of them'. But Locke's use of the term 'idea' is not the everyday one. It is a philosophically highly-charged one. For with the one word 'idea' he identifies the things we are said to be employed about when we think, with the things supposedly passively received by the mind in perception, otherwise called 'sense-impressions'. According to Locke, sense-impressions are ideas are the things we are employed about in thinking. And translating our thoughts (Locke: 'mental propositions') into sentences ('verbal propositions') is a matter of 'signifying' ideas with words.

There has to be more to it than this, of course. Otherwise a sentence would be at best a string of proper names.[2] There must be general words, and hence, if words have meaning by standing for ideas, general ideas. But how can there be general ideas if ideas are impressions on, or in, the mind? Surely impressions come in the category of particulars, not universals.

To meet the difficulty Locke invokes the doctrine — or, rather, doctrines — of abstraction. There are two doctrines, one of which is invoked for words for sensible qualities, like 'white', the other for words like 'man'. The doctrine of abstraction for words like 'white' is as follows. In external objects such qualities as colour and shape are 'united and blended', but the ideas they produce in the mind enter by the senses

---

1   The term 'sense-impression' — or 'impression', for short — has its origin in the assimilation of the passivity of the mind in perception to that of wax in receiving an impression from a seal. See Descartes, *Rules for the Direction of the Mind*, Rule 12.

2   I say 'at best' because of the problem, with sense-impressions, of satisfying the conditions for the use of a proper name, e.g. that the thing named should be re-identifiable.

'simple and unmixed'. For example, if I am looking at something white and round, like a snowball, the idea of white and the idea of round enter the mind separately. There are two separate ideas, one of white and the other of round. And I can consider them as such. This act of considering an idea as separate from other concomitant ideas is called 'abstraction'. In addition to being able to abstract ideas (i.e. consider them in their simple and unmixed state), I can notice that other ideas conform to, or agree with, the idea so abstracted (now called an 'abstract idea'). In virtue of this ability to notice agreement of ideas I can lay up the abstract idea in my memory to serve as a pattern or standard for all ideas of that sort. I can use it, in my thoughts, as a representative of all such ideas. So used, it may be called a 'general idea', though it is still a particular; its generality consists in the use to which it is put. The general word 'white' signifies the general idea of white. The use of the word by someone else excites, by a process of association of the word with the idea, the appropriate idea in my mind.

The doctrine of abstraction for words like 'man' is different. It has to be, since 'man' is not a word for a sensible quality, and it would be too implausible to hold that the idea of man enters the mind simple and unmixed. 'Abstraction' now comes to mean something more than a mere act of considering an idea that is already separate from other ideas. It becomes the act of separating out, from a number of complex ideas, what they 'have in common'. Abstract ideas, in this sense, are 'the workmanship of the understanding'. I have a number of complex ideas, of Peter and James, Mary and Jane, observe what they have in common, and accordingly frame an abstract idea in which what is peculiar to each is left out and what is common to them all is retained.

Locke recognised some of the difficulties in his account. He wrote, for instance, of 'the pains and skill required to form the general idea of a triangle' which 'must be neither oblique nor rectangle, neither equilateral, equicrural, nor scalenon; but all and none of these at once'. He even said that such an idea is, in effect, 'something imperfect, that cannot exist; an idea wherein some parts of several different and inconsistent ideas are put together'. I suppose he meant that it could exist *only* as an idea, not as a real thing; but even as an idea its existence may be questioned. Or it might be better to say that what may be questioned is that Locke can mean by the term 'idea' in talk of 'the general idea of a triangle' what he means by it when he identifies an idea with a sense-impression. Without continuity of meaning here, the pass of empiricism is sold. As Hume was to put it, an idea must be shown to be derived from an impression if it is not to be dismissed as fictitious.

A second problem Locke recognised was that arising from the 'privacy' of sense-impressions. If ideas are impressions how can two people be said to have the same idea? And so, how can two people mean the same by what they say? His solution was that in the case of colour words it would not matter if they did not. If the idea that a violet produced in one man's mind were the same as a marigold produced in another man's, and *vice versa*, it would not affect the ability of either of the men to distinguish between violets and marigolds. But he did not extend this argument to cover more complex qualities; and he remarked, more than once, that if a word did not excite in the hearer the same idea as it stood for in the speaker the hearer would not have understood the speaker, and the chief end of language in communication would not have been served.

A third problem concerns perception. When I see something I see it as having certain qualities or features, which it could have in common with other things. I see it as having a certain colour, a certain shape, and so on. That is, I see it as something to which *some* description, vague or precise, is applicable on the basis of my perception of it. In other, more philosophical, words, perception is of the universal in the particular; it is an epistemic concept. On Locke's account, however, perception is of the particular alone, for that is the declared status of sense-impressions. So there is a problem, for Locke, of explaining away what, on his account, must be an illusion, 'the illusion of the universal in perception'. I do not think that Locke ever recognised this problem. The nearest he came to recognising it was in recognising another problem about perception. If we set before our eyes a round globe we seem to *see* it as convex (that is, as having a curvature that bulges towards us). But, Locke says, 'it is certain that the idea thereby imprinted in our minds is of a flat circle'.[1] Strictly, the convexity is not something we *see*, it is something we *think*. But we perform the act of judgement 'so constantly and so quick, that we take that for the perception of our sensation which is an idea formed by our judgement'.[2] Had Locke recognised the problem of explaining 'the illusion of the universal in perception' then I suppose he would have tried to solve it on similar lines.

Part of Locke's theory is about the source of our ideas of what he calls the 'operations' of minds, such as remembering. The source, he says, is one which 'every man has wholly in himself: and though it be not sense, as having nothing to do with external objects, yet it is very like it, and might properly enough be called internal sense'.[3] In other words, I know what remembering is by introspecting an operation of remembering in which I am engaged. Norman Malcolm, Professor of Philosophy at Cornell University, is concerned, in his contribution to this volume, with the controversy between those who hold that memory is a direct awareness of

---

[1] *Essay*, bk II, ch. 9, section 8.
[2] Ibid., section 9.
[3] *Essay*, bk II, ch. 1, section 4.

the past and those who say that we remember by means of a representation of what is remembered, a 'memory-image'. He thinks that what generates the controversy is a mistaken assumption, the assumption that in genuine remembering there is an act, experience or event of remembering. If there is such an act it must have a content. And so the question arises: is the content the thing remembered (in which case what is past must exist now, since I am remembering it now, and so it cannot be past) or is it something which merely represents the thing remembered (in which case there is the problem of saying what it is that makes the act one of remembering)?

We may feel inclined to ask Malcolm: But if remembering is *not* an introspectible act, what is it? Do you mean that to say someone remembers something is to say something not about his *inner* state but about his *outer* state, his behaviour (along with his dispositions to behave in certain ways)? But he holds that the mistake is deeper than one of mistaking the outer for the inner. It is the mistake of asking, in the first place, in what remembering consists. 'People remember things; but nothing that occurs, either inner or outer, *is* the remembering'. I shall not attempt to summarise what he says in explanation of this remark. Let it suffice to say that his inspiration, at least in part, is Wittgenstein's treatment of a similar question about meaning (see page 21).

Malcolm attacks the Lockean notion of mental operations, of which we are aware by an internal sense. In the paper by P. M. S. Hacker, Fellow of St John's College, Oxford, it is the view that colour words have meaning by standing for 'subjective modifications of a perceiver's mind' that is under attack. If we hold this view then such possibilities may occur to us as that what one person means by the colour word 'red' may be what another person means by the colour word 'green'. We may then try, and fail, to think of reasons for saying that what is possible is not actual. Hacker is concerned to show, by means of 'a surview of our use of colour predicates, a description of our linguistic practices which will display what is involved in explaining the meaning or sense of colour predicates, and what is requisite for possession of colour concepts', that what, if we follow Locke, we might suppose to be possible is not in fact possible. To be possible something must be intelligible, and the intelligibility of 'my assertion that something looks red to me . . . presupposes cognizance of the criteria for asserting that something looks red to another'. The difficulty is that of explaining what 'cognizance of the criteria for asserting that something looks red to another' means, if the explanation is not to lead us into either scepticism or behaviourism.

Malcolm and Hacker find inspiration in the later writings of Wittgenstein for their attacks on the Lockean notion that the words 'remember' and 'red' have meaning for us by standing, respectively, for an introspected mental act and a sense-impression. Oswald Hanfling, Lecturer in Philosophy at the Open University, on the other hand, finds a point of resemblance between Wittgenstein and Locke's empiricist successor, David Hume. The resemblance is in the references, to be found in both philosophers, to human nature. Instead of trying – and, of course, failing – to find a rational justification for what we do, we should be content, as philosophers, to recognise that we do things naturally, instinctively. We should be content to *describe*, and not search for an explanation, a justification, an answer to scepticism. But side by side with this, in Hume, is his commitment to the empiricist programme, 'the matching of each word with some item of experience, until the whole stock of our concepts would be accounted for'. Hence the big difference between the two philosophers. It can be described as a difference in what they regard as 'given':

> For Hume, what is given . . . is always some simple thing that is sensed or felt; something like what he called 'impressions of the senses or memory', or some 'internal impression' such as Hume conceived the will to be.
> Wittgenstein wrote: 'What has to be accepted, the given, is – so one could say – *forms of life.*' This sentence reflects his rejection of the whole machinery of sense-data, and the atomism that went with it.

Hanfling draws a parallel between Hume and Wittgenstein on the postulation of occult qualities, processes and substances. He says that one of Wittgenstein's main objectives 'is to cure us of the urge to suppose that whenever something mental is predicated of a person, there must be something *in* his mind to make that predication true'. Malcolm, in what he says about remembering, clearly shares this objective. The position of D. M. Taylor, Senior Lecturer in Philosophy at the University of Kent at Canterbury, is less clear to me. He invites us to acknowledge that mental states are in some sense private, and that statements about one's own mental states are authoritative, and he proposes to enquire as to the origin, or source, of these characteristics. 'Is it that mental states and events are peculiar, even spooky, or is there a more mundane explanation?'

Malcolm describes (but does not explain) the phenomenon which interests Taylor, in a paper entitled 'Behaviourism as a Philosophy of Psychology'.[1] He writes:

> The testimony that people give us about their intentions, plans, hopes, worries, thoughts, and feelings is by far the most important source of information we have about them. This self-testimony has, one could say, an *autonomous* status. To a great extent we cannot check it

---

[1] In T. W. Wann (ed.), *Behaviourism and Phenomenology* (Chicago, 1964).

against anything else, and yet to a great extent we credit it. I believe we have no reason to think it is even a theoretical possibility that this self-testimony could be supplanted by inferences from external and/or internal physical variables . . . Within the whole body of language the category of first-person psychological sentences has crucial importance. Man's puzzling status as a subject and a person is bound up with these first-person utterances, having the two striking characteristics I have tried to point out: First, that for the most part, they are not made on the basis of any observation; second, that they are 'autonomous' in the sense that, for the most part, they cannot be 'tested' by checking them against physical events and circumstances, other than the subject's own testimony. If we want to know what a man wants, what he is thinking about, whether he is annoyed or pleased, or what he has decided, the man himself is our best source of information. We ask *him* and he tells us. He has a privileged status with respect to information about himself. . . . I have argued that behaviourism fails to perceive self-testimony in a true light. It mistakenly assumes that when a man tells you what he wants, intends, or hopes, what he says is based on observation, and, therefore, he is speaking about himself as if he were an *object of observation*. Behaviourism also assumes that these first-person utterances, since they are observational in nature, could theoretically be replaced by the observations of another person, although this might require 'technological advances'. Behaviourism, in other words, fails to perceive that self-testimony is largely autonomous, not replaceable even in principle by observations of functional relations between physical variables. Perhaps the best way to sum up behaviourism's shortcomings as a philosophy of psychology is to say that it regards man as solely an object.[1]

In some respects Taylor's position is very similar to Malcolm's anti-behaviourist one. Like Malcolm, he is opposed to 'having the question what one thinks or wants answered for one, by others'. He says that 'humiliation results in such cases from the sense of being treated as a thing to be talked about and pronounced upon but not worthy of talking, or pronouncement', and he talks of a person being 'reduced to the status of an object'. Where Malcolm says that a person's first-person utterances are 'autonomous' Taylor says that 'there can be no criteria, or sufficient condition, of thoughts or wants, independent of what a man says'.

In line with this one might take Taylor's answer to his question whether mental states are 'peculiar, even spooky' to be as follows. Some philosophers embrace the view that thinking, wanting, and so on, are things we know about by introspection because they think the only

---

[1] Ibid, pp. 153–4.

alternative is behaviourism, which involves the denial that a person's statements about his own mental states are authoritative. But there is a third alternative, which is neither introspectionist nor behaviourist, and which allows a person's statements about his own mental states to be authoritative.

The reason why I say I am unclear as to Taylor's position is that this third alternative is a *non*-empirical account of mind — self-testimony is not based on observation, either inner or outer — and yet Taylor claims to be giving an empirical account of mind.

I mentioned, above, the problem, for someone who holds that perception is the passive reception of sense-impressions, of explaining how it is that perception seems to be not of the particular alone, but of the universal in the particular. Locke, I suggested, did not recognise this problem. But his treatment of another problem — that of our seeming to see a globe as convex — suggests that, had he recognised the more fundamental problem, he might have tried to solve it in terms of our confusing (or 'fusing') what we think with what we see. Somehow we impose our thoughts, our concepts, on what is given to us to perceive, so that instead of *sensing* an 'unconceptualised' sense-impression, and *thinking* 'something is yellow', we seem to *see* something *as* yellow. But what, precisely, is this act of 'conceptualisation' whereby sense-impressions are converted into meaningful perceptions? Someone wanting to understand empiricism as a theory of perception will look to the empiricist for a theory of 'conceptualisation' as well, of course, as for reasons to suppose that there are such things as sense-impressions to be conceptualised. Will he look in vain?

D. J. O'Connor, Professor of Philosophy at the University of Exeter, provides a recognisably empiricist account of perception, though he uses the term 'sense-datum' in place of 'sense-impression' or 'idea'. (I think his only use of the term 'idea' is in his rather Lockean remark that 'language is pre-eminently a device for the storage and retrieval of structures of ideas'.) Sense-data, he says, are parts of sensory fields, which are the 'basic unconceptualised raw material' of our perception of the world. He says that any expression in language of a visual experience, even 'I see yellow', is 'already conceptually tainted'. What account does he give of conceptualisation? And what reason does he give to suppose that there are such things as sense-data?

To the first question the answer is that he gives an account which is exclusively metaphorical. It is in terms of the metaphors of weaving, moulding, clothing, and endowing. He writes of the complex conceptual network 'woven' into our sensory fields, of sensory fields being 'moulded' by concepts, of choosing the right set of concepts to 'clothe' the raw data (and of raw sensory fields being clothed with a variety of conceptual 'apparel'), and of concepts 'endowing' sense-data with meanings.

To the second question the answer is that he defines 'sense-data' as 'parts of sensory fields', and gives a reason for holding that sensory fields are 'ontologically distinct' from material objects, namely that their features do not match those of material objects. For example, because of limitations in the sensitivity of our sense-organs we may see two things as being the same shade of yellow which are in fact reflecting light of slightly different wavelengths to our eyes. Or, because of drunkenness or failing eye-sight a pencil may appear blurred which in fact is not blurred. (In the sense of 'an indistinct blurred appearance' a blur is essentially in the realm of appearance, not in that of reality.) As an argument for the existence of sense-data defined as parts of sensory fields this seems to me unassailable. But I do not see how it can be an argument for sense-data defined as the 'unconceptualised raw material' of perception. I do not see how sense-data can have features which can be contrasted with those of material objects unless they have features, i.e. are *not* 'unconceptualised'.

I take the primary meaning of 'interpret' to be that in which a sentence in one language is translated, by someone who understands it, so as to provide a sentence, with the same meaning, in another language. There are bi-lingual people engaged in this activity, called 'interpreters'. A readily intelligible secondary meaning of 'interpret' is that in which there is only one language involved, and we talk of an ambiguous sentence (e.g. 'He was drawing on the bank') being given two different interpretations. Interpretation in this secondary meaning is different from interpretation in the primary meaning in that one does not first understand the ambiguous sentence (with a 'neutral' meaning, so to speak) and then think of two alternative meanings for it. Interpreting in this secondary meaning is something we do in the sense in which, say, winning or losing a race is something we do, not in the sense in which running is something we do. It is not an activity in which we can be engaged, as is interpreting in the primary meaning. We talk of 'interpreting' not only ambiguous sentences but also ambiguous drawings. We can interpret a duck-rabbit figure as a drawing of a duck or as a drawing of a rabbit. Suppose it is asked: 'We interpret it differently. Do we also *see* it differently?' This is a question Wittgenstein asks, and which is discussed by P. B. Lewis, Lecturer in Philosophy at the University of Edinburgh. He says that one way of taking this question is as inviting the Lockean reply that what is really seen is a visual impression, and that anything else is the result of an act of judgement, and so, strictly speaking, not something that is seen. This way of taking it accords with thinking of interpreting as an activity (if *treating* a duck-rabbit figure as a drawing of a duck can properly be called an 'activity'), but if the answer to 'Do we also *see* it differently?' were to be 'Yes' then the Lockean reply would entail that there must be a visual experience which distinguishes the duck-appearance of the figure from the rabbit-appearance and which can be described *directly*, that is, in purely visual terms and not by reference to ducks and rabbits.

I remarked that the philosophical theory of empiricism has fruits in epistemological problems about how we can possibly know things it does not ordinarily occur to us to question, such as that tables and chairs continue to exist when unperceived. One way of dealing with this particular problem is to say that statements about unperceived objects are to be analysed as hypotheticals. To say that the table I write on exists when I am out of my study is to say that *if* I was in my study I might perceive it. The germs of this 'phenomenalist' solution of the problem are to be found in Berkeley; its full fruition, in J. S. Mill. Alan Hobbs, Lecturer in Philosophy at the University of East Anglia, writes, not about phenomenalism, but about what he calls 'new phenomenalism'. He is at pains to dissociate himself from the presuppositions of old-style phenomenalism:

Locke, Berkeley, and Hume, to different degrees and with varying emphasis, all contend that meaningful utterances and empirical beliefs must be traced back to simple sensory impressions. These sensory impressions are held to provide an exit from word-word expositions of meaning, and an escape from the regress of belief-belief justifications. At the ground-level of meaning and of belief, the subject simply confronts his sensory impressions and thereby acquires both basic meanings and basic beliefs. Crucial to these theories is the notion of a sense-impression as an unconceptualized, non-epistemic particular. Without such a notion, the distinctive character of these analyses of meaning and of basic belief would collapse. The hybrid of phenomenalism which this paper sets out ignores these traditional doctrines. The connections which it claims to trace are between one type of belief-reporting statement and another; not, as with traditional Empiricism, between a type of belief-reporting statement and some non-epistemic state.

The belief-reporting statements which are regarded as basic in new phenomenalism are, roughly, disjunctions of perception and hallucination claims. Accordingly, Hobbs says, 'the resultant explanation can be expected to clarify the status of perceptual knowledge, but it cannot constitute what has been traditionally called "an analysis of perception".'

Hobbs says that new phenomenalism is a 'rag-bag construction from a number of contemporary philosophers'. He quotes from P. F. Strawson and Jonathan Bennett. In the discussion which followed his lecture I asked him whether he regarded me as a new phenomenalist. He said that he did. Re-reading my now ancient paper 'Unthinking Assumptions and their

Justification'[1] I think there is some justification for this. The point at which I part company with Hobbs — and with present-day empiricists like Ayer — is in the use of the word 'hypothesis'. Hobbs says that 'the new phenomenalist must admit that the hypothesis of a-world-perceived *is* an hypothesis, . . .' If a new phenomenalist *must* admit this, then I am not a new phenomenalist. In my *Mind* paper I was explicitly attacking use of the word 'assume', in talk of our unthinkingly assuming that there are things which exist unperceived. But my remarks would apply equally to 'hypothesize', and I did, in fact, quote a passage from McTaggart in which the word 'hypothesis' occurs, to illustrate the kind of philosophising I was criticising.

Hanfling, in a passage contrasting Wittgenstein with Hume, says that Wittgenstein rejects 'the whole machinery of sense-data'. The implication is that Hume's 'impressions' are sense-data. If sense-data are what O'Connor calls 'the unconceptualised raw material' of perception, then R. J. Butler, Professor of Philosophy at the University of Kent at Canterbury, would disagree with this interpretation of Hume. He says that ideas and their antecedent impressions resemble one another in 'conceptual content', and something which is unconceptualised can hardly have conceptual content. Another way of saying that for Hume impressions have conceptual content is, it would seem, saying that Hume thought of them 'propositionally'. Butler cites such reasons for thinking this as that Hume speaks of them as thoughts, and as possible objects of belief.

Locke wrote: 'Our observation, employed either about external sensible objects, or about the internal operations of our minds, perceived and reflected on by ourselves, is that which supplies our understandings with all the materials of thinking'.[2] It does not follow that all our ideas are real, that is, conform with the real being and existence of things. We can misuse 'the materials of thinking' to create complex ideas which are 'fantastical or chimerical', ideas which lack that correspondence with the constitution of real beings which our simple ideas have.[3] Suppose we then make up sentences containing words which signify these ideas. What are we to say about such sentences? We might say that no truth can correspond to them, or that they are not 'factually' or 'cognitively' meaningful. Asked to formulate a principle about this, we might say that for a sentence to have factual or cognitive meaning it must express a statement that can, at least in theory, be confirmed or disconfirmed by making observations. We would then be in the vicinity of the most distinctive doctrine, the 'Verifiability Principle', of the twentieth-century heirs of British empiricism, the logical positivists.

1 *Mind*, LXIII (1954) pp. 226–33.
2 Locke, *Essay*, Bk I, ch. 1, Section 2.
3 Ibid, Bk II, ch. 30, Section 1–2.

Is there some formulation of the Verifiability Principle which we can accept without accepting the empiricism that lies behind it? Stuart Brown, Senior Lecturer in Philosophy at the Open University, thinks there is, though it is a formulation which makes it no longer a criterion of meaningfulness. But, Brown argues, it had already ceased to be such a criterion in Ayer's 'weak verifiability' formulation. Rather, it had become a criterion for demarcating science from non-science. In Brown's formulation the principle is about the conditions of our having beliefs:

> If there are no considerations which count as tending to determine the truth or falsity of an hypothesis (H) as opposed to that of any apparently competing hypothesis, then no assertion put forward as an independent judgement about H can be an expression of *belief* or doubt as to the truth or falsity of H.

Brown defends this formulation with an analysis of 'expression of belief': someone's assertion 'will not be recognisable as an expression of belief unless further clarification tends in the direction of answering the question "What makes him believe that?" with something which is recognisable as a *reason* for believing it.'

Errol E. Harris, Professor of Philosophy at Northwestern University, sees the main tenets of philosophical empiricism as being (i) that the original source of all knowledge is passively received sensations, and (ii) that all sensuous impressions, and the ideas derived from them, are particular existences, with no evident connection between any two of them. The consequence of philosophical empiricism for scientific methodology has been that it is either deductive or inductive. This raises the problem as to how science makes discoveries. The relation between observation and theory cannot be what traditional empiricism holds it to be:

> Observation may never be merely random and haphazard if it is to be scientific; but, without a prior hypothesis, random and haphazard is all it could be. Experiment is actually the question that the scientist puts to Nature, and no question arises unless some theory is already being entertained. Further, all observation, even the most naive, is an interpretation, in the light of prior knowledge, of presented 'data' (though I use that word with reservation, because nothing intelligible is ever merely 'given').

Harris is not satisfied with Popper's view that new theories are pure conjectures. Hypotheses, he says, 'are prompted by rational considerations', so 'some kind of logical account of them should be possible'. It will be an account which exhibits the origin of new theories as a step in the successive adjustments of an explanatory system, so as to remove contradictions. The reasoning involved is constructive, rather than in-ductive or deductive, and, he says, 'seems to demand a logic akin to both at once and yet identical with neither'. But, in the end, Harris admits to not knowing what the precise logic of this form of reasoning may be.

L. Jonathan Cohen, Fellow of The Queen's College, Oxford, examines possible ways in which what he calls 'criterial empiricism' may be defended. Criterial empiricism is the thesis that all beliefs about the structure and contents of the natural world are ultimately to be appraised for their truth, soundness or acceptability in terms of the data afforded by perceptual acts of seeing, hearing, smelling, tasting, or touching. Cohen dismisses five possible defences of this thesis. He dismisses the two classical arguments for criterial empiricism, giving reasons for not accepting the premisses of the arguments. The first is that since the elements composing our thoughts are copies of previous perceptions, the truth of a thought must always be apprehended by reference to the perceptual realities it purports to represent. The second is that since phenomenalism is true, every statement about existent entities must be a statement about perceivables and thus exposed to empirical checks. Cohen then proceeds to a lengthy discussion of the verification principle as a defence of criterial empiricism, a discussion which bears interestingly on some of the issues raised by Brown and by Harris. (In particular I see a similarity between what Harris says about the reasoning involved in the origination of theories being 'constructive', and Cohen's remark that 'it is not empiricism that sets permanent limits to science, as the phenomenalist claims, but science that progressively extends the horizons of empiricism'.) He concludes that verificationism can afford no support or defence for criterial empiricism. The two remaining defences Cohen dismisses are based on the apparent success that has attended the orientation of science towards criterial empiricism, and the need for scientists to employ interpersonally acceptable standards of evidence. He ends by advancing a defence of his own, the essence of which is that 'the need to invoke empirical criteria for the validity of our fundamental explanations is forced on us by the desire to make our explanations as unified and comprehensive as possible'.

Someone who is a criterial empiricist because he is a phenomenalist will analyse statements about an object's dispositions in terms of hypothetical statements about its observable properties or manifest behaviour. R. S. Woolhouse, Senior Lecturer in Philosophy at the University of York, contends that whilst hypotheticals are involved in the analysis of many dispositional statements, they are not invoked in the way the empiricist supposes. He argues that the notion of a disposition involves that of a 'tensed necessity', and therefore that empiricism fails in its attempt to bring things 'down to earth'.

A related question is taken up by Guy Robinson, Senior Lecturer in

Philosophy at the University of Southampton. 'Do the modalities of necessity and possibility attach to individuals or only to our classifications of them?' Robinson is interested in this for its bearing on determinism. If there are only *de dicto* modalities, he holds, determinism seems to lose its grip. He brings to bear on the question the writings of philosophers as various as Aristotle, Leibniz, Popper, Quine, David Lewis and Plantinga. Aristotle, with Robinson's help, and Leibniz, with God's, survive to fight another day.

A thoroughgoing empiricist will not be content to limit the application of his empiricism to the subject matter of the natural sciences. He will want to extend it into all areas of human concern. In ethics, empiricism may take a variety of forms. It may, as in utilitarianism, take the form of identifying the right action with that which is conducive to the production of certain states thought to be empirically definable. Or, when utilitarianism is rejected as an ethical theory because it commits the 'naturalistic fallacy', empiricism may take the form of a denial that there are 'non-natural qualities' and the assertion that moral utterances are not descriptive, but 'emotive'.

Stephan Körner, Professor of Philosophy at the University of Bristol and at Yale University, finds reasons for rejecting utilitarian, contractual and emotivist empiricist theories of ethics. (A contractual theory holds that an action is morally good if it conforms to the regulations of a well-regulated system of social institutions.) He advances a theory of his own, which, he claims, enables him (i) to acknowledge the fundamental difference between moral and non-moral attributes, and (ii) to account for it otherwise than 'by identifying moral with non-empirical attributes of a special kind'. The key to his 'new empiricist ethical theory' is the recognition of 'a feature which, though familiar in one's practical experience, has been strangely neglected by moral philosophers, namely the possibility of a person's having practical attitudes towards his practical attitudes'. There are, thus, attitudes at different levels: a person may, for example, have an anti-attitude to his pro-attitude towards smoking (that is, he may wish he didn't like smoking). This would be a case of a first level attitude being 'negatively dominated' by a second level one. A necessary characteristic of moral, as opposed to all other practical attitudes, Körner says, is that the practical attitude of second level is undominated. But for it to be a moral attitude something more is necessary: the second level attitude of a person must be 'directed not merely towards possession of the first level attitude by himself, but towards possession of the first level attitude by every human being and thus *eo ipso* by himself'. Körner claims for this account of the general structure of morality that it exhibits 'an aspect of the systems of practical attitudes which as a matter of empirical fact are discovered by introspection and the observation of others'. Whether he is right about the nature of moral attitudes is, then, for you, the reader, to decide — by the empirical method.

GODFREY VESEY

Honorary Director
Royal Institute of Philosophy

Professor of Philosophy
and
Pro-Vice-Chancellor, Academic Policy
The Open University

1

MEMORY AS DIRECT AWARENESS OF THE PAST

Norman Malcolm

The philosophy of memory has been largely dominated by what could be called 'the representative theory of memory'. In trying to give an account of 'what goes on in one's mind' when one remembers something, or of what 'the mental content of remembering' consists, philosophers have usually insisted that there must be some sort of mental image, picture, or copy of what is remembered. Aristotle said that there must be 'something like a picture or impression';[1] William James thought that there must be in the mind 'an image or copy' of the original event;[2] Russell said that 'Memory demands an image'.[3] In addition to the image or copy a variety of other mental phenomena have been thought to be necessary. In order for a memory image to be distinguished from an expectation image, the former must be accompanied by 'a feeling of pastness'. One has confidence that the image is of something that actually occurred because the image is attended by 'a feeling of familiarity'. And in order that you may be sure that the past event not merely occurred but that *you* witnessed it, your image of the event must be presented to you with a feeling of 'warmth and intimacy'. When all the required phenomena are put together, the mental content of remembering turns out to be, as William James says, 'a very complex representation'.[4]

A few philosophers have resisted the notion that when we remember a past incident or experience there must be in our minds a representation of it. They have wanted to say things of this sort: that in memory we are 'directly acquainted' with a past event; that it is the 'immediate object' of our mind; that we have a 'direct vision' of the past. Thomas Reid, for

---

[1] Aristotle, *De Memoria et Reminiscentia*, 450b.
[2] William James, *Principles of Psychology*, II, 649.
[3] Russell, *The Analysis of Mind*, p. 186.
[4] James, *Principles of Psychology*, I

example, says the following:

> Suppose that once, and only once, I smelled a tuberose in a certain
> room, where it grew in a pot, and gave a very grateful perfume. Next
> day I relate what I saw and smelled. When I attend as carefully as I can
> to what passes in my mind in this case, it appears evident that the very
> thing I saw yesterday, and the fragrance I smelled, are now the
> immediate objects of my mind, when I remember it . . . . Philosophers
> indeed tell me, that the immediate object of my memory and
> imagination in this case, is not the past sensation, but an idea of it, an
> image, phantasm, or species of the odour I smelled: that this idea now
> exists in my mind, or in my sensorium; and the mind, contemplating
> this present idea, finds it a representation of what is past, or of what
> may exist; and accordingly calls it memory, or imagination. This is the
> doctrine of the ideal philosophy . . . . Upon the strictest examination,
> memory appears to me to have things that are past, and not present
> ideas, for its object . . . . I beg leave to think, with the vulgar, that,
> when I remember the smell of the tuberose, that very sensation which I
> had yesterday, and which has now no more any existence, is the
> immediate object of my memory; and when I imagine it present, the
> sensation itself, and not any idea of it, is the object of my imagination.[1]

Now it is, or should be, a truism, that when I remember an odor, it is the
odor itself, and not a representation of it, that I remember. In fact, this
truism is really denied by some philosophers, as we shall see. But in regard
to the purely negative part of Reid's critique, his position is certainly
correct. I have the impression, however, perhaps unjust, that Reid wants to
say this further thing – that the odor I smelled yesterday *now* 'exists in
my mind' or 'in my memory'. If nothing else were meant than that I
remember *that odor*, then well and good. But one wonders whether Reid
was struggling to say something more – namely, that yesterday's odor, or
the sensation of it, is there, in my mind, *now*.

Samuel Alexander says that when I remember some past object, it is
'before my mind, bearing on its face the mark of pastness, of being earlier
than those objects which I call present'. 'The pastness of the object is a
datum of experience, directly apprehended. The object is compresent with
me *as past*'.[2] When Alexander says that the object I perceived in the past is
'before my mind', bearing a character of pastness, again one wonders what
this could mean. Like Reid, Alexander wants to deny that a representation
is substituted for the object. Our consciousness of a past object is 'direct',
he says, 'and is not the alleged artificial process of first having an

[1] Thomas Reid, *An Inquiry Into the Human Mind*, ch. 2, section 3.
[2] S. Alexander, *Space, Time and Deity*, (London, 1920) I, 113.

experience of the present and then referring it by some method to the past or future'.[1] That is certainly right. And although Alexander says that the past object 'is compresent with me', on the other hand he seems to insist that it does *not* exist at the time it is remembered:

> The truth is that remembering and expecting do occur at the present moment; but we are not entitled, therefore, to declare their objects simultaneous with the present. To be apprehended as a memory in the act of remembering simultaneously with an act of present perception is not to be apprehended as simultaneous with the 'present' object. The simple deliverance of experience is that it is apprehended as past.[2]
>
> The remembering is present, but both its object and what we may call its mental material (the past act of mind which experienced it) are past.[3]

The last remark would seem to be unambiguous: the object of memory does not belong to the present remembering. But only a page later one is again thrown into doubt. 'The past object of memory', says Alexander, 'is the appearance to me of the past thing in the present act of remembering'.[4] Does this mean that the past object puts in an appearance? The past act of mind, which experienced that past object, *does* 'persist into the present', says Alexander, although 'it persists as past'.[5]

I cannot obtain a clear grasp of Alexander's view. It is my impression that Alexander was torn between conflicting inclinations. He wanted to say two things, one being that when I remember something I previously experienced, that thing reappears to me, or is 'compresent', or 'persists into the present', although when it is thus present it bears the character of being past. The other thing Alexander wanted to say was that when I remember something from my past, that past thing is in no sense present.

A more recent writer, William Earle, maintains that memory is a 'direct vision' of the past. Earle emphatically repudiates the notion that in remembering there is a copy or representation:

> When I recall a past event, there is, I believe, no sense in which I can be said to form an *image, copy,* or *representation* of anything.[6]
>
> What I remember, then, cannot appear to me, the rememberer, as a copy of the past, but must appear as the past event itself.[7]

1 Ibid., p. 133.
2 Ibid., p. 117.
3 Ibid., p. 126.
4 Ibid., p. 127.
5 Ibid.
6 William Earle, 'Memory', *The Review of Metaphysics*, (Sep 1956) p. 5.
7 Ibid.

Earle holds that we do not remember objects or events *simpliciter*, but only objects or events *as experienced*! A person does not just remember a burning building, but he remembers himself looking at a burning building. I believe this particular claim is wrong, but I will not go into it now. The important point for us here is not the view that the memory of past events is always the memory of experiences. What concerns us is the claim that in remembering a past experience we do not have a representation of it but are 'directly aware' of the past experience. Earle says: 'I am now directly aware not of a copy of the past experience with its object, but of that past experience itself'.[2] He rejects Alexander's conception that the object of memory bears the mark of the past. 'If we turn to the intrinsic character of what it is we are remembering', says Earle, 'it is clear, I think, that it does not and cannot contain within itself the predicate "past" . . . nothing remembered can carry the predicate "past" stamped on its face . . . If we should suppose, for a moment, that the event recalled had as one of its internal properties the fact that it was past, we should find ourselves in the ludicrous position of remembering an event which is past with respect to itself . . .[3] Earle says that "Memory declares itself to be memory by its own intrinsic character of being precisely an immediate awareness of the past . . . an immediate vision upon the past'.[4]

Earle rejects the view that since 'the past does not exist now' it 'has no being whatever' and, therefore, that what 'exists for inspection' is only a present image and not the past experience itself.[5] He allows that 'the past does not exist *now*', but he denies that it does not exist *at all*. He argues as follows: 'As past, it is the subject of true propositions, and precisely what would such propositions be *about* if their subject matter had fallen back into pure nothingness . . . The past must be what true propositions assert it to be; the past therefore has its own distinctive and determinate mode of being'.[6]

If a man shaved off his beard last week then, according to Earle's reasoning, that beard has a 'mode of being' since it is true, for example, that it was a *red* beard. The trouble with this 'argument' is that one doesn't know what it *means* to say that the beard the man formerly wore '*has* a mode of being' although it was destroyed last week. The only clue I have to the understanding of this odd locution lies in Earle's argument: to say that the no longer existing beard '*has* a mode of being', just means that various propositions about it *are* true, which in turn just means that the beard *had* various properties. On this interpretation, Earle's obscure claim

---

1　Ibid., pp. 10–11.
2　Ibid., p. 11.
3　Ibid., p. 12.
4　Ibid., p. 18.
5　Ibid., p. 22.
6　Ibid., p. 23.

turns out to be a redescription, misleadingly in the present tense ('has'), of the undisputed fact that the beard *was* red, shaggy, etc.

To turn to the main point, I find it hard to make much sense out of the attempt to explicate memory as the 'direct awareness' of a past event or object. As philosophers have used the expression 'direct awareness' (also 'immediate acquaintance', 'direct apprehension', and so on) one thing they have tended to mean is that if a person, *B*, is 'directly' aware of something, X, then B's knowledge of the existence of X is not based on any inference or any mediation by or through something other than X.[1] This part of the meaning of 'direct awareness' *does* have an appropriate application to memory. To remember last week's bonfire is *not* to *infer* its past existence.

Another important feature of the customary usage given by philosophers to the expression 'direct awareness', is that B is 'directly' aware of X only if B's assertion that he is aware of X *could not be mistaken*. I do not believe that anyone ought to claim that memory comes up this requirement of 'direct awareness'. It certainly is not a logical or conceptual truth that if anyone asserts that he remembers that p, or that he remembers X, he could not be mistaken.

A third implication, I believe, of 'direct awareness', in its philosophical use, is that if B is 'directly' aware of X, then B and X *coexist*. Philosophers like to speak of 'direct awareness' of pains and mental images; but this direct awareness is thought to apply only to *present* pains and mental images. This implication makes hard sledding for any interpretation of memory as direct awareness. Although a person can be said to remember someone who is standing right before him, it is also true that we speak of remembering last week's bonfire or earth tremor. The bonfire is not now burning nor the earth now trembling. Furlong, for example, remarks that it seems 'absurd to say that we can be acquainted with what is no longer present'.[2] This remark illustrates the philosophical use (but not the ordinary use) of the expressions 'acquaintance', 'direct acquaintance', 'immediate awareness', etc.

Earle declares that memory is 'an immediate awareness of the past'. The implication, in philosophical language, of this would be that if Robinson *now* remembers last week's earth tremor, then the tremor *now* exists. Earle explicitly repudiates this consequence ('the past does not exist now'). Yet he is pushed toward that consequence by the idea of 'immediate awareness'. The result is a meaningless compromise. The earth tremor stopped; 'it does not exist *now*; but still it *has* a mode of being'.

It seems to me that the only intelligible part of the half-articulate notion that memory is a form of immediate acquaintance or direct

---

1   See my essay, 'Direct Perception', section II, in my *Knowledge and Certainty* (Englewood Cliffs, N.J., 1963).

2   E.J. Furlong, *A Study in Memory*, London 1951, p. 40.

awareness, lies in its rejection of the conception, more commonly favored by philosophers, that when we remember some past object, the remembering is done by means of a present image, copy or representation of the object. This negative criticism is sound. The positive aspect of the notion, the striving to say that in remembering the object of memory is 'compresent', or 'persists into the present', or 'has a mode of being' , presents nothing more than vague pictures. I think it just to remark that the intelligibility of the direct awareness doctrine consists exclusively in its saying 'No!' to the representative theory of memory.

Several proponents of the representative theory have thought the doctrine of direct awareness to be of sufficient interest to require a fairly painstaking rebuttal. Broad, for example, regards the remembering of events, places, persons, things, as closely analogous to sense perception — so much so that he calls it 'perceptual memory'. In his treatment of sense perception, Broad, as is well-known, rejects the view, which he calls 'naive realism', that the sensum, or sense-datum, of which we are 'directly aware', is identical with the perceived physical object or any part of it. Similarly, he undertakes an elaborate refutation of 'naive realism' concerning *memory*, which is the view that the 'mnemic datum' (as we might call it) or the 'objective constituent of the memory-situation' (as Broad calls it), that which one is supposed to be directly aware of when one remembers a past event, is identical with all or part of the remembered past event.[1] Price, too, devotes careful attention to the view that the so-called 'image' which, according to him, has to be present in 'cognitive' remembering, and which is presumably an object of direct awareness, is identical with the remembered past event. Price finds formidable difficulties in that view, as would be expected.[2] Furlong devotes a chapter to the doctrine of 'direct acquaintance with the past', and rejects the doctrine.[3]

I think it is possible to understand what it is that generates the controversy between the representative and the direct awareness theories of memory. First of all, we start with the assumption that when genuine remembering occurs, there is something that is variously called a 'memory-act', 'memory-event', 'memory-process', or 'the present occurrence in remembering'. The next step is to ask, What is the *content* of this act, event or process? It is as if we thought of the memory-act or memory-process as being a *container* (something like a box); and then we ask, What is *in* this container? What are its contents?

Now since the act or process is *remembering something*, it would be natural to suppose that a description of the content of the container would be a description of what is remembered. We remember many kinds

---

[1] Broad, *Mind and Its Place in Nature*, ch. 5.
[2] Price, 'Memory-Knowledge', *P.A.S.*, Suppl. vol. 15.
[3] Furlong, *A Study in Memory*, ch. 3.

of things: events, person, books, remarks, facts, situations, names, melodies, smiles, and so on. We are tempted to think of what is remembered as *present* in the 'container' of the memory-act or memory-process. This way of thinking immediately gets us into trouble. For example, Robinson remembers his wife's putting her car keys into the kitchen drawer. We feel an absurdity in saying that this past incident is *present* in the act of remembering. We are tempted to say, in such a case, that what Robinson really remembers is the *fact* that his wife put the keys in that drawer; for the fact has no date, and therefore it does not seem *quite* so absurd to say that the fact is 'present in Robinson's remembering'. But in many cases the translation into a fact-locution is not plausible. Robinson remembers his father's smile: we do not want to render this as, Robinson remembers that his father smiled. Thus we feel driven to hold that what is present in this memory-act is not the thing that is remembered, his father's smile, but some substitute for it, an image or mental representation of his father's smile. Since we have 'a craving for generality', we postulate that in *all* cases the 'content' of remembering is a substitute for what is remembered. This solution leaves us dissatisfied, however, precisely because the substitute is *not* what is remembered. This dissatisfaction produces the protests against the representative theory.

In *The Blue Book* Wittgenstein gives a nice diagnosis of these conflicting inclinations. In the passage I am going to quote he is speaking, not of remembering, but of *wishing*; yet the diagnosis is appropriate for remembering as well. He is speaking of the inclination to feel that when we wish for something to happen, there must be, in our wish, a *shadow* (as he calls it) of what we wish for.

> The idea that that which we wish to happen must be present as a shadow in our wish is deeply rooted in our forms of expression. But, in fact, we might say that it is only the next best absurdity to the one which we should really like to say. If it weren't too absurd we should say that the fact which we wish for must be present in our wish. For how can we wish *just this* to happen if just this isn't present in our wish? It is quite true to say: The mere shadow won't do; for it stops short before the object; and we want the wish to contain the object itself.[1]

In an earlier passage Wittgenstein mentions a similar problem about *expecting*. We expect something that has not yet happened. If we compare *expecting* with *shooting*, and of course we realise that we cannot shoot something that isn't there, this gives rise to the question, How can we *expect* something that is not there? Wittgenstein remarks that, just as with

---

[1] Wittgenstein, *The Blue Book*, (London, 1958). p. 37.

wishing, 'The way out of this difficulty seems to be: what we expect is not the fact, but a shadow of the fact; as it were, the next best thing to the fact'.[1] And, he says, 'The shadow, as we think of it, is some sort of picture; in fact, something very much like an image which comes before our mind's eye; and this again is something not unlike a painted representation in the ordinary sense'.[2]

The motivation for insisting on the presence of a representation, in expecting, wishing, and indeed, in all *thinking*, is not difficult to grasp. All of us are influenced by it. We can think of a friend who is far away, or one who is no longer alive. It seems that our friend himself cannot be present in our thought of him. We feel forced to hold, as did Descartes, Locke, and Hume, that what is there in our thought is an *Idea* of our friend; and we are strongly inclined to conceive of the *Idea* as a picture or image of him. With regard to *belief* (for example, the belief that it was Jones who stole the money) we have an overwhelming inclination to suppose that the object, or the 'immediate' object, or the 'content' of the belief, or 'what is believed', is not the *fact* that Jones stole the money, nor the event of his stealing it, but is a *proposition*. This is 'the shadow' of the fact or event. In *The Analysis of Mind*, Russell says, in regard to his belief that Caesar crossed the Rubicon:

> This event itself is not in my mind when I believe that it happened. It is not correct to say that I am believing the actual event; what I am believing is something now in my mind, something related to the event . . . but obviously not to be confounded with the event, since the event is not occurring now but the believing is . . . What is believed, however true it may be, is not the actual fact that makes the belief true, but a present event related to the fact. This present event, which is what is believed, I shall call the 'content' of the belief.[3]

Russell goes on to call the present event, which is the 'content' of the belief, a 'proposition'.[4] In his paper of 1919, 'On Propositions: What They Are and How They Mean', he divides propositions into two categories, those composed of images and those composed of words. He regards propositions of the first kind as primary: 'The primary phenomenon of belief consists of belief in images . . .'[5] Image-propositions are more fundamental than word-propositions: 'A word-proposition, apart from niceties, "means" the corresponding image-proposition, and an image-

[1] Ibid., p. 36.
[2] Ibid.
[3] Russell, *The Analysis of Mind*, pp. 233–4.
[4] Ibid., pp. 241, 242.
[5] Russell, *Logic and Knowledge*, ed. R.C. Marsh (New York, 1956) p. 308.

proposition has an objective reference dependent upon the meanings of its constituent images'.[1]

It is inevitable that we should be drawn to the same conceptions in regard to memory. We may recall how Augustine declares that it is by images that we remember the things perceived by sense: 'For surely the things themselves are not let into the memory, but the images of them only are with an admirable swiftness catched in . . .'[2] The feeling that since we cannot have the presence of the things themselves we do want to have 'the next best thing', is wonderfully expressed by James Mill, in his saying that when he remembers a previous sensation, there is present in him something that is not identical with the sensation, yet is 'more like' it, 'than anything else can be'.[3]

We noted Russell's view that when one believes that Caesar crossed the Rubicon, *what* one believes, or the *content* of one's belief, is not 'the fact that makes the belief true', but is a *proposition*. In the most fundamental cases, according to Russell, the proposition is an image or a configuration of images. Russell held that one can have different 'attitudes' toward one and the same propositional content − that is, one can expect it, or remember it, or want it, or believe it, or be afraid of it, or be in doubt about it, or just 'entertain' it, and so on.[4] With regard to the 'cognitive' attitudes of expectation, memory and mere 'assent', they may have exactly the same 'content', and will differ only in the nature of the 'belief-feelings' that are directed toward that content. Thus the expectation that it will rain, the memory that it did rain, and the belief or 'mere assent' that it is raining, may have the same propositional content, namely, a visual image of rain.[5] Or, to take Russell's favorite example, when I remember what I ate for breakfast this morning, 'The process of remembering will consists of calling up images of my breakfast, which will come to me with a feeling of belief such as distinguishes memory-images from mere imagination-images'.[6]

An interesting consequence of Russell's view that the 'content' of an expectation and of a memory may be the same, is that the 'content', i.e., the proposition believed, contains no *tense*. This is an inevitable development of his theory that 'in the most fundamental case' the content, or proposition, is just a complex image, since it is difficult to see how *tense* could be indicated by an image. Russell says that 'it is clear that the images may be the same for a memory and an expectation, which are nevertheless different beliefs . . . If this is so, difference of tense, in its

1   Ibid., p. 309.
2   Augustine, *Confessions*, bk 10, ch. 9.
3   James Mill *An Analysis of the Phenomena of the Human Mind*, I, 51−2.
4   Russell, *The Analysis of Mind*, p. 243.
5   Ibid., p. 250.
6   Ibid., p. 175.

psychologically earliest form, is no part of what is believed, but only of the way of believing it.'[1]

Future tense, or past tense, is supplied by the particular belief-feeling. If the image were of rain, the image-proposition might be expressed by the words 'rain' or 'raining'. The particular kind of belief-feeling called 'expectation' turns this into 'It will rain'; memory belief-feeling turns it into 'It did rain'. Rain is expected, and rain is remembered; so *rain* or *raining* is the 'content' of belief in both cases. Many different 'propositional attitudes' may be directed upon the same content. Suppose, says Russell, that you have 'a visual image of your breakfast-table':

> You may expect it while you are dressing in the morning, remember it as you go to your work; feel doubt as to its correctness when questioned as to your powers of visualizing; merely entertain the image, without connecting it with anything external, when you are going to sleep; desire it if you are hungry, or feel aversion for it if you are ill.[2]

Russell's position presents a feature that is distinctive in its boldness. This is the doctrine that what any propositional attitude is attached to, is some occurrence in the mind of the person who has the attitude. What I remember or expect 'is something now in my mind', 'a present event'.[3] What I remember is in all cases, something that is simultaneous with the remembering; it is the content of the remembering. Thus the truism, affirmed by Reid, that when I remember today the fragrant flower that I smelled yesterday, it is that flower and that odor I remember, and not an image or an idea — this truism is denied by Russell's view that what is remembered is 'a present event'. Aristotle was puzzled as to how we *can* remember an absent thing, if what we are aware of in remembering is only a present picture. Russell's response to this puzzle is to *deny* that we can remember an absent thing! What we remember *is* the present picture.

Russell is, however, not entirely single-minded on this point. He holds that an occurrence of genuine remembering contains the judgement 'this occurred', and that the reference of the demonstrative 'this' is neither clearly the past event, nor clearly the present image, but is vaguely *both*. He declares that 'if the word "this" meant the image to the exclusion of everything else, the judgement "this occurred" would be false.' This statement is plainly opposed to his other doctrine that what we remember *is* the present image. In view of the absurdity of this doctrine it is not surprising that Russell himself should contradict it.

We are faced with two conceptions of the nature of remembering. One

---

[1] Russell, *Logic and Knowledge*, p. 308.
[2] Russell, *Analysis of Mind*, p. 243.
[3] Ibid., pp. 233, 234.

conception is that memory is a direct awareness of what is remembered; the other is that we remember by means of a representation of what is remembered. These conceptions are opposed to one another, and neither seems satisfactory. I suggested that the following imagery may influence us: We assume that in genuine remembering there is an act, experience, or event of remembering. We think of this act or event as having a *content*. When we try to say what this content *is*, we are forced to choose between two alternatives. Either the content of the memory-act or memory-event is the occurrence, situation, or thing that we observed or learned about in the past; or the content is an image, copy or representation of the past occurrence, situation or thing. We tend to think of the memory-act or memory-event as a container; and then we have a question as to what is *in* the container.

I want to propose that there is an error in the intitial assumption. It is wrong to think that there is a 'memory-act' or 'memory-event' in the meaning that philosophers have attached to those terms. If we resist this assumption then we shall not be confronted with the imagery of a container, nor with the problem of deciding what is *in* the container. Thus this motive for choosing between either of the two conceptions of memory would be removed.

If we go back to the example of Robinson's remembering his wife leaving her car keys in the kitchen drawer, and try to pick out the memory-act, or the memory-event, or the remembering, we are completely frustrated. In response to his wife's query, 'Do you remember where I put my car keys?', the most relevant thing that may have occurred was Robinson's going over to the kitchen drawer and fetching out the keys. The philosophers who assume the existence of an act or event of remembering, and then are worried as to what the *content* of it is, will *not* want to say that this action of Robinson's *was* the remembering, or was the memory-event or memory-act. Why don't they want to say that? Because an action of that sort is capable of having many different *meanings*. We can imagine an action of that description occuring in circumstances where it would not be an expression of Robinson's remembering that his wife put her keys in that drawer. Suppose that Robinson had, in response to his wife's query, shrugged his shoulders and said 'I'm sorry'; but then had walked over to the drawer, opened it (in order to get something to eat) and, surprised at seeing the keys there, had handed them over to her. In the situation as originally described, Robinson's action was a manifestation of his remembering where his wife put the keys. In the second situation it was not. An action described as 'Robinson's walking over to the kitchen drawer, taking out the car keys and handing them over to his wife', obviously can mean different things in different situations. We could say that such an action is *potentially* ambiguous. But the philosophical belief in a 'memory-act' or 'memory-event' is a belief in something that is thought of as being *intrinsically unambiguous*. The act of memory, whatever it is, is supposed to be an act of memory *whenever* it occurs. It is a definite act with a definite, fixed, nature. It differs from perception, imagination, decision, or anything else. As Thomas Reid says:

> We may remember anything which we have seen, or heard, or known, or done, or suffered; but the remembrance of it is a particular act of the mind which now exists and of which we are conscious.[1]

The conception is the same that Hume had when, in speaking of 'the will', said:

> By the *will*, I mean nothing *but the internal impression we feel and are conscious of, when we knowingly give rise to any new motion of our body, or new perception of our mind.*[2]

The conception clearly is that when you do something 'willingly', there is a definite phenomenon of willing it: whenever *that* phenomenon occurred you would be willing that same thing. Similarly, Reid assumes that when you remember today the odor of a rose smelled yesterday, there is a particular act of the mind which, whenever it occurs, can be nothing other than *the memory* of that odor; it could not, for example, be *the anticipation* of it, or *the desire* for it.

I think it is unquestionable that when philosophers try to describe 'the experience of remembering', when they seek to find out 'What exactly happens when we remember some past event', they assume that something must take place, which always and whenever it occurs, is the remembering of that event. This is why memory-theorists have striven so hard to give a fine, exact, account of 'what happens' in memory. William James thought that a necessary component of memory was 'the revival in the mind of an image or copy of the original event'.[3] But James also thought that this resembling image is not nearly enough. For one thing, the image must be 'referred to the past'. This requires not only 'a general feeling of the past direction in time', but also that we think of some name or symbol of the event, or else think of some contiguous events.[4] But, furthermore, in order for *me* to remember the event as occurring in *my* past, it must be attended with a feeling of 'warmth and intimacy.' Thus a memory-event is, as James said, 'a very complex representation'.[5]

1   Reid, *Essays on the Intellectual Powers*, essay III, ch. 1.
2   Hume, *Treatise*, bk II, pt III, section 1.
3   James, *Principles*, I, 649.
4   Ibid., p. 650.
5   Ibid., p. 651.

Russell spells out the composition of the memory-event in still greater detail. The first component is, of course, an image which is a copy of the past event. Then there is some component which makes us not only refer the image to the past, but also to place the remembered event in a time ordering with other events. Russell is not sure what this component of the memory-event is, but he makes three conjectures. One is that there is a specific 'feeling of pastness'; another conjecture is that there is a succession of images 'in the same order as their prototypes'; a third suggestion (the most remarkable one!) is that there is a set of simultaneous images which gradually *fade*, and 'by fading, acquire the mark of just-pastness in an increasing degree as they fade, and are thus placed in a series while all sensibly present'.[1]

It is instructive to note how completely and explicitly *theoretical* is Russell's treatment of the problem of how we achieve the right temporal ordering of remembered events. He says the following about 'memory-images':

> They must have some characteristic which makes us regard them as referring to more or less remote portions of the past. That is to say if we suppose that A is the event remembered, B the remembering, and t the interval of time between A and B, there must be some characteristic of B which is capable of degrees, and which, in accurately dated memories, varies as t varies. It may increase as t increases, or diminish as t increases. The question which of these occurs is not of any importance for the theoretic servicability of the characteristic in question.[2]

Russell says both that the characteristic in question belongs to the 'memory-images' and that it belongs to 'the remembering' — which is confusing, since he does not want to just identify the two. It is best to regard this alleged characteristic as simply one component of the total 'memory-occurrence'. Russell's remarks make it completely clear that he is not giving an introspective report. He doesn't even know what the 'characteristic' is; but he thinks he knows that it *has* to be there. Why? Obviously, because if it were not there, then we should not be *able to do* something that we do every day, namely, remember the temporal order of various events.

In order to account for this same ability, James Mill produced the most remarkable hypothesis in the whole literature of memory. He employs the example of his remembering an occasion of George III's addressing the two Houses of Parliament. Mill remembers not only the person of the King but

---

[1]   Russell, *Analysis of Mind*, p. 162.
[2]   Ibid., p. 162.

HUNT LIBRARY
CARNEGIE-MELLON UNIVERSITY
PITTSBURGH, PENNSYLVANIA 15213

also the sound of his voice; and also he remembers the audience. But there is combined with these 'objects' the 'idea' of himself as both having witnessed the scene and as now remembering it. Mill says:

> Now in this last-mentioned part of the compound, it is easy to perceive two important elements; *the idea of my present self*, the remembering self; and *the idea of my past self*, the remembered or witnessing self. These two ideas stand at the two ends of a portion of my being; that is, of a series of my states of consciousness, intervening between the moment of perception, or the past moment, and the moment of memory, or the present moment. What happens at the moment of memory? The mind runs back from that moment to the moment of perception. That is to say, it runs over the intervening states of consciousness, called up by association. But 'to run over a number of states of consciousness, called up by association', is but another mode of saying, that 'we associate them'; and in this case we associate them so rapidly and closely, that they run, as it were, into a single point of consciousness, to which the name *Memory* is assigned.[1]

It is probable that Mill's belief in this high-speed mental process was motivated more by a desire to explain how one *could remember* any past event, rather than by a desire to explain how we can remember its correct temporal order, although the hypothesis (if it were any good) would explain the latter as much as the former. Of course it is incredible that anyone should testify that he *recalls* having ever performed the feat that Mill thinks we must always go through when we remember anything. This theory would possess no plausibility whatever unless one supposed that this rapid transiting of states of consciousness is something that either 'the mind' or the brain does for us without our being conscious of the process.

To return to Russell's account of the components of 'the memory-event', an additional feature of it is a 'feeling of familiarity' that accompanies the images and makes us 'trust' them. Finally, there is yet another component of the total memory-experience, namely, a distinctive 'feeling of belief', which is not present when one is merely imagining something; this belief-feeling is 'the distinctive thing in memory.'[2]

My aim is not to display Russell's ingenious inventions, but to point out that his intention, and that of most other memory theorists, is to assemble a package that *is and can be nothing other than the remembering* of some particular event. This is strikingly shown by the fact that Russell does not even require that what is remembered should have *occurred*. As G. E. Moore noted, Russell seems to assume that whether a person

---

1   James Mill, *op. cit.*, pp. 330–1.
2   Russell, ibid., p. 176.

remembered something 'depends only on what his state was at the moment, never at all on whether what he thought he remembered actually occurred'.[1] This is one significance of Russell's famous 'sceptical hypothesis' that the world might have been created five minutes ago 'complete with memories and records'.[2] The point is that if a person had a visual image of dogs fighting, together with 'a sense of pastness', 'a feeling of familiarity', and 'a feeling of belief', then he would be *remembering* a dog fight, regardless of what else was or had been the case, even if there had never been any dog fights nor any dogs!

In reviewing these attempts by philosophers to describe the mental content of remembering, one should be impressed by the implausibility or even incredibility of their proposals. A still more important thing to be noted, is the crucial assumption that of course there is a 'memory-act' or 'memory-event'. What do I mean by calling this an 'assumption'? Surely Robinson remembered, when asked, where the keys had been put. His remembering this was an event, a happening in the world. This is true. The assumption I am talking about is the assumption that whenever it is true that a person, A, remembered X, at time t, then at t A did something, or something took place in his mind, *which was the remembering*. This assumption may appear to be obviously true, but in fact it is profoundly false.

I believe that if we study the actual details of examples of memory, not viewing them through the veil of theory, not assuming that something or other *must* be the case, we shall come upon nothing whatever that has the powerful property of being *the remembering*. What we do find is nothing other than various actions, gestures, utterances, images, and thoughts, which, in some contexts, are 'manifestations' of remembering, but when placed in other contexts are not.

An idea that greatly influences our thinking about the psychological concepts in general is the idea that when a person expects, wants, intends, or remembers X (and so on, through the whole range of psychological concepts) there is some state or event that in some vague sense is present 'in' him, and whose *intrinsic* nature is such that whenever *it* is present in a person, that person expects, wants, intends, or remembers X. The full-blown conception at work here is that remembering where you parked your car is a distinct state of consciousness, and remembering your dental appointment is a different and equally distinct one; deciding to water the lawn is a unique conscious impression, and deciding to trim the rose bushes is another one; expecting Mike to visit you is a definite mental

---

[1]   G.E. Moore, *Philosophical Papers* (New York, 1959) p. 217.
[2]   Russell, *An Outline of Philosophy* (New York, 1927) p. 7. I study this 'hypothesis' in the first of *Three Lectures on Memory*, in *Knowledge and Certainty*, supra.

phenomenon, and expecting Nancy is a different but equally specific one. For every different particular thing that is wanted, hoped for, expected, regretted, believed, remembered (and so on), an absoluteley specific and different mental content occurs.

My attempt to characterise this philosophical idea is pretty rough; but it is adequate if the vague picture comes through. Indeed, the idea *is* nothing more than this vague picture – and it is this that dominates our philosophical thinking at every turn.

I believe that an even more fundamental picture forces itself on us when, as philosophers, psychologists, neuropsychologists, or psycho-linguists, we want to learn more about thinking, intending, expecting, wanting, remembering, and the other psychological phenomena. We want to know what these phenomena *are*, what they *consist in*. Since the human organism has an inside and an outside, it is a natural idea that remembering, intending, etc., occur either inside or outside: they must be either something *inner* or something *outer*.[1] I think one tends to regard it as self-evident that remembering, for example, either consists in the outward manifestations of memory (e.g., the smile of recognition; the utterances, gestures, and actions that display correct remembering), or possibly in propensities and dispositions toward such outward manifes-tations; or, on the other hand, remembering consists in some *inner* states or events. That remembering is either something inner or something outer seems to be an exhaustive disjunction.

When we explore these alternatives, however, we are frustrated and baffled. Consider a case in which you recognise someone whom you meet on the street. Let us suppose that you smile at him and say 'Hi'; and then you add, 'You look very brown!'. 'Been at the seashore', he says. The two of you continue on your separate ways. Did the recognition 'consist in' your smile and your utterance of 'Hi'? Surely not. Some people greet absolute strangers in that way. A very friendly person may say to a complete stranger, 'My, you look brown!'

A philosopher might hasten to propose that the recognition did not consist in any *actual* behaviour, but in a propensity or disposition to say or do certain things. But one is hard put to make this plausible. A propensity or disposition to do *what*? To answer 'Yes' to the question, 'Do you know that man?' The Apostle Peter, fearing for his life, had no propensity to acknowledge that he knew Jesus. His fear was a so-called 'countervailing' condition. To accommodate this obvious kind of objection a philosopher may seek to define a complex set of conditions, such that if *all* of them were satisfied, then recognition would have occurred. But these attempts are always unsatisfactory: either some circumstance has been neglected,

---

[1]   See my 'Wittgenstein on the Nature of Mind', *Amer. Phil. Quart.*, Monograph no. 4 (Oxford, 1970) pp. 17 ff.

thus providing for the possibility of a counter-example; or else the definition has become so complex that no one, perhaps not even the author, can understand it. A more fundamental consideration is that there is no definite set of *all* the conditions that would be relevant to the question of, say, whether a person *A* had recognised a person *B*. In a particular context of circumstances it may be absolutely clear that *A* recognised *B* when he smiled at him and greeted him. This does not imply, however, that there is a non-trivial description of those circumstances that *logically entails* that *A* recognised *B*. With a little inventiveness we can imagine some further logically possible circumstance, such that if it were added to the description of the context it would be wrong, or at least no longer clearly correct, to say that *A* recognised *B*. There is no point at which we could rightly say, 'Given *this* set of conditions, nothing else whatever would have any bearing on whether *A* recognised *B*'. Gottlob Frege held that a concept 'must have a sharp boundary'. 'A concept that is not sharply defined is wrongly termed a concept'.[1] This is not true of most of the concepts we employ in ordinary life. We are not taught to use them, and do not intend to use them, in conformity with some rigid set of necessary and sufficient conditions. As Wittgenstein remarks: 'If someone were to draw a sharp boundary I could not acknowledge it as the one that I too always wanted to draw, or had drawn in my mind. For I did not want to draw one at all'.[2]

These reflections may make us turn away from the attempt to define recognition in terms of behavior or behavioral propensities, and to move to the other alternative, namely, to hold that recognition is an *inner* state or occurrence. The same for intending, believing, wanting, remembering, and so on. The difficulty here, of course, is to *specify* what the inner something is. In the case of memory we surveyed the variety of candidates that various authors have proposed: images; feelings of pastness, familiarity, fittingness; a belief-feeling that belongs uniquely to remembering; and so on. Some of these items are preposterous inventions; others are things that sometimes occur but often do not. And sometimes these latter occur in cases that are not examples of remembering.

Since attention to the phenomenology of remembering does not produce any specifiable item that will qualify as the remembering we may feel inclined to make the most stultifying move of all, namely, to conclude that remembering something (e.g., a dental appointment) is an indescribable, unspecifiable, event or state. We feel that we *know* what it is, but we cannot *say* what it is. We are inclined to exclaim, with a special intonation, 'It is just a *particular mental event*!' We feel that it *had* to be

---

[1] *The Philosophical Writings of Gottlob Frege*, ed. Geach and Black, p. 159.
[2] Wittgenstein, *Philosophical Investigations*, section 76.

there, since we certainly did remember the dental appointment. We want to say that it was 'a *definite, inner, occurrence*'. We can almost *see* it![1]

This desperate resort to an unspecifiable inner event reveals the intensity of our metaphysical belief that when, at a particular time, a person remembers something, the remembering is an occurrence *in* him at that time. The idea that remembering consists in an indescribable, inner event, results in a host of unanswerable questions. On this general view there would be a *multitude* of indescribable, inner events, corresponding to the multitude of psychological concepts. How could one *learn* which of them is *remembering*? If one could not learn this, would one ever be *entitled* to say, 'Oh, I have just remembered that I have a dental appointment'? Or suppose that a person who did, in some way, come to know which particular, inner event, his remembering a dental appointment is, but also happened to have a bad memory, and consequently *mistook* some *other* inner event for it – but yet said, correctly, 'Oh, I have a dental appointment today!', and showed up at the dentist's office at the right time! Here I am paraphrasing and adapting Wittgenstein's remark:

> 'Imagine a person whose memory could not retain *what* the word 'pain' meant – so that he constantly called different things by that name – but nevertheless used the word in agreement with the usual indications and presuppositions of pain' – in short he uses it as we all do. Here I should like to say: a wheel that can be turned though nothing else moves with it, is not part of the mechanism.[2]

I will not dwell any further on the untenability of the idea that remembering something (or wanting it, expecting it, believing it, and so on) is an indescribable inner event.[3] I believe that a philosopher who clings to this idea is ultimately forced to hold of these unspecifiable inner events that all of them *show* their nature to us in such a way that we do not have to, and indeed cannot, *learn* what they mean, nor can we *forget* what they mean; they have their meanings 'written on their face' in such a way that we *cannot* mistake them for anything else; they are entities that logically cannot have more than a single interpretation.

I will just say, somewhat dogmatically, that there is not, and cannot be, anything in the world that has this super-magical property. No image or

---

[1] Cf. Wittgenstein, *Philosophical Investigations* (Oxford, 1953) section 305.
[2] Ibid., section 271.
[3] I have studied this notion in several writings. Among them are the following: 'Wittgenstein's *Philosophical Investigations*', in my *Knowledge and Certainty* (Englewood Cliffs, N.J., 1963); 'Behaviourism as a Philosophy of Psychology', in *Behaviourism and Phenomenology*, ed. T.W. Wann (Chicago, 1964) pp. 148–9; 'Wittgenstein on the Nature of Mind'. *op. cit.*, 'Memory and Representation'. *Noûs*, IV no. 1 1970; *Problems of Mind* (New York, 1971).

configuration of images, no word or sentence (whether spoken aloud or to oneself), no gesture, facial expression, or bodily movement, is such that it is logically impossible for it to be understood in more than one way.

Those philosophers who have tried to identify and analyze 'the act of remembering' or 'the present mental occurrence in remembering', have been engaged in a hopeless enterprise. No image, feeling, thought, utterance, or action, is intrinsically and regardless of circumstances, the remembering of a dental appointment. There are gestures, utterances, and pieces of behavior that, in the human contexts in which they occur, are expressions of memory. A smile and a greeting would reveal *recognition* in one context, but just friendliness in another. Wittgenstein speaks of trying to remove the temptation to suppose that there *must* be a mental event of sudden understanding, or of hoping, or wanting, or believing, etc., alongside or underneath the *expressions* of understanding, hope, belief, and so on.[1] He suggests the following 'rule of thumb': 'If you are puzzled about the nature of thought, belief, knowledge, and the like, substitute for the thought the expression of the thought, etc.' When we reflect on the futile endeavors of the memory theorists, perhaps the best way to sum up the reason for their failure, is that the memory event or act they are trying to pinpoint is nothing that does or could exist. People remember things; but nothing that occurs, either inner or outer, *is* the remembering. The question, 'In what does remembering consist?', should be answered in this way: It doesn't consist in anything!

Now here we may think of an alternative. Why not identify the remembering, in each context, with the *expression* of memory that occurs in that context? Thus, in one case, Robinson's remembering where his wife put the keys would consist in his walking to the right drawer and taking them out; in another case, his remembering this would consist in his uttering the words, 'You left them in the kitchen drawer'; in still another case, it would consist in his having an image of his wife dropping the keys in that drawer; and so on.

Stanley Munsat endorses this suggestion. He speaks of the phenomenon of *suddenly* remembering something, and he addresses himself to the traditional question, *What happens when a person suddenly remembers something?* He discusses this matter with acuteness. He remarks that:

> We know perfectly well what things or what sorts of things occur when someone suddenly remembers something. Sometimes, for example, the person who suddenly remembers something snaps his fingers and then charges off to do something, like taking the pot off the stove. And if these seem to be only 'outward manifestations' of the *real* 'suddenly remembering', perhaps we might mention such things as feelings of

[1] Wittgenstein, *The Blue Book*, pp. 41–2.

excitement, mental pictures, a sudden intake of breath. Have we now gotten to what is essential to suddenly remembering? Have we now penetrated the superficial 'side effects' of suddenly remembering and gotten down to the real hard-core of the occurrence or progress known as suddenly remembering? But none of these things can be what we are after either, for all of these might occur yet it be a case not of suddenly remembering, but, for example, suddenly realizing or suddenly figuring out that, or its suddenly occurring to one, or simply suddenly being struck by the fact that . . . We are inclined to feel that a football, wherever it is and whatever is done to it, is a football; and, so too, a phenomenon which we point to as an example of suddenly remembering, wherever and whenever it should occur, is suddenly remembering . . . But it is precisely because this is the sort of thing that we want to find that we will never find it . . . And the reason why we will not settle on any one or combination of these as composing the essence of suddenly remembering is that none of these phenomena are in themselves or in combination either necessary or sufficient for the occurrence of the phenomenon of suddenly remembering.[1]

These remarks are perceptive and precisely right. Munsat then goes on to say something puzzling:

'Suddenly remembering' does indeed name a mental occurrence or episode. When I say 'I just remembered . . .', I am giving voice to something which just happened. What 'just happened' *may* be, for instance, that I just had a mental image, and nothing else. I see no reason not to say that in such cases, the suddenly remembering consisted of the having of a mental image. However, it must be realized that this same image, occurring in a different context, could *not* be taken as a case of suddenly remembering.[2]

It seems to me that here some of the previous insight is lost. When I exclaim, 'Oh, I just remembered that I have a dental appointment!', what 'I am giving voice to' (to use Munsat's phrase) is not that I had an image of a dental chair (if I did have one). What I am giving voice to (if my memory is correct) is just this — that I suddenly remembered a dental appointment. It appears to me that Munsat was yielding here to the inclination to picture sudden remembering as something 'inner' or 'mental'. Why else does he say that it is 'a mental occurrence'? Is he thinking that one time it might be one mental occurrence and, another time, a different mental occurrence? The fact is, however, that there might be no mental

---

[1]   S. Munsat, *The Concept of Memory* (New York, 1966) pp. 41–3.
[2]   Ibid., p. 47.

occurrence at all in a case of sudden remembering. For example, you and I are groping to recall the name of a mutual acquaintance: suddenly you exclaim, 'Prince!', and I say 'Right!' Perhaps all that happened when you suddenly remembered the name was that you uttered the name. Was just that, by itself, a 'mental' occurrence? I doubt that anyone will want to say so.

In addition to the mistaken claim that the expression 'suddenly remembering' *names* 'a mental occurrence', Munsat seems to me to be ill-advised in his apparent willingness to say that when, in suddenly remembering my dental appointment, if what happened was that I had an image of a dental chair, then the sudden remembering *consisted of* my having that image. If what happened was that I snapped my fingers and said 'Dentist!', it would be equally permissible to say that the sudden remembering consisted of *those* occurrences. Munsat is well aware that the meaning of such occurrences depends on their contexts. He is also aware that the typical philosophical urge to uncover the nature of sudden remembering is a desire to penetrate to some event or state that is *intrinsically* sudden remembering, a phenomenon such that 'wherever and whenever it should occur' it would be sudden remembering. I think that the cleanest way to react to this philosophical urge is to brand it as an illusion, arising from a misconception about the concept of memory and the other psychological concepts. It puts matters in the clearest light to say that sudden remembering does *not consist in anything*, rather than to say that one time it consists in a certain expression of memory, another time in a different one, and so on.

It would appear that when Wittgenstein dictated *The Blue Book* he did not have as clear a perception of this matter as he did subsequently. He says there, for example, that in a particular case 'the experience of thinking *may* be just the experience of saying, or may consist of this experience plus others which accompany it'.[1] But writing later (in *Zettel*) and speaking of such an example as your calling 'Please come here', in the direction of two people, A and B, but meaning that *B* should come, not *A*, he has a deeper and truer insight when he remarks that it is in error to say that your meaning B *consists in something*.[2] He further remarks that ' "Meaning" does not stand for an activity which wholly or partly consists in the outward expressions of meaning.'[3] Nor, on the other hand, is it something *inner* that accompanies those expressions. The same holds for sudden remembering.

Let me try to summarise the position I have been taking. There have been two opposed views about the 'content' of remembering. One view is

[1]   Wittgenstein, *The Blue Book*, p. 43.
[2]   Wittgenstein, *Zettel* (Oxford, 1967) section 16.
[3]   Ibid., section 19.

that in memory we are 'directly aware' of the events and objects that we witnessed in the past. The other view holds that this cannot be, and that 'the immediate given' of remembering is a present representation. The proponents of both positions seem to have the idea that when a person remembers a certain thing, X, something occurs that is 'intrinsically' the remembering of X. This occurrence is called the 'experience', 'act', or 'event' of remembering. The question that the two positions quarrel over is, what is 'contained' or 'present' in the event of remembering? Is it 'the past event which we are *said* to be remembering',[1] or is it a representation in the form of some 'present mental occurrence'? My own belief is that the assumption of an intrinsic memory-event, when closely considered, simply fades away, no longer felt to be intelligible. With its disappearance one is freed from the necessity of choosing between these two rival 'theories' as to what its *content* is, and *a fortiori* from the necessity of thinking that since the past occurrence cannot be there in the memory-event, therefore what *is* there is a representation. In this way I try to remove *one* source of the assumption that there has to be a representation in remembering.

---

[1] Russell, *Analysis of Mind*, p. 164; emphasis added.

2

LOCKE
AND THE MEANING
OF COLOUR WORDS*

P. M. S. Hacker

While thinking philosophically we see problems in places where there
are none. It is for philosophy to show that there are no problems.[1]

1. INTRODUCTION

Those of us who are not colour blind have a happy command of colour
concepts. We say of trees that they are green in spring, that they are the
same colour as grass and a different colour from the sky. If we shine a
torch with a red bulb upon a white surface, we say that the surface looks
pink although it is white. And if we suffer a bout of jaundice we
(allegedly) claim that white things look yellowish to us, although they are
not yellow, nor do they (publicly) look yellow. We employ this tripartite
distinction unworriedly and unthinkingly. But when, in doing philosophy,
we are called upon to elucidate colour concepts it becomes evident that
these elementary concepts present intricate problems to the philosophical
understanding. It is extraordinarily difficult to obtain a proper surview of
colour grammar, and the temptations of philosophical illusion are legion.
We go wrong before the first step is even taken, and hence do not notice
our errors, for they are implicit in every move we make. We multiply
impossibilities *seriatim*, getting better, like the White Queen, with practice.
We then either slide into scepticism, or alternatively exclude it on
empirical grounds — appealing, as is so popular in American philosophical
circles, to the wonders of science, in particular physics and neuro-
physiology, to keep the *malin genie* from the door.

* I am grateful to many colleagues with whom I discussed earlier drafts of this paper,
especially Professors R. Arrington, J. Bennett and J. Kim from the U.S.A. Mr. D.
Isaacson, Dr. A.J.P. Kenny and Dr. J. Raz showed similar tolerance and helpful-
ness at Oxford. I am particularly indebted to Dr. G.P. Baker for his advice, criticisms and comments.
1   Wittgenstein *Philosophical Grammar* p. 47.

The main problem I wish to deal with in this paper is the inverted spectrum supposal. It is only one of a host of perplexing philosophical problems about colour, but it is instructive. Indeed if it can be resolved, the solution may point the way to resolving further vexed questions. In particular, the method I shall adopt to tackle it throws light upon the doctrine of subjectivity of secondary qualities, and I shall briefly discuss that issue in passing. My central concern, however, is to explore the suggestion that suppositions of inverted spectra are logically incoherent, that the alleged possibilities are illusory, and that the fact that they are thought to be imaginable shows no more than the dangers of relying upon what we think we can imagine as a criterion of logical possibility.

One can no more imagine a logically impossible state of affairs than one can draw one, but one can be under the illusion that one imagines a state of affairs which is impossible, that a form of words preceded by 'I can imagine that' makes sense, and hence that the resultant sentence makes sense. And if we so think, we may foolishly infer from apparent imaginability to logical possibility. Our imagination, foxed by the grammar of colour, leads us astray. Yet one can imagine only what can be described. Whether spectrum inversion can be coherently described is to be read off, not from our imaginings but from the grammar, the rules of use, of colour predicates. Escher's wonderful etchings are not pictures of logically impossible objects but, as it were, 'logically impossible pictures' i.e. pictures which violate the 'logical syntax' of pictorial representation, and so make no 'pictorial sense'. Usually we can quickly spot what is awry with Escher's pictures. But when faced with the logical syntax of colour predicates, particularly when indulging in uncontrolled imaginings, we lack the clear surview which is readily obtainable in the case of conventions of perspectival two-dimensional representation of 3-dimensional objects. So we go hopelessly wrong. What follows is primarily an essay in the 'Dialectic of Pure Colour', an attempt to explore the illusions of Reason with respect to colour concepts in the particular case of spectrum inversion.

2. THROWING UP CLOUDS OF DUST

In *An Essay Concerning Human Understanding* Locke suggests that by the different structure of our sensory organs things might be

> so ordered, that *the same object should produce in several men's minds different ideas* at the same time; v.g. if the idea that a violet produced in one man's mind by his eyes were the same that a marigold produced in another man's and *vice versa*. For, since this could never be known, because one man's mind could not pass into another man's body, to perceive what appearances were produced by those organs;

neither the ideas hereby, nor the names, would be at all confounded, or any falsehood be in either.[1]

In the sequel Locke coyly remarks

> I am nevertheless very apt to think that the sensible ideas produced by any object in different men's minds, are most commonly very near and undiscernibly alike. For which opinion, I think, there might be many reasons offered: but that being besides my present business, I shall not trouble my reader with them.

I shall take this supposal as the first alleged possibility. My present business will be to offer reasons for its being not an unactualised possibility, but an impossibility.

Other apparently conceivable cases of spectrum inversion are more difficult to handle, and call for more tentative judgement. A second possibility, not envisaged by Locke, is a sudden spectrum inversion. Here we are asked to imagine a person, A, waking up one morning to find that his experience of colour is strikingly different from what it has been hitherto. Grass now appears to him to be the same colour as tomatoes were (and appeared to him to be) yesterday, and so for all other colours. Has everything overnight changed colour? Is it logically possible for everything to change colour thus? Comparison with the avowed perceptual experience of others relieves A of the need to explore this tantalising philosophical question, for they observe no change. So he concludes that his colour perception has suddenly become inverted. Distressing though this is, it is no barrier to communication as long as A remembers to switch colour predicates symmetrically in his descriptions. If he does so he will simply reproduce the situation described in the first case, and no misunderstanding will occur.

The scrupulous philosopher may still worry. Perhaps what happened overnight was not a colour inversion, but an inversion of my use of colour predicates, coupled with an odd feeling that things are awry (as indeed they are!). To help our philosopher's flagging imagination, let us introduce a further case which does not invoke memory, and does not rely on a past shift. This is the alleged possibility of contemporaneous repeatable inversion. When I have both eyes open things are with me (apparently) as with everyone else. But when I close one eye the inversion phenomenon occurs. Now — is this not imaginable?

Here then we have a range of alleged possibilities. Of course, no one thinks such things ever happen. The cases involving change are open, allegedly, to verification. The Lockean case, however, is not. But

---

[1]   Locke, op. cit., bk II chp. XXXII section 15.

philosophers whose imaginations are so fertile are prone to be 'scientistic' in these matters. Science informs us, some philosophers claim, that we are all 'wired up' much the same way. Our retinal structures are similar, the cones and rods of the retina respond in the same way to light of such and such wavelength, our optic nerves operate in similar fashion and our brains (which are more or less, give or take an argument or two, identical with our minds) have a common physiological structure. And all this suggests that it is a good *hypothesis* to suppose that the Lockean case never occurs.

The trouble about such fertile imaginations as produce these examples of 'evident' possibilities is, paradoxically that they are not sufficiently rich. What we need is not stories that *sound* plausible but patient philosophical analysis. We need a surview of our use of colour predicates, a description of our linguistic practices which will display what is involved in explaining the meaning or sense of colour predicates, and what is requisite for possession of colour concepts. The strategy to be employed involves two thrusts, firstly to clarify the way in which colour predicates have a sense (in order to block the idealist or subjectivist drift), secondly to approach the examples by a constructivist or anti-realist route, to raise in each case the question of the satisfaction of the assertion conditions for the ascription to the subject of colour perception on the one hand and relevant linguistic competence on the other. I shall, however, restrict myself to the first two cases — they provide ample material for discussion and if the arguments are correct they should be applicable with only marginal variation to the third imagined case.

Before proceeding further, however, I should like to digress to a related topic. Locke's supposition of spectrum inversion was made plausible in part by the fact that it was entertained in the context of the doctrine of the subjectivity of secondary qualities. This classical doctrine, though still current in the philosophical world, has been much criticised of recent years. I think, however, that a novel kind of criticism can be directed against it which links it attractively with the inverted spectrum supposition and finds a common root to both in a misapprehension of conceptual articulations.

3. A DIGRESSION — PRIMARY AND SECONDARY QUALITIES

It was, of course, no accident that Locke posed the problem of the inverted spectrum in the sharp way he did. Espousing the New Way of Ideas, derived from Descartes, he believed that names had primary reference to, and were given sense in terms of, subjective mental items. If the primary sense of colour predicates involved reference to subjective modifications of a perceiver's mind (how things look, in respect of colour, to him), then the colour inversion hypothesis would indeed make sense. However, not only did Locke invert the order of logical priority between 'ξ looks *C* to me' and 'ξ is *C*', but, notoriously, he thought that perceived colours are no more than ideas of secondary qualities which are objectively only powers in objects to affect perceivers in certain ways. The doctrine of the subjectivity of secondary qualities of course reinforces the temptations of the inverted spectrum supposition.

The sources of the subjectivity thesis are diverse, stemming in part from the Neo-Platonist antecedents of the new sciences, in part from the revival of atomism, and in part from the metaphysical interpretation the philosopher-scientists of the seventeenth century imposed upon the achievements of mathematical physics. Kepler, much influenced by Neo-Platonism, distinguished between primary and secondary qualities, not in terms of objectivity and subjectivity, but in terms of degrees of reality. The primary qualities, he thought, possessed a superior degree of reality because they are amenable to mathematical treatment. The real world is quantitative in character, and qualitative differences in the sensible world must be explicable in terms of underlying quantitative ones. Secondary qualities such as colour, taste, sound, heat, etc. are not subjective, but less real than primary metrical ones. In a transposed form the same argument was misguidedly utilised by Descartes to prove the subjectivity of secondary qualities. In the third Meditation he argues that primary qualities can be perceived clearly and distinctly, secondary qualities only confusedly and obscurely. By 'clear and distinct' here Descartes evidently means not resistance to hyperbolic doubt, but susceptibility to geometrico-mathematical analysis. Descartes misguidedly takes this as a proof of subjectivity of secondary qualities.

When Democritan atomism is fed into Keplerian Neo-Platonism a fresh impetus is given to the thrust towards subjectivity of secondary qualities and the attendant severance of appearance from reality, of the humanly perceptible world from things as they are. Atoms were conceived as lacking secondary qualities. This alone would not show that secondary qualities are subjective, but only (and unobjectionably) that they are not absolutely dissective. However, atomism was invoked to provide a corpuscularian explanation of the physiology of perception. So Galileo takes it that if corpuscles have only primary qualities, and if perception of secondary qualities is physiologically explicable in corpuscularian terms, then secondary qualities, as they appear, are no more than modifications of the mind, and as they are, are no more than powers. A similar argument occurs in Descartes, who, while rejecting atomism (matter being infinitely divisible) adopted the corpuscularian account of perception. Needless to say, the fact that the mechanism of perception is explained in terms which involve no reference to secondary qualities does not show that the objects of perception are not qualified by secondary qualities.

The corpuscularian theory of perception was wholly speculative. But the concrete achievements of mathematical physics involved, with respect to body and matter, nothing other than primary qualities of extension, figure, motion and weight (the latter constituting an embarrassment to the reductionist, and disregarded by Descartes). It was therefore plausible to take the concept of a material object to be defined in terms of primary qualities alone, and it is only one small step − or rather, slip − to think that the alleged inessentialness of secondary qualities is tantamount to their subjectivity. Galileo slipped in this direction, and Locke slid after him.

The Cartesian revolution, with its novel characterisation of the mind, its sharp delimitation of the domain of science, and its radical bifurcation of mind and nature, posed the philosophical problem of the relation of appearance to reality with peculiar urgency. The New Way of Ideas reinforced the scientifically motivated drift to subjectivity. Sensations and perceptions were both classified as ideas, and objects of perception duly assimilated to sensations. Hence we find both Locke and Boyle following Descartes in observing that pain, a sensation, does not resemble its cause, and as a result misguidedly querying with what right we should assume that the idea of red should resemble its causal ancestor. Likewise Locke argues from the subjectivity of pain to the subjectivity of heat, blithely disregarding the distinction between a (possibly painful) heat indicative sensation, feeling hot, and heat.

Other Lockean arguments, derived largely from Boyle, turn on the dependency of perception upon the state of the perceiver (hot and cold hands in tepid water), upon conditions of observation (porphyry being claimed to be, not invisible, but *colourless* in the dark), upon the causal dependence of secondary qualities on primary ones (alterations to the texture of an almond produce alterations in colour) and upon the merely relative dissectivity of determinate secondary qualities (blood under a microscope does not consist exclusively of red particles). None of his arguments bear any weight.

A striking feature about the classical arguments in support of the subjectivity thesis is that individually they are poor. Only in the context of the struggle to come to philosophical grips with the new scientific world picture and the resultant conception of the mind does it become intelligible that they were accepted as even persuasive. Why then does the subjectivity thesis retain such a powerful grip upon the philosophical imagination?

No doubt there are many reasons, some of them as firmly associated with misunderstandings of the scientific enterprise as were those of the seventeenth century philosopher-scientists. But deep philosophical error is commonly associated with misapprehension of conceptual articulations. In this case the subjectivist thrust stems unwittingly from a very natural assimilation of what I shall call 'anthropocentric' qualities to subjective ones. A quality is anthropocentric, but in no sense subjective, insofar as the sense of an expression designating it is conveyed by an ostensive definition by reference to a sample which sample is only usable (and hence the definition only fully intelligible) by someone who can perceptually discriminate it in the requisite way. Of course, this in no way *distinguishes* primary from secondary qualities, since 'metre' no less than 'red' is thus defined. But, as I shall try to show in the sequel, the role of ostensive definition and of paradigmatic samples in explanation of the sense of predicates of sensory qualities can, if misunderstood, very readily reinforce any inclinations one may have to adopt the subjectivity thesis. Moreover, the very same misunderstandings lie at the heart of the inverted spectrum supposal.

When considering the use of colour predicates it is reasonably clear that lexical definition is valueless in explaining their sense. Of course we can coin artificial colour words, such as 'gred', which are defined in terms of disjunctions of other colour words e.g. 'either green or red', and hence define 'green' as 'gred but not red'. And we can play Goodmanian games with non-projectible predicates such as 'bleen'. But these 'artificial' terms presuppose command of ordinary colour concepts and can throw no light on what is involved in mastery of a colour vocabulary. Similarly we can define 'red', as dictionaries do, by citing typical objects which normally are of that colour — so 'red' is defined as 'the colour of blood, rubies, fire etc.'. Of course this presupposes that we know what 'the colour of ξ' means, and that we know what colour blood, rubies etc. are. In fact, such a definition merely tells us what objects can be employed in the role of paradigmatic samples in an ostensive definition. It is at least plausible to suppose that the age-old tradition that colours are simple ideas, and hence both indefinable (lexically) and (more confusingly) 'given' in experience, is correct in so far as it points to the necessity of ostensive definition.

One prominent kind of ostensive definition involves the use of paradigmatic *samples*; not, it must be stressed, examples. It was upon this kind of ostensive definition that Wittgenstein lavished most careful attention — for it is the source of a multitude of philosophical confusions. We can distinguish canonical samples — such as the standard meter, or gram, from optional samples. Canonical samples are unique, and the object whose length or weight provides *the* standard for being e.g. a meter long or one gram in weight, has a privileged role in judgments of length or weight in the metric in question. Optional samples, however, involve no such unique object — and it is they which are pertinent for an understanding of colour predicates, taste, smell, odour and sound predicates. We neither have nor need standard sepias or acrids or C-flats in Paris. Rather we explain the meanings of these expressions by reference to any object which standardly exemplifies such properties and which is generally agreed to exemplify them. When so teaching, or explaining, the meanings of predicates of perceptual determinates we employ an object as a paradigm which, unlike the canonical paradigm, we may, upon a subsequent occasion, describe as having the property. The object is used now as a sample, later as an object for description.

Wittgenstein recurrently stresses a point not hitherto apprehended about such methods of explaining the sense of an expression: the ostensive definition 'This is red' is not a description of an object, and the sample used is not an object described by the sentence 'This is red', but rather belongs to the method of representation. It is not a description because the 'logical form' of the sentence is 'This *colour* is red', not 'This object (apple, piece of paper, etc.) is red'. If 'This colour' were not red, it would not be 'This colour'. The sentence is accordingly not bipolar, and does not express a genuine proposition. By the same token the sample employed is not described by the ostensive definition but belongs to the method of representation — its introduction is not 'a move in a language-game' but a preparation for such a move. If the ostensive definition is understood (and to be sure much more needs to be grasped than can be overtly conveyed by the mere ostension) then the hearer can go on to say of things that they are red — they resemble in the requisite way (i.e. the way which we — the standard users of the language — accept as criterion of sameness of colour) the sample used in the ostensive definition.

Since the role of the sample is to provide a standard of comparison it must be usable. In what way is it a standard of comparison, and in what sense must it be usable? It is a standard of comparison in so far as the predicate defined by reference to an optional sample is truly applied to an object to the extent that the colour of the object is that of the sample i.e. satisfies the criteria *we conventionally accept* for sameness of colour. To that extent the sample provides a standard. But we do not carry around a table of samples for comparison, either in our pockets or in our heads. What we teach a learner of the colour grammar is to be able to make colour judgements without comparing what he sees with a sample, although of course acquisition of the ability in question must be such that his non-comparative judgements coincide (more or less) with the judgements he (and we) would make if a table of samples were available. The availability of such a prop is not the same as the use of an available prop — and the ability we wish to train is the ability to make judgements in normal conditions without the support of a table. Only in very special cases do we fall back on such support. Nevertheless it is very easy to think that acquiring the ability to use colour predicates is a process of transferring a table of colour samples from hand to mind.

This temptation runs very deep. We are prone to think that a private, mental, sample can fulfil the role of a public one — that knowing the meaning of a word defined by reference to a sample in an ostensive definition consists in an ability to produce a mental surrogate for it. To be sure we cannot display the sample — but we can, we think, assure ourselves that we know what we mean. It is against this illusion that Wittgenstein argues in *Investigations*, section 265, in one of the most difficult passages in the book.[1]

The sample must be usable. Without broad agreement in discriminatory capacities, and wide constancy in colour properties on a background of regular conditions of observation we would have no colour vocabulary. The samples by reference to which sense is assigned to colour predicates are only usable, are only of help in conveying the sense of the predicate in question, to those who can see and discriminate appropriately. The blind cannot master colour concepts properly,[2] yet meaning is one thing and truth another, we rightly feel. So though a blind man cannot see whether an object is red or green, he ought to be able to understand what the words mean, because meaning must be independent of the facts. On the other hand, only someone who can see red and green things can learn what the words mean, so the meanings of the words must be the properties things which are red or green have, and which we see. Or, perhaps they must be the 'ideas' we obtain when we see these things — and the blind must be 'given' something. And we are thus torn between absurdities. In fact the ability to discriminate colour is a precondition for acquisition of the ability to use colour predicates, and it is the former the blind lack — samples are of no use to them. So too the colour blind man cannot distinguish samples which we use as paradigms for two quite distinct colours: red and green — there is simply something we can do which he cannot, and hence he cannot fully grasp the use of these words. Our samples are of no use to him, and hence he cannot learn what others can.

Possession of a common colour vocabulary by a linguistic group requires both agreement in definitions and agreement in judgements. We must agree on usable paradigms to fulfil the role of samples in teaching contexts — this provides a check on shared definitions of colour predicates. We must also be in broad agreement in our colour judgements — for this provides a check on shared methods of application of the terms defined in an ostensive definition. To that extent agreement in concepts (meanings, definitions) is not independent of agreement in truth (judgement). Both these kinds of agreement presuppose common discriminatory capacities.

[1]   The passage should be collated with *Investigations*, sections 53, 73; *Zettel*, sections 546–8, 552; and *Blue and Brown Books*, p. 89. For discussions of the issue see J. Hintikka, 'Wittgenstein on Private Language: Some Sources of Misunderstanding' *Mind*, lxxviii (1969), pp. 423–5; A. J. P. Kenny, *Wittgenstein*, (Allen Lane, 1973) pp. 190 ff; P. M. S. Hacker, *Insight and Illusion: Wittgenstein on Philosophy and the Metaphysics of Experience* (Oxford, 1972) pp. 234 ff.

[2]   This is not to say that the blind cannot have a partial grasp of colour concepts. They may apprehend aspects of their logical form, i.e. their combinatorial possibilities, their kinship to e.g. heat predicates, their aesthetic significance, etc. (Cf. P. T. Geach, *Mental Acts* (London, 1957) pp. 35–6). But possession of a concept is a capacity, and the blind lack an essential element involved in possession of colour concepts, namely the ability to apply them non-evidentially to experience.

Hence the criteria for whether a person has grasped a particular colour concept e.g. 'red' consist of whether he will, when asked what 'red' means, pick out samples which *we*, standard speakers of the language, would also be willing to pick out, and also whether, when asked to bring something red, or to collect all the red things in the room, he will do so in a way in which we likewise would. In short we check his conceptual ability precisely by reference to agreement in judgements and in definitions.

It is noteworthy that contrary to Locke's idealist semantics colour predicates are logically prior to colour appearance predicates (i.e. ξ looks such-and-such a colour) and that the latter are quite different from, though related to, 'ξ looks such-and-such a colour to X'. The concepts of being a certain colour (e.g. red), looking thus, looking thus to a person (as well as looking thus to me), normal conditions of observation and normal observer are tightly interwoven. But being such-and-such a colour is the fundamental notion.[1] We teach a normal observer i.e. a child with normal discriminatory capacities, what it is for something to be e.g. red, by presenting him with samples in normal conditions of observation. But we do not define 'being red' by reference to any specification of normal observers or to specification of normal conditions of observation. These are the background conditions for teaching the meanings of these expressions, not part of what is taught. Similarly, in these conditions the red things we present will look red to the learner, but what he learns in the initial situation is 'ξ is red', not 'ξ looks red'. Not only are 'normal conditions of observation' and 'normal observer' not part of the meaning of 'ξ is red', as might be supposed by someone who defined being red as looking red to the normal observer in normal observation conditions, but 'normal conditions of observation' and 'normal observer' are themselves defined by reference to the logically prior concepts of being a given colour and looking a given colour. Normal conditions of observation are those conditions, whatever they may be, under which, e.g. red things look red, and the normal observer is he who can, under normal conditions of observation, pick out e.g. red things i.e. he to whom red things in normal circumstances, look red. Hence the necessary truth that red things normally look red − or more generally that things normally appear the way they are.

This is not to suggest that we could not teach the colour vocabulary by reference to things which only look thus but are not. We could do this by covertly using a whiteboard and differently coloured spectacles, or colour projections. But this would invite confusion when we came to teach the distinction between being and looking. What is that distinction, and how is

[1]   This Wittgensteinian line of thought has been recently discussed in the philosophical literature; see e.g. G. E. M. Anscombe, 'The Intentionality of Sensation', in R. Butler (ed.), *Analytical Philosophy*, 2nd series pp. 172 ff.; D. W. Hamlyn, 'Seeing Things as They Are', Inaugural Lecture, Birkbeck College (London, 1964).

it to be explained? It might be thought that the correct move here would be to claim that looking C is looking as a thing that is C looks to normal observers in normal observation conditions.[1] The claim is true, indeed tautologous. Moreover I shall utilise the formula at a later stage; but it is not, I think, helpful for present purposes. For it invokes normality conditions in explaining the concept of looking thus and so; but, if the above suggestion is correct, the concept of normality conditions itself is anchored in the internal relation between appearance and reality. Furthermore the claim presupposes an independent grasp of the notion of 'the way a thing looks'. Is there an alternative route which will preserve the insight intact?

The dominant use of 'looks C' non-logically implies the fulfilment of a doubt-or-denial condition, which condition is, as Grice has shown, cancellable.[2] The concept of looking thus and so makes room for the possibility that things should be other than they look; the possibility — but, just because the doubt-or-denial condition is cancellable, not the necessity. This feature is worth examining.

The assertion conditions of categorical colour ascriptions are trivial, involving mere recognition. Of course, the circumstances in which such underived ascriptions are appropriate include such facts as that normal conditions obtain, that the speaker is a normal perceiver, that the object in question looks (and looks to him) as he says it is. But these facts do not have to be subsumable under concepts available to the speaker prior to the possibility of his mastering the use of colour predicates.

To be sure, rightfully asserted immediate colour ascriptions are still defeasible. One obvious ground for denial is the obtaining of an aberrant circumstance e.g. a coloured light shining on the object in question. Recognition of such a condition is indeed a ground for employing appearance statements of the kind which are our present concern. It is not surprising that the standard way of teaching the novel concept of looks C to someone who has mastered the concept of being C is by presenting him with a relatively aberrant circumstance of observation which, despite appearances, leads us to withold the predicate 'ξ is C' and apply 'ξ looks C'. We do not teach the learner the normal conditions — we rely on them; we teach him to identify the abnormal conditions which justify the assertion that something looks C but is not. Yet though this line of investigation seems promising, we must budget for the fact that the doubt-or-denial condition is defeasible, and that one may correctly apply 'ξ looks C' not only when aberrant conditions defeat the assertion 'ξ is C', but also when it is undefeated.

---

1   G. E. M. Anscombe, *loc. cit.*
2   H. P. Grice, 'The Causal Theory of Perception', *Proceedings of the Aristotelian Society*, suppl. vol. (1961). Grice's discussion is not, of course, confined to colours, but the above remarks are.

In the case of immediate perceptual (recognitional) colour judgements there is no gap between believing that one is in a position to judge what colour a thing is, and rightfully (but not necessarily truly) believing it to be C. The fact that a speaker makes such a colour judgement implies that he believes that he is in a position to make that judgement. Given the way colour predicates are explained, *actually* to be in a position to make an underived colour judgement requires that normal observation conditions obtain. For if these conditions were not normal, he would not be in a position to assert, on the basis of recognition alone, that the object is C (for it would not look C, nor, other things being equal, would it look C to him). Of course, he might believe himself to be in such a position.

By contrast an immediate judgement of colour appearance does not require that normal conditions of observation obtain, nor that the speaker believes they do. Nor does it require that they do not obtain, or that they be believed not to obtain. Colour appearance statements are assertable whether or not colour statements are assertable. The defeat of the assertion conditions for a colour statement by presence of a recognised aberrant condition does not defeat the corresponding objective appearance statement. The latter is defeated only by subjective aberrant conditions, necessitating retreat to statements of subjective appearances (*infra*). Despite the fact that the propriety of asserting a colour appearance statement is not affected by presence or absence of normal observation conditions, asserting 'It looks C' rather than 'It is C' suggests that the speaker has some specific reason for preferring to assert the weaker appearance statement rather than the stronger colour statement. Hence the attachment of the doubt-or-denial condition. But this is cancellable, and if cancelled (as in 'This looks red, and indeed it is red') *does* imply that the speaker believes that *no* aberrant conditions obtain. Hence we teach the language learner to use 'ξ looks C' not only when recognising aberrant conditions defeating the assertion 'ξ is C', but also when the conditions are appropriate for a straightforward colour statement.

The way things look is as public as the way things are. But having added this first articulation to the language we can add another – the further concept of the way things look to a person. Again we must beware of confusing the background with the foreground. The initial learning situation in which the meaning of 'red' was taught could only succeed if what was presented looked red (and indeed looked red to the learner), but what was taught was (part of) the use of 'ξ is red'. So too when we taught the use of 'ξ looks red', we relied on the object's looking red to the learner – but we were not teaching him the more sophisticated concept of looking red to a person. The latter, like all person referring psychological predicates, must involve a double-pronged move. For what must be learnt now is both 'ξ looks red to A' and also 'ξ looks red to me'. And this involves a new set of moves – for hitherto what was taught was mere recognition of circumstances which justify a criterionless assertion of 'ξ is red' or 'ξ looks red'. But the assertion 'ξ looks red to A' requires learning grounds for its assertion. These lie in the behaviour and circumstances of A — paradigmatically A's behaviour (discriminatory behaviour) and his utterances when confronted by something that either is, or looks red — and later his behaviour and utterances independently of being so confronted. As in all such cases self-ascription presupposes the possibility, in virtue of command of the justifying criteria, of other-ascription. My assertion that something looks red to me is criterionless but its intelligibility presupposes cognizance of the criteria for asserting that something looks red to another. Likewise, although what is red normally looks red, and what looks red normally looks red to me, the new articulation makes room for the possibility of my asserting that some thing looks red to me although it does not look red (because I know of some subjective aberrant condition), and *a fortiori* for my rightfully asserting that something looks red to me, although unbeknownst to me it neither looks red nor is red.

If this outline of the *ordo essendi* of compound predicates of the kind in question is correct it is easy to see how the doctrine of the subjectivity of secondary qualities inverts the conceptual structure. The anthropocentricity of the secondary quality i.e. the fact that the concept of the quality presupposes a human perceptual discriminatory ability, is confused with subjectivity. The link with a paradigmatic sample which must be discriminable is, *via* the idealist semantics of seventeenth century representationalism, misunderstood to yield the doctrine of private ostensive definition. The fact that the sample is best conceived to belong to the method of representation is distortedly reflected in the thought that the sample is mental — i.e. belongs to the content of the mind rather than to its structure. Consequently the logical order is inverted, and the private i.e. subjective appearance is taken to be prior to the public i.e. both objective appearance and objective quality.

Thus far some lessons to be learnt from Wittgenstein. But it is well to be warned of the difficulties inherent in seemingly simple problems. Of the thrust towards subjectivity in respect of colour Wittgenstein wrote:

> The atmosphere surrounding this problem is terrible. Dense mists of language are situated about the crucial point. It is almost impossible to get through to it.[1]

4. CLEANING UP

Let us employ the material furnished to us by Wittgenstein to see whether

---

[1]   Wittgenstein 'Notes for Lectures on Private Experience and Sense Data' *Philosophical Review* (1968) p. 306.

the 'imagined' possibilities of inverted spectra are coherent or not. I shall turn first to Locke's suggestion.

Objects $X_1 \ldots X_n$ are the class of red objects, $Y_1 \ldots Y_n$ that of green ones. A identifies Xs as red, Ys as green. So does B. A contends that Xs normally look red and that Ys normally look green. So does B. But we are asked to entertain the possibility that what A calls 'looks red to me' is the same ('experiential content') as what B calls 'looks green to me'. So A's language, if translated into B's, would yield the result that whatever looks red to A looks green to B. Or — to put it another way — the kind of experience A has when he sees an X is the same kind of experience as that which B has when he sees a Y. To be sure, A's identifying Xs as red involves a similar predicate switch (he means by 'red' what B means by 'green'). For we are not asked to entertain the thought that A claims that oddly enough red things look green to him, but rather that he claims that red things look red, only in fact — from God's viewpoint — it is evident that 'looking red' for A is 'looking green' for B.

We can examine this supposal by following Wittgenstein's guidelines. The anchor which will hold us secure is what A understands by colour expressions. Does A know what 'red' means? We ask him what the word means and he points at the colour of an X, saying 'This is red'. We ask him to bring a red object, and he brings an X. When he asks us to bring a red object, and we bring an X, he is satisfied. So he does know what 'red' means.

Nevertheless, we may feel, the question is — how does red look to him? And that question, we think, must somehow be unanswerable by everyone except A. For to know how red looks to him we should have to be able to 'look into his mind'. It is here that we become confused, conflating the logical privacy of ownership of experience with a putative epistemic privacy. To be sure only he can have the experience of something looking red to him — B cannot have the experience of something looking red to A. Or rather — the only sense we can give to this deformed expression is that B can, of course, have the experience of seeing A look at (and notice) something that looks red (and perhaps hear him say 'That looks red'). But if A knows that X looks red to him, then he can tell B, and then B will know too. For A to know this he must not only know the meaning of colour words, but also of the more complex expressions built up out of them.

We have seen that A knows what e.g. 'red' means. Does he know what 'ξ looks red' means? We must call upon him to manifest his knowledge of its meaning i.e. his ability to use the expression 'That looks red' correctly. Since he knows what 'ξ is red' means, nothing could be simpler. A must point to an X, and say that Z, which he claims looks red, looks the way X looks (in normal conditions of observation). And that, barring any further aberrations, suffices. Command of concepts of appearances rests firmly upon prior mastery of concepts of actualities. Given that we now know that A can use both 'ξ is red' and 'ξ looks red' correctly, and that he is confronted in normal conditions either by a red object, or an object that looks red but is not, and asserts that it looks red (or that it looks red to him), we are in a position to assert that the object looks red to A. What more could we want?

What then remains of the alleged possibility that the experience A calls 'looking red (to me)' is in fact the same kind of experience as that which B calls 'looking green (to me)', only A (unlike B) has that experience when he looks at Xs? Nothing at all. The very supposition derived from confusing logical with epistemic privacy, sample belonging to the method of representation with object represented thereby, discriminability of sample which is requisite for its usability with its subjectivity and linguistic capacity with mental state. Once the threads are disentangled and kept apart the Lockean supposition is clearly empty. The case of Lockean inversion gives no grounds at all for asserting any perceptual or conceptual differences. The most we can budget for is the supposition that red things should *sometimes* look green to A (i.e. look to him the way green things do) and that he should say so. This is indeed possible.

Lockean inversion traded on the notion that the meanings of colour words are in some sense hidden, that only A knows that 'ξ looks red to me (A)' means, and that what he means cannot be fully conveyed to another, just because it is so well hidden — what better hiding place could be found than the mind? The other envisaged possibilities present different problems, for they allow us past confirmation of A's previous mastery of colour grammar, recognise that this is an ability, and argue that the ability is unimpaired by the perceptual accident of a sudden inversion. Tackling this proves more difficult.

Overnight spectrum inversion suggests that it makes sense to suppose that grass should look green to A yesterday, but red today, that poppies should look red to A yesterday and green today, and so too symmetrically for all other coloured objects, even though objects have changed neither colour nor objective appearance. The wrong way to handle the supposition is to use the notion of subjectively looking C as a lever. If we ask how grass looked to him yesterday, A will reply 'the way that looks to me now' pointing at a poppy. Contrariwise, if we ask how poppies looked to him yesterday, A will reply similarly, pointing at grass. From this we might conclude that A's 'subjective spectrum' has become 'inverted'. But is the conclusion so obviously correct?

It is given that A's perception was normal, his mastery of colour grammar firm and his memory unimpaired. The crucial question is whether the behaviour he is evincing now is compatible with the assumption that his mastery of colour grammar is constant. It is acknowledged that normal perceptual competence is a prerequisite for mastery of colour grammar.

But once acquired, it seems, why should the perceptual abnormality involved in the alleged inversion impair the linguistic competence, especially when the abnormality does not impair the structure of the discriminatory capacity?

The first move to try is to test *A*'s use of the elementary colour terms. *Prima facie*, mastery of colour concepts is shown, *inter alia*, by picking out the right paradigms. *Ex hypothesi*, *A* will err systematically and symmetrically. Should we judge that he does not know what 'red', 'green' etc. mean? After all, every non-inductive identification he makes (when given a simple colour chart which precludes inductive correlation) is wrong.

Against this hasty judgement, however, the following considerations may be pitted. A person wearing coloured sunglasses will similarly misidentify samples, yet we do not judge his conceptual competence to be affected while wearing sunglasses. To this the reply is that we do not judge his discriminatory capacity to be affected either, merely that it is impeded. One's ability to run is not impaired by e.g. being tied up — when one is tied up one cannot exercise it, but the ability is unaffected. An extrinsic limitation upon the exercise of an ability, whether by way of coloured glasses or by way of ropes, is not tantamount to loss of the ability. But the spectrum inversion is, in some sense, an intrinsic limitation. To this the riposte is that a person suffering from jaundice does (allegedly) suffer an intrinsic, if temporary, impairment of his discriminatory capacities, but is his command of colour terms impaired? Certainly his non-inductive identifications will be awry. But it is noteworthy that his errors will not be uniform. Rather, he will be unable to discriminate colour differences which normal perceivers can. In this respect he will resemble the colour blind, and differ from the inverted spectrum case. However, unlike the colour blind cases, we confidently claim (so it seems), that it is yellow that e.g. white looks to him. Whereas to the red-green colour blind red-and-green does not look uniformly red nor uniformly green, only uniform. So it seems that we can either agree that his command of some colour terms e.g. white, is impaired, because 'he does not know the difference between white and yellow', or, affirm that though he cannot distinguish white from yellow, he does know what the words mean. If we take the latter option the question is whether the fact that the impairment *is* an impairment of discrimination *together with* retention of constant points in the range, makes a crucial difference. It is tempting to think so. For the baffling feature of the spectrum inversion is precisely that discrimination is not structurally affected at all. A distinguishes colours exactly as everyone else does. In his case *nothing* looks to him the way it is. The question is whether the conceptual connection between how things subjectively appear and how they are can tolerate this degree of pressure even in the case of a particular person. I shall return to this point below.

A different line of inquiry is worth exploring. A cannot non-inductively identify colour samples. But it is claimed that he does nevertheless know what colour terms mean (he knew yesterday). This must be claimed, since A must know this in order to know that it is red that grass now looks to him and that it is green that poppies look. How does he know this? Such knowledge is not evidential, all that is requisite is mastery of the use of expressions of the form 'ξ looks C to me'. Does A possess this? He should, in explaining e.g. 'ξ looks green to me' point to paradigms for 'green', and claim that for a thing to look green is to look the way these paradigms now look (i.e. in normal conditions). If he does then what does he mean by claiming that poppies look green, or look green to him? Does he mean that they look the same colour as grass, that he cannot distinguish grass from poppies in respect of colour? This is ruled out *ex hypothesi*, for it would be a case of colour blindness, not of colour inversion. So A cannot explain either 'ξ is C' or 'ξ looks C' or 'ξ looks C to me' in the standard way, using an immediately identifiable sample as a fulcrum.

The case of Lockean inversion surreptitiously invoked a mental sample to secure correctness of use of colour terms. The present case finds an equally secure hiding place in the past. To say that poppies, rubies and post boxes look green to him, A explains, is to say that they look to him now the way grass looked to him yesterday. Superficially this is plausible. But it invites the response – how did grass look to you yesterday? A can move in one of two ways. Either he can respond by claiming that it looked the way it was, namely green, in which case he is no better off, since he cannot explain what 'green' means in the requisite way. Alternatively he may reply that grass yesterday looked the way poppies look (to him) today. But this circle is too tight. 'ξ looks C (to me)' must finally be explained by reference to 'ξ is C', and 'ξ looked C (to me) yesterday' must be explained in terms of 'ξ looks C (to me) now', otherwise all leverage is lost. So 'ξ looked green yesterday' must be anchored to the use of the present tense and to the use of the simple colour predicate. A can only vindicate his claim that he is using the expression 'ξ looked green to me yesterday' correctly if, when challenged to explain his meaning he can connect past subjective appearances with present ones, present ones with objective appearances and these in turn with things being thus and so. The latter must in turn be tied to a usable paradigm which A must be capable of picking out directly. If A cannot jump these hoops, he needs a lesson; and if he can, his worries are groundless. If he persists in thinking that something has changed, all we can do is to give him a tranquilliser.

Yet another way to put pressure upon the intelligibility of the supposition is to reflect upon the fact that 'ξ looks C to me' is non-inductive evidence for 'ξ is C',[1] that the concept of how things appear is logically related to that of how things are. Among those philosophers who are willing to toy with the notion of a criterial nexus it is generally accepted that criterial support is defeasible, but equally that a global breakdown of criterial support is unintelligible. So, for example, while pain behaviour is a criterion for pain, some pain behaviour may be pretence and some pains may be concealed. But it is not intelligible that all pain behaviour be pretence, or all pains be concealed. And this, if true, seems true of each person, as well as of the totality of persons in a language community. For, if it made sense for A's pain behaviour never to be more than pretence, or for A to be in constant pain but never show it, it is difficult to see how to prevent generalisation. Analogically we might extend the argument to our case. It is not intelligible that things should never appear as they are — for then we would have no conception of how they are, and hence none of how they appear. But is it then intelligible that in one person's case things should, from a certain time, never appear as they are, that red things never look red, green things never look green and so on and yet that the relevant conceptual abilities be retained? For if it be intelligible in the one case how is generalisation to be blocked? A second, intimately related, worry is over the intelligibility of systematic disruptions of the internal relation between 'ξ looks C to me' and 'ξ is C' for insofar as 'ξ looks C to me' will never provide criterial evidence for A's asserting 'ξ is C' is this breakdown consistent with the retention of sense of 'ξ looks C to me'? Why should we be so confident that it is red that green looks to A, when nothing red looks red?

Each of these lines of exploration can be probed much farther, and many further thrusts and ripostes can be exchanged. I shall, however, abandon them and turn to an attempt to outflank the general strategy in the arguments hitherto examined.

5. BLOCKING A DIFFERENT ROUTE

The strategy employed in trying to show the two main suppositions of spectrum inversion to be incoherent rested primarily upon the availability of conventional paradigms which play an essential role in our criteria of identity for colours and in our grounds for ascribing mastery of colour concepts to people. It is by reference to agreed paradigms that we can give

---

[1]   This form of connection between the relevant kinds of statement is itself open to question. Wittgenstein adopted such an analysis in the *Blue Book*, but silently dropped it in the *Investigations* for good, though not obviously conclusive /reasons. More recently the form of the analysis provides the core of P. F. Strawson's illuminating defence of the causal theory of perception, *Freedom and Resentment and Other Essays* (Methuen, 1974) ch. 4.

sense to the expressions 'same colour' and 'different colour', as well as to 'red', 'green' etc. We can then give sense to 'ξ looks C' as well as 'ξ looks C to A' and 'ξ looks C to me'. These in turn enable us to use the more complex expressions 'ξ looks the same colour as ζ' as well as 'ξ looks the same colour as ζ to A as to B (or to me)'. Moreover, the use of the past tense locutions likewise depends upon the availability of criteria of identity for the corresponding present tense ones.

This point can be brought out clearly by consideration of an ingenious manoeuvre which attempts to by-pass the main thrust of the previous arguments. Could we not imagine a person with normal colour discriminatory capacity who possesses the concepts of being coloured, being colour indiscriminable and colour discriminable, but who lacks any concepts of colour determinates? If so, cannot we imagine such a person suffering a sudden spectrum inversion? Let us suppose that the class of objects $X_1 \ldots X_n$ is a complete class of colour indistinguishable objects, and so too for $Y_1 \ldots Y_n$, but, of course, any X is colour-distinguishable from any Y. Why could this person – A – not wake up one morning to find that although all Xs and all Ys are still symmetrically distinguishable, Xs now look (to him) colour indistinguishable from Ys yesterday, and Ys now look (to him) colour indistinguishable from Xs yesterday, and so too symmetrically for all other classes?

The ingenuity of this supposition of spectrum inversion derives from the fact that it deprives us of one of our main strategic weapons in combatting the persistent empiricist, namely the possibility of exploiting the role of samples in explaining the sense of colour words, in determining the understanding of those words, and in determining via our conventions of application criteria for sameness of colour. In so doing, however, it likewise deprives us of our ordinary criteria for identity and difference of colour over time. But it appears to compensate for this by giving us criteria for colour indistinguishability.

The general idea is that A knows what it is for two objects to be colour indistinguishable – any pair of objects which we would take as indistinguishable in colour A would too. When asked to collect exactly matching pairs, he successfully does so. He *a fortiori* also knows what it is to be coloured – he rightly says of ordinary glass, or of clear water, that they are colourless, and of other extended objects that they are coloured.

It is not obvious that the concept of colour does not presuppose the concepts of determinate colours, that 'colour' is not akin to a variable of which the specific colours are values. Indeed, this must be demonstrable if one wants to argue, as I think is most plausible, that every colour grammar is complete, and that it makes no sense to speak of discovering new colours (although perhaps not new shades). But I shall not explore this difficult route now.

The path I should like to suggest as leading to the conclusion that this form of the supposition of the possibility of spectrum inversion is incoherent involves the availability of criteria of identity of colour over time. Just as 'ξ is C' is logically prior to 'ξ looks C' which is in turn prior to 'ξ looked C', so too 'ξ is colour-indistinguishable (or distinguishable) from ζ' must be logically prior to 'ξ looks colour-indistinguishable from ζ'. So I shall begin by examining 'ξ is colour-indistinguishable from ζ', and defer 'ξ looks colour-indistinguishable from ζ' until later.

What are the grounds for asserting that X_1, and X_2 are the same colour? Simply that they both fall within the extension of some colour predicate C i.e. that the statements $C X_1$ and $C X_2$ are true, and hence that X_1 is the same colour as X_2, namely C (note that we are talking of sameness of colour, not of indiscriminability). What are the grounds for asserting that X_1 is now the same colour as it was at t_1 and a different colour from Y_1 at t_1? Simply that X_1 is now C and was, at t_1, C too, and of course that Y_1 at t_1 was not C ('t_1' indicating some past moment of time).

It is plausible to think that the capacity to make diachronic statements of colour identity presupposes the capacity to make synchronic statements of colour identity, which in turn involves a capacity to make simple statements of colour. Given all this, a speaker can go on to make the same moves with 'ξ looks C'.

But if we are deprived of the use of colour predicates, and the use of colour paradigms to provide an anchor whereby to check the former, are the envisaged moves in our final story coherent? It *seems* that we have grounds in the use of pairs of samples, for assertions of current colour-indistinguishability and distinguishability. And *if* that is correct, it seems that we can make sense of past tense assertions of colour-indistinguishability i.e. 'X_1 was colour-indistinguishable from X_2 at t_1' can be asserted by anyone with mnemonic ability who has mastered the present tense assertion and who has, in general, a grasp of the use of tenses. So far, at any rate, there appears to be no difference between him and the person who has full command of the colour vocabulary and asserts that X_1 was C at t_1. But how can we give sense to the expression: X_1 now is colour-indistinguishable from X_1 at t_1 (or from Y_1 at t_1)? X_1 at t_1 is no longer available for display.

Of course, it seems that the situation is no different in essentials from asserting that X_1 now is the same, or a different, colour from yesterday. For here too X_1 yesterday is no longer available for display – we rely on memory (and of course on our knowledge of relative colour constancy, and on confirmatory judgements of others). And so too it seems in the problematic case – we have given an application to 'ξ is colour-indistinguishable from ζ', to its past tense version, to 'ξ is coloured', and we know what an X (be it what object it may) is. But, as Wittgenstein ironically remarks

> Perhaps a logician will think: The same is the same — how identity is established is a psychological question (High is high — it is a matter of psychology that one sometimes *sees*, and sometimes *hears* it).[1]

The difficulty, of course, is that we have so far only explained 'ξ is colour-indistinguishable from ζ' in the present tense, and hence in the past tense, but have not explained its use in statements of the form 'ξ at t_1 is colour-indistinguishable from ζ now'.

In our colour grammar the use of 'X_1 is now the same colour as it was yesterday' presupposes the use of 'X_1 is now C', 'X_1 is the same colour as Y, (namely C)' and 'X_1 was C yesterday'. The resources of the story give us 'X_1 is now colour-indistinguishable from Y_1' and 'X_1 was yesterday colour-indistinguishable from Y_1' and their negations. Will this allow us to give sense to 'X_1 today is colour-indistinguishable from ξ yesterday'?

Again, at first glance it *seems* so. If we are in a position to assert 'X_1 was colour-indistinguishable from Y_1 yesterday' and also to assert 'X_1 is now colour-distinguishable from Y_1' it would seem that we *must* conclude that either X_1 has changed colour overnight or that Y_1 has changed colour overnight (or that both have changed (albeit in different ways)). Hence it *seems* that we can conclude either that X_1 is now colour-indistinguishable from X_1 yesterday and hence that Y_1 is now colour-distinguishable from Y_1 yesterday or that X_1 is now colour-distinguishable from X_1 yesterday and hence that Y_1 is now colour-indistinguishable from Y_1 yesterday. And *if* we can do this, why can't we claim that X_1 was yesterday colour-distinguishable from Y_1 yesterday, and is also so today, but that X_1 today is colour-distinguishable from X_1 yesterday and colour-indistinguishable from Y_1 yesterday, and so too for Y_1?

Note that so far we have not even budgetted for spectrum-inversion. All we are exploring is symmetrical colour change overnight, and the possibility of expressing it in the limited colour grammar of the story. But let us continue to explore the matter further, and defer for a moment the spectrum inversion which supposes not that things have changed colour, but that the way they look to me has changed in the now familiar supposed fashion.

Are things as the superficial analysis suggests? I think not. Let us take first colour change which is not symmetrical (subscript 't' will indicate yesterday, 'n'-now). We are given that $X_t = Y_t$ and that $X_n \neq Y_n$. Note that it is *only* by reference to this that we can make sense of statements of

---

[1] *Philosophical Investigations*, section 377.

diachronic colour-distinguishability or indistinguishability. We are obviously inclined to infer a complex disjunction – either X has changed, or Y has changed or both have changed differently i.e.

$(X_n \underset{c}{=} X_t \ \& \ Y_n \underset{c}{\neq} Y_t) \ v \ (X_n \underset{c}{\neq} X_t \ \& \ Y_n \underset{c}{=} Y_t) \ v \ (X_n \underset{c}{\neq} X_t \ \& \ Y_n \underset{c}{\neq} Y_t \ )$ or

more briefly $(X_n \underset{c}{\neq} X_t) \ v \ (Y_n \underset{c}{\neq} Y_t)$. We want to infer this on the grounds that given the premise of prior indistinguishability and current distinguishability, it cannot be the case that $(X_n \underset{c}{=} X_t) \ \& \ (Y_n \underset{c}{=} Y_t)$. But can we so infer? It is noteworthy that the inference is valid in classical logic, but is not in intuitionistic logic. According to intuitionistic logic the inference from $-P \ v \ -Q$ to $- (P \ \& \ Q)$ is valid, but the converse: $- (P \ \& \ Q) \vdash (-P \ v \ -Q)$ is not, for if we are not in a position to assert one of the disjuncts, we are not in a position to assert the disjunction.

This is not the place to debate the comparative merits and demerits of classical and intuitionistic logic. Independently of this matter it can be seen that with the given resources we can only assign sense to statements of diachronic colour-distinguishability and indistinguishability by reference to contrasts between current and past distinguishability and indistinguishability. But if we now move from non-symmetrical change to symmetrical change, we saw off the branch upon which we are sitting. For now it is being suggested that $X_t \underset{c}{\neq} Y_t$ and $X_n \underset{c}{\neq} Y_n$, but that $X_n \underset{c}{=} Y_t$ and $Y_n \underset{c}{=} X_t$. But we can give no sense to this claim in this context, for the assertion of diachronic colour-discriminability and indiscriminability can, with the limited available conceptual resources, rest on nothing other than the contrast between past distinguishability and present indistinguishability (or vice versa) – which does not obtain in this case.

A striking feature of the story is that colour-indiscriminability was introduced to fulfil the role of sameness of colour. 'The substitution of "identical" for "the same" . . .', Wittgenstein remarked, 'is another typical expedient in philosophy'.[1] But criteria of identity for colours are provided by our use of samples. In the absence of concepts of determinate colours we lack criteria for sameness and difference of colour. The story tried to compensate by giving us paired samples by reference to which we assign sense to 'ξ is colour-indiscriminable from ζ'.[2] But this arguably fails to give us grounds for assertion of diachronic statements of colour-distinguishability and indistinguishability and certainly fails to fulfil this role in the case of alleged symmetrical change. And it fails to do so precisely through lack of concepts of colour determinates with their attendant criteria of identity.

If the argument so far is correct then the suggestion of possible

---

[1]   *Op. cit.*, section 254.
[2]   It is noteworthy, incidentally, that indiscriminability, unlike identity, is not transitive – a further chink in the armour of our adversary that might be explored.

spectrum inversion in this case can be quickly dismissed: 'ξ looks to me colour-indiscriminable from ξ' is parasitic upon 'ξ looks colour-indiscriminable from ζ'. The past tense expressions are parasitic upon the present tense ones. But how can we budget for 'ξ looked to me yesterday colour-indistinguishable from the way ζ looks to me now'? Clearly only by reliance on the logically prior expressions already discussed. If X_n looks to me colour-indistinguishable from Y_n (i.e. looks to me the way two objects which *are* colour-indistinguishable look) and if X_t looked to me colour distinguishable from Y_t, then *if* our anti-realist scruples can be put aside, we can *perhaps* give sense to diachronic statements of apparent, subjective, colour-distinguishability and indistinguishability. But this is not enough for the supposition of an inverted spectrum. For this alleges that it is intelligible that X was colour-distinguishable from Y, still is colour-distinguishable from Y, and that X now is colour-indistinguishable from X yesterday, Y now is colour-indistinguishable from Y yesterday, but that it should appear to me that X now is colour-distinguishable from X yesterday and indistinguishable from Y yesterday, and also that Y now looks to me colour-distinguishable from Y yesterday but colour-indistinguishable from X yesterday. But the *only* conditions we could establish as giving sense, with these limited conceptual resources, to diachronic statements of colour-distinguishability and indistinguishability depended upon the fact that if two objects were colour-indistinguishable and are now distinguishable one or both must have changed, and since this condition is *not* met in this supposal of inverted spectrum, we *cannot* give any sense to the corresponding diachronic statement of looking colour-indistinguishable. And so the supposal is quite literally senseless.

If the foregoing arguments are correct then the inverted spectrum supposition is incoherent. The Lockean case is, I think, decisively refuted. The subsequent cases of sudden inversion are highly dubious and although the arguments I have brought against them are perhaps inconclusive, they are, I hope, suggestive; at any rate sufficiently so to arouse our suspicions. The alternative route which by-passed the controls furnished by samples proved to be illusory.

Locke concludes his discussion by reminding his reader that the supposition of actual spectrum inversion

if it could be proved is of little use, either for the improvement of our knowledge or conveniency of life, and so we need not trouble ourselves to examine it.

We have troubled ourselves to examine it in some detail, not its actuality, but its logical possibility and so intelligibility. If the argument is right, or at least points in the right direction then we may rest assured that its actuality cannot be proved because it is not logically possible. To be sure, it is of little use for the improvement of our knowledge or conveniency of our life. At best it may improve our knowledge of our knowledge, by helping us to understand the concepts we use. Ought one to ask more of philosophy?

3

HUME AND WITTGENSTEIN

Oswald Hanfling

It is well known that Wittgenstein's reading of the philosophical classics was patchy. He left unread a large part of the literature which most philosophers would regard as essential to a knowledge of their subject. Wittgenstein gave an interesting reason for his non-reading of Hume. He said that he could not sit down and read Hume, because he knew far too much about the subject of Hume's writings to find this anything but a torture.[1] In a recent commentary, Peter Hacker has taken this to show that 'Wittgenstein seems to have despised Hume'. Hume, he adds, 'made almost every epistemological and metaphysical mistake Wittgenstein could think of'.[2]

There is a good deal to be said for this contrast. To understand what the later Wittgenstein was arguing against, we can, in many cases, do no better than turn to the writings of Hume. And often we can best understand the nature and implications of Hume's views by considering them in the light of Wittgenstein's later philosophy. But perhaps this is not what Wittgenstein had in mind when he gave his reason for not being able to read Hume. Perhaps what he meant was that Hume was *too close* to his own position. Is this conceivable? In what follows I shall try to show that it is.

In presenting my argument I shall, inevitably, be selective; preferring those passages from the two philosophers which favour my thesis to those that go against it. I have no desire, however, to dispute the validity of the contrasts that are usually drawn between Hume and Wittgenstein. My aim is only to show that they also had certain fundamental things in common, and that these things are important enough to be worth bringing out.

To begin with, consider some general points of style and attitude, for

---

[1]   In a conversation with Karl Britton. See 'Portrait of a Philosopher', in *Ludwig Wittgenstein, The Man and his Philosophy*, ed. K. T. Fann, p. 61.

[2]   P. M. S. Hacker, *Insight and Illusion*, p. 218.

example the way in which Hume *wrestles* with his material. It is true that he has many long passages of 'straight' exposition, in which he seems to reach definitive conclusions with confident ease. But against this there are the well-known passages, especially in the Appendix to the *Treatise*, and in the Conclusion of Book I, in which he reveals his uncertainties, confesses the shortcomings of his work, and imparts to us a sense of intense struggle. These features bear comparison with what we find in the work of the later Wittgenstein. So also does the way in which certain key topics come up again and again in different parts of the work; in Hume's case, topics like belief and causality; in Wittgenstein's, topics like the idea of a mental process or entity. The sense of struggle that we find here is not a mere device for developing the argument in a more interesting way. We are made to feel that the problems of Hume and Wittgenstein really are, for them, problems of great difficulty and of central importance.

Both Hume and Wittgenstein were concerned with what we might call the 'mental welfare' of the philosopher. They saw and described the bizarre mental states which lay in wait for anyone who engaged in philosophical reflection along certain very tempting lines. And they saw that what was needed was not (as G.E. Moore sometimes thought) the refutation of a wrong conclusion, but rather some kind of therapy. It was not that the sceptical philospher, for example, had simply made an error in his reasoning, and could therefore be corrected; it was rather that his view, though in a sense unassailable, was set in the wrong light. What was needed was to be rescued from seeing things in a false perspective, from attaching the wrong sort of significance to the premises and conclusions of the sceptic's argument.

SCEPTICISM

Only a superficial or biassed reading of Hume's work could lead anyone to conclude that Hume was little more than a sceptic, that scepticism is his main conclusion. Such an interpretation is hardly conceivable since the appearance of Kemp Smith's essay on Hume in 1905.[1] Perhaps it would be an exaggeration to say that Hume was no more a sceptic than Wittgenstein; but I hope to show that there would be *something* in such a claim.

Hume's great aim was to show that beliefs and morals had their basis in facts of human nature, and his scepticism was intended to further this aim. 'My intention', he wrote,

---

[1]   *Mind* (1905). See also his book, *The Philosophy of David Hume.* I have made much use of these two works. I have also found very useful Richard H. Popkin's essay 'David Hume: His Pyrrhonism and His Critique of Pyrrhonism', *Philosophical Quarterly* (1951) reprinted in *Hume*, ed. V. C. Chappell.

in displaying so carefully the arguments of that fantastic sect [of scepticism], is only to make the reader sensible of the truth of *my* hypothesis.[1]

Again and again Hume makes it clear that his object is not to destroy beliefs and certainties, but rather to lay bare their true nature. He shows that as long as they are disputed on the kind of grounds taken for granted both by the sceptic and by his opponent, the sceptic is bound to win. The moral, for Hume, is not that we must abandon belief, but that we must revise our conception of it. He drives home the sceptical argument as vigorously as he does in order to bring out the need for such revision.

As experience will sufficiently convince anyone, who thinks it worth while to try, that tho' he can find no error in the foregoing [sceptical] arguments, yet he still continues to believe, and think, and reason as usual, he may safely conclude, that his reasoning and belief is some sensation or peculiar manner of conception, which 'tis impossible for mere ideas and reflections to destroy.[2]

The question to be asked is not how scepticism can be refuted, but

how it happens, that even after all we retain a degree of belief, which is sufficient for our purpose, either in philosophy or common life.[3]

Compare now Wittgenstein's treatment of solipsism in *The Blue and Brown Books*. First of all, there is the same dismissal of attempts to refute the solipsist on his own ground.

The trouble with the realist is always that he does not solve but skip the difficulties which his adversaries see.[4]

Wittgenstein drives home the sceptical argument just as vigorously as Hume. It is no answer to say 'that things are as they appear to common sense'.[5] How can I even form the hypothesis 'that anyone else has personal experiences?' Doesn't this, as far as I am concerned, 'transcend all possible experience?' Yet, on the other hand, what do these arguments show about the nature of belief and doubt concerning the reality of other people's experiences? 'Does a realist pity me more than an idealist or a solipsist?'[6]

---

[1] Selby-Bigge edition of Hume's *Treatise*, p. 183. Italics added.
[2] *Treatise*, p. 184.
[3] *Treatise*, p. 185.
[4] *The Blue and Brown Books*, p. 48.
[5] Ibid., p. 46.
[6] Ibid., p. 48.

In these sections Wittgenstein brings out the cast-iron nature of the solipsist's case by considering a variety of examples which might be thought to falsify it (examples of sharing other people's experiences); and rejecting those examples because they do not apply to what the solipsist 'really means'.[1] Thus in the course of Wittgenstein's discussion the solipsist's meaning is refined; we can see what his case really amounts to, and at the same time we learn some important truths about how that which he questions — our ordinary beliefs — may, and may not, be vindicated. We arrive at a conception of them which is, in Hume's words, 'the only one upon which they can stand with any security'.

Of course there are important differences between the two philosophers. Hume's argument is roughly of the following form. If our basic beliefs were founded on reason, then they would be destroyed by philosophical scepticism; therefore they are not founded on reason.[2] There is nothing here, as there is in Wittgenstein, to bring out the peculiar and dubious nature of the sceptic's 'language-game'. Part of the great interest of Wittgenstein's discussion of private languages, and of what he says about meaning and use, lies in its implications for scepticism. By contrast, the philosophy of language is almost entirely lacking from the works of Hume. Nevertheless there are *some* well-known passages in Hume which at least suggest that there is something queer about a use of language which has no effect in any language game that is actually played. It was this lack of an effect, rather than any flaw of reasoning, which in Hume's view devalued Berkeley's arguments.

> That all his arguments, though otherwise intended, are, in reality, merely sceptical, appears from this, *that they admit of no answer and produce no conviction.* Their only effect is to cause that momentary amazement and irresolution and confusion, which is the result of scepticism.[3]

The same idea is evident in a passage from the *Treatise.*

> Shou'd it here be asked me, whether I sincerely assent to this argument, which I seem to take such pains to inculcate, and whether I be really one of those sceptics, who hold that all is uncertain, and that our

[1] 'An innumerable variety of cases can be thought of in which we should say that someone has pains in another person's body', p. 50. On pp. 52–3 he considers an example of feeling pain in another person's tooth, and points out that this is not the kind of thing that the solipsist is denying.

[2] In Hume's moral philosophy the argument runs: If moral judgements were founded on reason, then they would be vulnerable to the moral sceptic; for " 'tis not contrary to reason to prefer the destruction of the whole world to the scratching of my finger" (*Treatise*, 416); therefore they are not founded on reason.

[3] Selby-Bigge edition of Hume's *Enquiries*, p. 155.

judgement is not in *any* thing possest of *any* measures of truth and falsehood; I shou'd reply, that this question is entirely superfluous, and that neither I, nor any other person was ever sincerely and constantly of that opinion . . . Whoever has taken the pains to refute the cavils of this *total* scepticism, has really disputed without an antagonist.[1]

To 'dispute without an antagonist' is, in Wittgenstein's words, to operate a wheel that is not connected to the mechanism.

DESCRIPTION V. JUSTIFICATION (i)

I said earlier that Hume's objective was to establish the true foundations of belief, in place of the kind of spurious foundations which are prey to the attack of the sceptic. What are these true foundations? This takes us to a central and very difficult aspect of Hume's philosophy. It is also a central and very difficult aspect of Wittgenstein's philosophy. What is at the bottom of our basic beliefs — about causes, about the future, about the external world, about morals?

> All these operations are a species of natural instincts, which no reasoning or process of the thought and understanding is able either to produce or to prevent.[2]

A common criticism of Hume has been that he confuses philosophy with psychology, that he answers with psychological facts a question which is not about the fact of belief, but about its justification. There is a genuine difficulty here, a difficulty that Hume's philosophy shares with that of Wittgenstein. But it is important to understand the difficulty correctly, and not to attribute to Hume a gross confusion between things which are, fairly obviously, distinct.

There are two points to be made. In the first place, the kind of 'psychology' that is involved here is not that of an empirical science; Hume is not committing the fallacy of answering conceptual questions by means of empirical research. His 'psychology' is introspective and in that sense *a priori*. He wants us to *notice* that certain things are as he says, not to learn it from him. In this respect Hume's 'psychology' is on the same footing as

---

[1] *Treatise*, p. 183; from the section 'Of scepticism with regard to reason'. Although Hume is better known for his concern about the foundations of inductive inference, his 'Pyrrhonian scepticism' is first directed against the 'demonstrative sciences'. Wittgenstein also is concerned with the foundations of both types of reasoning, and in both cases appeals to facts of nature as ultimate. (See, for example, *Remarks on the Foundation of Mathematics*, p. 63.) I have not thought it useful to keep the two types sharply distinct for the purpose of my discussion.
[2] *Enquiries*, pp. 46–7.

Wittgenstein's 'natural history':

> What we are supplying are really remarks on the natural history of human beings; we are not contributing curiosities however, but observations[1] which no one has doubted, but which have escaped remark only because they are always before our eyes.[2]

The second thing that Hume is not doing is to say that human nature (natural instincts and the like) is something that stands *behind* our basic beliefs and certainties, in such a way as to provide an independent justification for them. His invocation of psychological fact is not intended to answer the demand for justification, but rather to block it. To hold, as Hume does, that basic beliefs are determined by nature is not to say that there is something 'there', behind those beliefs, which stands to them in some kind of relation (whether of justification, causality or whatever); it is simply to say that we do hold these beliefs and hold them in a regular and predictable way. 'That's how we do it.'

The rejection of 'explanation' and 'justification' in favour of 'description' is a fundamental and recurrent theme in Wittgenstein's philosophy. He concludes Part I of the *Brown Book*: 'Our method is *purely descriptive*; the descriptions we give are not hints of explanations.'[3] His aim is to cure us of the urge to go beyond the descriptions, where this can only lead to metaphysical nonsense. The positions of Hume and Wittgenstein are in many ways so closely parallel that it is easy and tempting to expound one with the help of quotations from the other. Thus we can gloss Hume's meaning in the passage from the *Enquiries*, quoted above, by means of Wittgenstein's remark about his certainty that the object before him is a chair:

> I want to conceive [this certainty] as something that lies beyond being justified or unjustified; as it were, as something animal.[4]

Or take the passage in which he speaks of the certainty one has of never having been on the moon.

> Perhaps someone will say 'There must be some principle lying behind our confidence', but what can such a principle achieve? Is it more than a natural law of 'taking for true'?[5]

---

[1]   The German *Feststellungen* does not have the empirical connotations of 'observations'.

[2]   *Philosophical Investigations*, 415. Cf. 109.

[3]   *Blue and Brown Books*, 125.

[4]   *On Certainty*, 359.

[5]   Ibid., 172; my translation.

Wittgenstein's mention of 'natural law' in this connection reminds us of a further aspect of Hume's position. Hume did not merely characterise our beliefs as being part of the workings of nature; he actually formulated some natural laws of "taking for true" ', describing how the mind is caused to hold such and such beliefs. Here again of course — as we shall see when discussing Hume's account of causality — the laws are not something *behind* the facts of nature; they are merely formulations of the observed regularities.

'What does man think for? What use is it?. . . Does man think because he has found that thinking pays?'[1] I can hardly think of a better way of dealing with Wittgenstein's question — and in Wittgenstein's spirit — than by means of a well-known passage from Hume: 'Nature, by an absolute and uncontrollable necessity has determin'd us to judge as well as to breathe and feel'.[2] That, of course, is to block the question rather than to answer it; it is in harmony with what Wittgenstein himself goes on to say: 'It often happens that we only become aware of the important *facts*, if we suppress the question "why?" '[3] This recommendation to suppress the question 'why?' is a central part both of Wittgenstein's and of Hume's outlook; in both philosophers it makes its appearance in a variety of contexts. In the passage I have quoted Wittgenstein is concerned to show that to press the question 'why?' in regard to the fact that man thinks can only lead to a distorted view of what thinking is. For how could such a question be answered (as opposed to being blocked)? 'What would show *why* he thinks?'[4] We must not take it for granted that the question 'why?' can always be asked sensibly. The answer 'man thinks because thinking pays' is a silly answer, given in reply to a silly question.

It is in just this spirit that Hume deals with the question on page 183 of the *Treatise*[5] :

Shou'd it here be ask'd me, whether I sincerely assent to this argument, which I seem to take such pains to inculcate, and whether I be really one of those sceptics, who hold that all is uncertain, and that our judgement is not in *any* thing possest of *any* measures of truth and falsehoood; I shou'd reply, that this question is entirely superfluous, and that neither I, nor any other person was ever sincerely and constantly of that opinion. Nature, by an absolute and uncontrollable necessity has determin'd us to judge as well as to breathe and feel.

---

[1] *PI*, 466—7.
[2] *Treatise*, p. 183.
[3] *PI*, 471.
[4] *PI*, 468.
[5] Previously quoted on pp. 50—1.

The attempt to provide a *general* justification for thinking and judging can only lead to accounts which, on the one hand, dodge the sceptical argument and, on the other, give a ludicrously false picture of the *facts* about thinking; facts of human nature which 'lie beyond being justified or unjustified'.

> The squirrel does not infer by induction that it is going to need stores next winter as well. And no more do we need a law of induction to justify our actions or our predictions.[1]

This assimilation of human nature to animal nature is also to be found in Hume.

> It is certain that the most ignorant and stupid peasants — nay infants, nay even brute beasts — improve by experience, and learn the qualities of natural objects, by observing the effects which result from them. When a child has felt the sensation of pain from touching the flame of a candle, he . . . will expect similar effects [in the future] . . . If you assert, that . . . the child is led into this conclusion by any process of argument or ratiocination, I may justly require you to produce that argument . . . It is not reasoning which engages us to suppose the past resembling the future . . .[2]

BELIEF AND FEELING; GROUNDS AND CAUSES

In the passage just quoted Hume uses the example of someone putting his hand into a flame. The same example is used by Wittgenstein in speaking of our belief in the uniformity of nature.[3] But the resemblance goes deeper than that. One of Hume's main conclusions about belief is his characterisation of it as a 'feeling, or sentiment'.[4] Thus he regards belief as something that happens to us, a 'passion', rather than something for which our reason is answerable. It is because of this that Hume's self-addressed question whether he really assents to the sceptical argument is 'superfluous'. His account of causality, for example, is based on a *causal* theory of belief; it says that certain sets of experiences cause ('determine') the mind to hold such and such beliefs.

Wittgenstein, in the passage about our belief in the uniformity of nature, considers how one might deal with questions about the general justification of beliefs based on past experience. A first move is to say that

---

[1]   *On Certainty*, 287.
[2]   *Enquiries*, p. 39.
[3]   *Philosophical Investigations*, 472 ff.
[4]   See, for example, *Treatise*, p. 624 and *Enquiries*, p. 48.

what 'justification' *means* in such contexts is 'supported by such and such past experience'. But now the question may be asked why we should operate with such a concept of justification. And here Wittgenstein falls back on the *facts* of human nature; he exchanges the vocabulary of grounds and reasons for that of cause and effect.

> If you are surprised at our playing such a game I refer you to the *effect* of a past experience (to the fact that a burnt child fears the fire).[1]
> [Do] I argue to myself: 'Fire has always burned me, so it will happen now too'? Or is the previous experience the *cause* of my certainty, not its ground? Whether the earlier experience is the cause of the certainty depends on the system of hypotheses, of natural laws, in which we are considering the phenomenon of certainty.
> Is our confidence justified? — What people accept as a justification — is shown by how they think and live.
> We expect *this*, and are surprised at *that*. But the chain of reasons has an end.[2]

Hume, as I said, regarded belief as being a 'feeling', or 'sentiment'. Wittgenstein wrote:

> The belief that fire will burn me is of the same kind as the fear that it will burn me.[3]

Like Hume, Wittgenstein regarded the *natural reaction* to the fire as being more basic than any reasoned belief about it. We do not *reason* from past experience, any more than do infants or animals, to arrive at a belief which then guides our reaction; the truth is, rather, that the facts of natural reaction determine what the concepts 'belief' and 'certainty' amount to in these contexts.[4] Wittgenstein's argument in these sections is akin to Hume's famous reversal:

> Perhaps 'twill appear in the end, that the necessary connexion depends on the inference, instead of the inference depending on the necessary connexion.[5]

Hume seeks to show that our inference (e.g. from fire to pain) is not a matter of reasoning from an independent 'necessary connexion'; the truth is, rather, that our association of fire with pain ('the fear that it will burn me') determines what such a 'necessary connexion' amounts to.

[1]   *PI*, 480.
[2]   *PI*, 325–6.
[3]   *PI*, 473.
[4]   *PI*, 474.
[5]   *Treatise*, p. 88.

THE GIVEN

'At the foundation of a well-founded belief lies belief that is not founded'.[1] 'The chain of reasons comes to an end'.[2] 'To be sure there is justification; but justification comes to an end.'[3] What Wittgenstein is saying here was also said by Hume; and we find the same idea of 'a chain of reasons' which cannot go on indefinitely. It is there both in Hume's epistemology and in his moral philosophy. Speaking about our belief that Caesar was killed in the senate-house on the ides of March, he claims that this belief is connected by a 'chain of argument' (which he traces) to certain impressions of the senses or memory. This is the stopping point, 'beyond which there is no room for doubt or enquiry'.[4] And in the *Enquiry Concerning the Principles of Morals* he writes:

> Ask a man *why he uses exercise;* he will answer, *because he desires to keep his health.* If you then enquire, *why he desires health,* he will readily reply, *because sickness is painful.* If you push your enquiries farther, and desire a reason *why he hates pain*, it is impossible that he can ever give any . . . It is impossible that there can be a progress *in infinitum*; and that one thing can always be a reason why another is desired. Something must be desirable on its own account.[5]

So far the parallel with Wittgenstein is striking. It is when we consider *what* constitutes 'the given' that we find a big difference between the two philosophers. For Hume, what is given as the terminus of the chain is always some simple thing that is sensed or felt; something like what he called 'impressions of the sense or memory', or some 'internal impression' such as Hume conceived the will to be.

Wittgenstein wrote: 'What has to be accepted, the given, is — so one could say — *forms of life*.'[6] This sentence reflects his rejection of the whole machinery of sense data, and the atomism that went with it. He rejected the empiricist dogma which equated the basic with the simple. In place of Hume's attempt to locate the foundations of knowledge in simple 'impressions', Wittgenstein says, of the *whole 'language-game'* of inductive reasoning, for instance, that

> it is not based on grounds, It is not reasonable (or unreasonable).
> It is there — like our life.[7]

1   *On Certainty*, 253.
2   *PI*, 326; *Zettel*, 301.
3   *On Certainty*, 192.
4   *Treatise*, p. 83.
5   *Enquiries*, p. 293.
6   *PI*, p. 226.
7   *On Certainty*, 559.

And the emotions, so far from being simply 'internal impressions', are described by Wittgenstein as 'modes of this complicated form of life'.[1]

So there is here an important resemblance, and an important difference, between Wittgenstein and Hume. Both of them stressed the need for an end-point in explanation and justification; something had to be accepted as 'given'. If anything was to be justified, then something had to be accepted without justification; something whose validity it would not make sense to question. It is in their conceptions of the nature of the given that a radical difference between the two philosophers shows itself.[2]

WORD AND OBJECT

One of the central things in Wittgenstein's philosophy is what he says about the meaning and the use of a word. Words do not have meanings in virtue of a one to one correspondence between words and objects. The question 'What is the meaning of a word?' is countered by the advice 'Don't ask for the meaning, ask for the use.' It is possible to say various things about the right and wrong uses of a word, and thereby one explains its meaning. But if the question 'What *is* the meaning?' is insisted on, then we are in for trouble. For example, we may be tempted to point to something that is there in front of us, like a piece of furniture, and to identify *it* as the meaning of a word, such as the word 'chair'. Or we may be tempted to *postulate* some entities to fill the role of 'meanings', entities like 'universals' or mental images. An immense amount of philosophical mystification has resulted, through the ages, from the postulation of such entities.

Now all this may seem to be stony ground in which to look for the seeds of a common view between Hume and Wittgenstein. The whole empiricist programme, as originally conceived, was the matching of each word with some item of experience, until the whole stock of our concepts would be accounted for. Was not Hume committed to this programme, and to this conception of the meanings of words? It seems to me that in one important respect Hume broke away from this conception. I am thinking of his treatment of causality.

Hume describes to us, vividly and repeatedly, his efforts to discover some object or quality which would constitute the meaning of 'cause' in a case in which *A* is causing *B*; some entity which stands to the word 'cause'

---

[1]   *PI*, p. 174.
[2]   In this paper I cannot do more than sketch the difference. I have not tried to do justice either to the empiricist notion of 'simple ideas' or to Wittgenstein's notions of a language game and a form of life. For a recent comparison of Hume's and Wittgenstein's ideas about ultimate certainties, see G. E. M. Anscombe, 'Hume and Julius Caesar', *Analysis* (1973).

as the objects *A* and *B* stand to the words '*A*' and '*B*'. He never found such an entity. Hume's way out of that difficulty was, in effect, to describe the *circumstances* in which we call something a cause. A cause, according to Hume, is not a certain item of experience corresponding to the word 'cause'; the truth is rather that we apply that word to an object if the object stands in a certain relationship, on the one hand, to other objects, and on the other hand, to the mind.[1]

That is one side of Hume's account of the concept of causality. But there is another. For Hume could not be content to leave the matter thus. If the cause was not there, in or beside the objects *A* and *B*, then where was it? It was just this kind of question that Wittgenstein kept fighting against. In *Zettel*, referring to our conceptual systems of colours and numbers, he poses the question: 'Do the systems reside in *our* nature or in the nature of things?' '*Not*', he replies, 'in the nature of numbers or colours.'[2] It would, of course, be a disastrous misunderstanding of Wittgenstein to take him to be implying that the systems must (therefore) 'reside in *our* nature'. The point of his negative and apparently evasive answer is to suggest that there is something wrong with the question.[3] Someone who has properly understood what Wittgenstein says about meaning and use will see that the question is 'badly framed'. We can – as Wittgenstein does – reject one of the offered alternatives as certainly wrong; but that doesn't mean that we have to be saddled with the other. There is no *need* for us to answer the question in the terms in which it is posed.

Now Hume does face, and answer, just such a question in connection with causality; and he answers it by coming down squarely on one side. Not being able to find any distinct quality of causation by examining billiard balls and the like, he concludes that it must reside in us; it is 'not in objects', but 'belongs entirely to the soul'.[4] Why must Hume say this? Why can he not be content with his account in terms of the *use* of causal words? The answer, and the other side, as I called it, of Hume's account, lies in the fact that he is not altogether emancipated from the one-to-one correspondence view of the relation between concepts and reality. This is made clear by the cast-iron principle which he repeats at the outset of the

---

[1]   See his two definitions of "cause", *Treatise* p. 170.

[2]   *Zettel*, 357.

[3]   In 358 he continues in a similar vein: 'Then there is something arbitrary about this system? Yes and no. It is akin both to what is arbitrary and to what is non-arbitrary.'

[4]   He reaches a similar conclusion in connection with arithmetic, and in connection with moral and aesthetic concepts. There is a comparison of causality with arithmetic in the *Treatise*, p. 166: 'Thus as the necessity, which makes two times two equal to four, or three angles of a triangle equal to two right ones, lies only in the act of the understanding, by which we consider and compare these ideas; in like manner the necessity or power, which unites causes and effects, lies in the determination of the mind to pass from the one to the other.'

section 'The idea of necessary connexion', and which forms the starting point of his problem: 'We must find some impression, that gives rise to this idea of necessity, if we assert we have really such an idea'.[1] Side by side, then, with his account of the idea of causality in terms of the circumstances for using causal words, we find a statement which satisfies empiricist dogma, namely that causal necessity is 'nothing but an internal impression of the mind . . .'.[2] Where you can't find an external entity to correspond to a given word, you have to postulate an internal one. The tension between the two conceptions is evident in the sentence in which Hume runs them together. After the words just quoted he adds: '. . . or a determination to carry our thought from one object to another'.[3] These two wordings are far from equivalent; the difference between them reflects the difference between the 'correspondence' and the 'use' conceptions of language. Behind the first (that causal necessity is 'nothing but an internal impression') lies the idea that the words must 'stand for' something – 'we must find some impression'; behind the second (the mind being 'determined' to 'carry its thoughts'), the idea that a word is explicable in terms of conditions for its use – in the case of causal necessity, a complex set of conditions involving (according to Hume) past objects as well as present ones, and mental occurences as well as external ones.

The two sides of Hume's account have fared very differently in terms of acceptance. Few have been satisfied with Hume's treatment of the causal nexus as 'an internal impression of the mind'. But there has been widespread acceptance of the view that to call something a 'cause' is to say something about regularities between sets of things, rather than to indicate the presence of a special entity or quality.[4]

OCCULT ENTITIES

One of the many slogan-like utterances for which Wittgenstein has become known is his advice to 'look and see': 'Don't say "There *must* be . . ." – but *look and see*',[5] In the passage from which this quotation is taken Wittgenstein is resisting the temptation to insist that whenever we apply the same word to a set of objects, they must have 'something in common',

---

[1]   *Treatise*, p. 155.
[2]   Ibid., p. 165.
[3]   'Determination' is here used in a passive sense, i.e. the mind being determined *by* the conjoined objects.
[4]   R. B. Braithwaite, in his *Scientific Explanation*, writes: 'The assertion of a subjunctive conditional may be regarded as a summary statement of this whole situation' – a situation, described by Braithwaite, in which the person making the assertion has come to hold certain beliefs in a certain way (p. 297). Braithwaite, who sees his account as a development of Hume's 'constant conjunction' view, explains our causal notions in terms of *the circumstances in which we use* causal language.
[5]   *PI*, 66.

in virtue of which we do so. But the advice to 'look and see' has been taken, rightly, to epitomise Wittgenstein's outlook in a more general way. Throughout his philosophy of language he resists the postulation of a variety of entities and procedures which are supposed to constitute or to confer meaning, by asking us to attend to what actually goes on in our language. And throughout his philosophy of mind (the two are closely connected) he invites us to consider the *facts* of consciousness, rather than to insist that such and such processes 'must be' there.

No doubt it would be paradoxical to describe Wittgenstein as an empiricist. It is no part of my purpose to play down the deep differences which separate him from the empiricist school. Nevertheless the maxim 'look and see', which plays a central role in Wittgenstein's philosophy, has obvious affinities with the programme of classical empiricism. It is, moreover, a maxim that Hume took to heart in his discussion of causality; in his repeated examinations of what is *actually there* in a case in which one thing is regarded as the cause of the other. What Hume is in effect saying is: 'Don't say there *must* be something there (in addition to the constant conjunction of the two things) in virtue of which we say that *A* causes *B*; but *look and see*.' The person who insists that there 'must be' something else 'need not', says Hume, 'put himself to the trouble of inventing any long reasonings; but may at once shew us an instance of a cause, where we discover the power or operating principle.'[1] He accuses his predecessors of giving way, in a 'prodigious diversity' of ways, to the pressure for postulating the presence of some special quality or 'power' and of arriving, consequently, at an altogether mistaken notion of causality.

Hume's argument has two strands. On the one hand, he shows that the supposed special quality cannot be found; on the other, that such unknown qualities, even if they exist, cannot possibly play the role for which they have been cast. 'I am indeed, ready to allow, that there may be several qualities . . . with which we are utterly unacquainted; and if we please to call these *power* or *efficacy*, 'twill be of little consequence to the world.'[2] The presence of the unknown qualities is irrelevant in the same sort of way as the presence of the beetle in the language-game that Wittgenstein describes in *PI* 293. This rejection of fictitious and irrelevant entities is a constant feature of Hume's argument. He demonstrates the uselessness of the notions of divine or human 'acts of volition' to supply the supposedly missing element of causal necessity.[3] And elsewhere he attacks the philosophical notions of substance, and of an immaterial self, on similar grounds.[4]

---

1   *Treatise*, p. 159.
2   Ibid., p. 168.
3   *Enquiries*, pp. 64–73.
4   *Treatise*, pp. 219–24, 259.

So much for the parallel between Hume and Wittgenstein on the postulation ('feigning', as Hume calls it) of occult qualities, processes and substances. In his philosophy of mind Wittgenstein is constantly trying to cure us of the assumption that whenever something mental is predicated of a person, there must be something *in* his mind to make that predication true. There is another kind of assumption, equally hard to resist, in connection with mental predicates, which Wittgenstein seeks to counteract in a discussion in *Zettel*. Consider the enormous scope of an average person's memory. People often wonder *where* all the contents of the memory are 'stored'. There is an almost irresistible assumption that there must be ('*must* be') some physical storehouse containing linkages between original experiences and present memories.

I saw this man ten years ago: now I have seen him again, I recognise him, I remember his name. And why does there have to be a cause of this remembering in my nervous system? Why must something or other, whatever it may be, be stored up there *in any form*? Why *must* a trace have been left behind?[1]

A certain conception of the world — a pre-Humean conception — underlies the feeling that something must be 'stored up'. Wittgenstein characterises this conception (in another context) as the idea that 'the causal nexus is the connexion of two machine parts by means of a mechanism, say a series of cog-wheels.'[2] Against this 'primitive conception' Wittgenstein asks: 'Why should there not be a natural law connecting a starting and a finishing state of a system but not covering the intermediary state?'[3] This attitude is in harmony with the constant conjunction view, and with Hume's slogan 'Anything can be the cause of anything.'[4] And when, in conclusion, Wittgenstein warns us not to think of '*causal efficacy*' in this context, he means the kind of notion that Hume meant when he spoke of 'qualities . . . with which we are utterly unacquainted' and to which his occultist opponents might try to attach such labels as 'power' and 'efficacy'.

---

[1]   *Zettel*, 610.
[2]   Ibid. 580; my translation.
[3]   Ibid., 611, 613.
[4]   I am aware that one of the conditions that Hume laid down for the causal relation was that of *contiguity*; and this might seem to favour the 'cogwheel' view. However, I believe that Hume's introduction of contiguity stems from other aspects of his philosophy, and is not an essential part of the 'constant conjunction' view of causality for which he is known. John Passmore (*Hume's Intentions,* p. 30) remarks that 'spatial contiguity fades away' from Hume's account of causality. See Passmore's book for a discussion of Hume's problems concerning spatial relations.

DESCRIPTION V. JUSTIFICATION (ii)

I have referred to the philosopher who postulates entities behind and between phenomena, which are supposed to explain those phenomena, as an 'occultist'. Now it might be objected that this is just the description that should be applied to the opposite view, the view which resists the postulation of such entities. For is it not an occultist attitude to say, as both Hume and Wittgenstein do, 'Let us stop looking for explanations and justifications and just accept that this and this is how things are'?[1]

Hume's attitude to the matter is summed up by what he says, in the opening pages of the *Treatise*, about the working of the mind.

> Its effects are every where conspicuous; but as to its causes, they are mostly unknown, and must be resolv'd into *original* qualities of human nature, which I pretend not to explain. Nothing is more requisite for a true philosopher, than to restrain the intemperate desire of searching into causes, and having establish'd any doctrine upon a sufficient number of experiments, rest contented with that, when he sees a farther examination would lead him into obscure and uncertain speculations.[2]

It is a common criticism of Hume that there appears to be no room, in his system, for distinguishing grounds for belief from causes of belief, and consequently, for criticising any beliefs as irrational. If all that we can do by way of accounting for a belief is to refer it to a law of human nature, then it would seem that justification or criticism in terms of reason is out of place. Hume himself appears to drive home this unwelcome conclusion when he writes of belief as being 'a species of natural instincts, which no reasoning or process of the thought and understanding is able either to produce or to prevent'.[3] Wittgenstein attached importance to the distinction between grounds and causes of belief, and in this respect there is a contrast between his position and that of Hume. In order, on the other hand, to bring out what they have in common, it is necessary to distinguish between the two rather different jobs that Hume's account of belief was intended to do. There was, on the other hand, the task of explaining what belief *is*; what the difference is between *believing* an object to exist, and merely imagining it. In this task Hume was constrained

---

[1]   Some degree of simplification is unavoidable in a broad discussion of this kind. Thus (a) I tend to run together the notions of *explanation* and *justification*, both of them being opposed to 'description', and (b) I do not attempt to do justice to the *variety* of contexts in which the opposition is made.

[2]   *Treatise*, p. 13.

[3]   *Enquiries*, pp. 46–7; previously quoted on p. 51. The passage is used in a criticism of Hume by A. Flew, *Hume's Philosophy of Belief*, pp. 96–9.

by the atomism which he inherited from Locke's 'way of ideas'. The only way he could find of fitting belief into that system was to regard it as a kind of additive to the idea of the object *simpliciter*. If belief were not to be a 'nothing', then it must be a 'something'; the task of the atomistic epistemology was to say what kind of something it was. This aspect of Hume's account of belief is quite foreign to the later Wittgenstein's views; it is also an aspect which, as is well known, led Hume into insoluble problems.

But the second job that Hume's account was designed for concerned not beliefs in general, but certain fundamental beliefs, namely, those which were the object of sceptical attack. Taken in *this* context, what Hume says about belief is closely akin to Wittgenstein's position.

Sceptical doubt, both with respect to reason and the senses, is a malady which can never be radically cur'd, but must return upon us every moment, however we may chace it away, and sometimes may seem entirely free from it. 'Tis impossible upon any system to defend either our understanding or senses; and we but expose them farther when we endeavour to justify them in that manner.[1]

Like Wittgenstein, Hume rejects the attempt to underpin our basic beliefs with more ultimate justifications, to 'justify them in that manner'; like Wittgenstein he speaks instead of a malady which needs a cure. In this context the distinction between grounds and causes will not help us.

At the foundation of grounded belief lies belief that is not grounded.[2]

The difficulty is to realize the groundlessness of our believing.[3]

The task of philosophy, as Wittgenstein saw it, lay not in discovering ultimate foundations of belief, but in coming to terms with the apparently incurable urge to postulate such foundations.

Here we come up against a remarkable and characteristic phenomenon in philosophical investigation: the difficulty — I might say — is not that of finding the solution but rather that of recognising as the solution something that looks as if it were only a preliminary to it . . .

This is connected, I believe, with our wrongly expecting an explanation, whereas the solution of the difficulty is a description, if we give it the

---

[1] *Treatise*, p. 218.
[2] *On Certainty*, 253; my translation.
[3] *On Certainty*, 166.

right place in our considerations. If we dwell upon it, and do not try to get beyond it.

The difficulty here is: to stop.[1]

Some basic beliefs and language-games have to be accepted as facts of nature; to see them in any other way can only lead to distortion.

The primitive language-game which children are taught needs no justification: attempts at justification need to be rejected.[2]

I want to conceive [basic certainties] as something that lies beyond being justified or unjustified; as it were, something animal.[3]

Compare the well-known passage from Hume's *Treatise*, about the sceptic's attitude concerning 'the existence of body':

Nature has not left this to his choice, and has doubtless esteem'd it an affair of too great importance to be trusted to our uncertain reasonings and speculations. We may well ask, *What causes induce us to believe in the existence of body?* but 'tis in vain to ask, *Whether there be body or not?* That is a point, which we must take for granted in all our reasonings.[4]

Well, who is the occultist, the philosopher who says there *must* be such and such a thing 'behind' what we believe and what we do, or someone who, like Hume and Wittgenstein, maintains that 'explanations come to an end'? Of course it would be monstrous if Hume or Wittgenstein were putting an embargo on the aquisition of new beliefs or the justification of existing ones; if, for example, they were advising mankind not to ask why the litmus paper turns red, but to be satisfied with the fact *that* it does so; not to look for justifications for a given belief, but merely to note that the belief is held. This would indeed be an occultist attitude; it would be opposing a justified quest for enlightenment. But Hume and Wittgenstein are, fairly obviously, not opposed to such research and enquiry; the place at which they draw the line is elsewhere. Well then, who decides where the line is to be drawn? Why should we accept that Wittgenstein's 'bedrock'[5] is indeed bedrock? There are two things to notice about these questions. One

1   *Zettel*, 314.
2   *PI*, p. 200.
3   *On Certainty*, 359; previously quoted on p. 52.
4   *Treatise*, p. 187.
5   'If I have exhausted the justifications I have reached bedrock, and my spade is turned. Then I am inclined to say: "This is simply what I do." ' *PI*, p. 217.

is that both philosophers are concerned with *a priori* and not scientific investigation. There is nothing in Hume or Wittgenstein to dissuade scientists from discovering *scientific* facts, and providing scientific explanations.

The other point to be noticed is that Hume and Wittgenstein are not after all arguing in a vacuum. They don't *begin* by asking us to accept some things without explanation and justification; this advice is, rather, their reaction to certain deep-seated philosophical problems. It is these problems which set the context for the advice that we should be content with description. For it is in relation to them that the urge to postulate occult entities arises, and that the spurious nature of certain explanations and justifications needs to be exposed.

4

AN EMPIRICAL ACCOUNT OF MIND

D.M. Taylor

What could an empirical theory of the Mind be? Surely one which demonstrated that questions about the existence of minds were empirical questions — to be decided by observation, by the senses. This in turn would require an explanation of the meaning of statements about *minds* or *mental* states in terms referring to observable events, states and objects.

It is of course possible that some, perhaps even a majority of mental statements are not reports of events or states at all, or at least that they are not simply this. They might for example be, or be in part, assessments or evaluations of observable events and states, or again, they might represent decisions, claims, or permissions. I shall return to this point later. For the moment it is enough to notice that such suggestions are in no way incompatible with Empiricism.

A major difficulty for an empirical theory is that many, though not all, mental states and events do not appear to be, in any straightforward sense, observable by means of the senses. They are, it would seem, not publicly observable, though their effects may be. There is too an awkward asymmetry between self knowledge and knowledge of the mental states of others. One appears to have incorrigible and certain knowledge of one's own mental states but only contingent and probable knowledge of the mental states of others. Often this second feature of mental concepts is held to be explained by the first. These two features, which I shall call *privacy* and *authority* might seem to rule out an empirical theory of mind. Indeed the ascription of them to mental states and mental statements is regarded by some as intolerable for this reason. They fear that to do so is to accept that mental states and events are immaterial, or non-physical. For if to be physical is to be observable by the senses, what can't be observed can't be physical and must, therefore, be spooky. For others the proposition that mental events and states are private and first person mental statements incorrigible is not just intolerable but logically impossible; a language which referred to logically private states or objects would, necessarily, be meaningless.

These difficulties would be removed if it could be shown that it is simply a mistake to suppose that mental states and events are private, or that one is in a specially privileged position when speaking about one's own experiences. Indeed there are theories which have this as a consequence; one such is Materialism, or the theory of Mind-Brain identity. This theory, however, has internal weaknesses. As an account of the meaning of mental statements it is false. But as an empirical hypothesis it depends on the discovery of an interpretation of mental statements which is consistent with the hypothesis that they may be used to refer to *physical* events and states. Thus, e.g. 'I see a red image' might be represented as 'Something is going on now which is the same as what goes on when I see a red thing'. Suppose, however, that I say that I see a red image although as a matter of fact there is no physical similarity between my present state and my state when I see a red thing. Would it follow that the image statement and its interpretation were false, that I was mistaken or lying? Clearly not. The apparently straightforward *general* statement used to interpret the *image* statement simply obscures the issue. If it could properly be taken *both* to represent the image statement and also to refer to physical events and states, then a *physiologist could* tell me what images I saw — *he* would be the authority. But he can't; for he isn't. In the end the original problem of finding an interpretation of mental statements consistent with empiricism remains unsolved.

The objection to such theories as materialism and behaviourism and indeed to the doctrines of some naive Wittgensteinians is that in order to avoid the difficulties raised by *privacy* and *authority* they imply that others are in exactly the same position with respect to knowing what I think, want or feel, as I am and that in both cases the knowledge is obtained in the same way — that is by observation of physiological, or behavioural, events and states. They imply that when I say, or express, what I think, or want, an appropriate and natural response would often be that I was mistaken about my thoughts and wants. This is false.

Instead of accepting that privacy and authority are intolerable or impossible attributes of mental states and judgements, let us acknowledge that mental states are in some sense private, and that statements about one's own mental states are authoritative, and go on then to enquire as to the origin, or source, of these supposedly objectionable characteristics of mental concepts. Is it that mental states and events are peculiar, even spooky, or is there a more mundane explanation?

Gilbert Ryle provides a model for such an investigation in his treatment of perception and, in particular, of images. Images are *private*; you can't experience mine, nor I yours. And statements about them by the person who has them are *authoritative*; you can't tell me what mine are like. Ryle's explanation of this is as follows. According to him, when I say 'I see a red sphere' and it is an image that I see, I am exercising my capacity to discriminate between colours and to identify the colour red — in the unusual circumstance that there is, in fact, no red sphere visible in front of me. We, and here I mean language users, *could* judge my statement, and indeed any such statement, false for that reason. Or we could take it as evidence of linguistic incompetence. But we do not and the fact that we do not is important.

For if saying 'I see a red sphere' in the absence of public red spheres, does not of itself imply that a mistake has been made either about the facts or in the use of words, then it *must make sense* to speak of someone exercising his capacity to identify a colour in the absence of an appropriate public object. Indeed there is special linguistic provision made for just this case in the language of images.

Now normally one may allow that someone possesses a linguistic capacity, e.g. uses colour words in correct identifications of colours, yet judge, on a particular occasion, that he has made a mistake and wrongly described a particular object. But when we speak of seeing images, since there is no object, this distinction between, on the one hand, having a discriminating capacity and, on the other, getting the description of a particular object right, cannot be made. The only requirement for the correct use of image statements, therefore, is possession of the *capacity* to identify colours and the only ground on which to attack such statements is incapacity in identifying them. It follows that to acknowledge that a man has the linguistic capacity to use colour words correctly, *is* to acknowledge that his statements about his images are invulnerable to criticism. Unless a man is judged linguistically incompetent, his image statements cannot be challenged. But the authority he has about his images is simply the authority of one who knows how to identify colours, and use colour words correctly; it is a necessary concomitant of his linguistic and discriminatory skill or knowledge.

Ryle's account also explains the *privacy* of images. To have an image is to exercise a capacity to discriminate. Others cannot perceive my images because the sentence, 'Jones perceives my image', would mean, 'Jones exercises my capacity to discriminate'. But while Jones can exercise his own capacities, he cannot exercise mine.

Ryle's analysis of images provides in these ways a completely innocent explanation of *privacy* and *authority* with respect to this mental concept.

I want now to show how, in the case of another important group of concepts, *thinking that p*, *wanting that q* and *intending to do x*, an explanation can be given of both *privacy* and *authority* which is equally innocent of spooks or indeed any other mysterious entities and in this way to make a further step towards an empirical theory of mind.

What do we mean when we say that a person thinks that p, or wants an x? What are these states; in particular what would we expect to observe, or have observed if we said of someone that he thought that p, or wanted that q?

Normally when someone or something enters a state we expect to observe some property, not observed beforehand, the presence of which distinguishes something which is in the state from something which is not. When a man catches a disease we observe symptoms associated with that state — there is thus an observable difference between those who are and those who are not diseased.

This is, however, not true of all states; in particular of legal and quasi-legal states, e.g. being a debtor, or under an obligation. No observable properties distinguish debtors from creditors, for to become a debtor is not to acquire or lose an observable characteristic. Being a debtor, like being married, or divorced, a widow, or an adult, is (all else being equal) simply a consequence of a particular type of event which is the necessary condition of being in the state in question, a loan, a wedding, a death, or a birthday. In each case being in the state consists of nothing but the occurrence of one event, e.g. of accepting a loan, and the non-occurrence subsequently of another, e.g. repayment.

Thinking that p and wanting an x are in my view states of this kind. When we say that A thinks that p we are not talking about patterns of behaviour, dispositions to behave, or physiological conditions of the brain. Insofar as we are asserting any matter of fact, the assertion is categorical and about a particular event or events. But what kind of event is it that can play for *thinking* the role *borrowing* has in relation to being a debtor? I shall argue that thinking that p and wanting an x are states logically constructed out of *linguistic* events, or sayings.

Thus when we say that A thinks that p we imply that A has said that p. But we imply the occurrence of no events other than sayings, and no present difference other than the fact that something has now been said.

When I say that thinking that p is a logical construction from sayings I am simplifying. For neither utterances nor sayings are in general necessary and sufficient conditions of thinking that p. They do, however, provide conditions which are necessary and which, in the absence of various excuses, or excluding conditions, are held to be adequate for saying of someone that he thinks that p.

Here again there is a link with concepts like being in debt.

There is no debt without borrowing. Yet a man may be held not to be in debt when he is acknowledged to have received goods (even to have borrowed goods) if he did not know he had received them or if he was a minor, or of diminished responsibility.

States of this kind, which I shall refer to as legal, or quasi-legal states, are apparently defined, on the one hand, by specifying conditions necessary for entry into the state and, on the other, by a set of rights and duties, privileges and obligations conferred, or acquired as a result of accession to the state. Fulfilment of the necessary conditions usually secures entry to states of this kind but there is, nevertheless in such cases, an implied rejection of the various possible claims by which the person might have escaped, or have been prevented from, having it said of him that he was in that state.

In a phrase once used in this context by P. F. Strawson one might say that *saying that p* was a logically adequate criterion of *thinking that p* in the sense that the addition of no *other*, or *further*, *facts* could produce a *more* logically adequate criterion of thinking that p. But one would have failed to grasp the point of saying that A thinks that p if one did not understand *also* the system of privileges and obligations activated by A's saying that p. In just the same way, knowing what it is to be a debtor involves more than knowing that it results, usually, from borrowing.

I want now to defend the thesis that thinking that p (and wanting an x) are quasi-legal states constructed out of actual sayings.

But before doing so I should explain that I include among actual sayings, things said to oneself. This presents no problems for empiricists. On the one hand the analysis suggested can be given without them. And, on the other, as Ryle has shown, things said to oneself, if they are private, are merely *contingently* private. For if something *can* be either public or private, it cannot be essentially private and anything which is said to oneself could have been said to others.

I shall begin by giving some reasons for believing that saying that p must be central to any analysis of thinking that p.

We often move as a matter of course from saying to thinking, or wanting. Indeed we standardly report what a man says as what he thinks.

A to B   : Jones is a villain
B to C   : A thinks that Jones is a villain.

But what kind of step is this? It seems plain, though there's no time to argue it here, that it cannot be an inductive step. Yet it cannot be deductive either, since the move from '*says that p*' to '*thinks that p*', may always be resisted. My own view is that it is a step which *must be allowed* and *may be insisted* upon unless one or other of a range of let-outs or excluding conditions is pleaded, or enforced.

The step may always be resisted but there seem to be only two grounds upon which to resist it.

C to B   : How do you know that A thinks that Jones etc.
B to C   : He says that Jones etc.
C   : Perhaps he doesn't think it though.
B   : Do you mean he was deceiving us?
C   : Or that he has changed his mind.

Now the last objection would not apply to the statement that A *thought* that Jones etc. In *that* case we are left with deceit as the only general ground on which to object to the step from *'saying that p'* to *'thinking that p'*. Consequently we may assert that,

'A said that p', implies 'A thought that p', unless there was deceit.

Moreover since both deceit and change of mind imply thought, though opposite in sense to what was said, we may also assert that,

'A says that p', implies 'Either A thinks that p, or A thinks that q where q is inconsistent with p.'

i.e. that A thinks something about what p asserts.

'Saying that p' then, is *at least* related to *'thinking that p'* in that we infer the latter from the former with provisos about deceit (and possibly change of mind). It is not however *in general* a sufficient condition of thinking that p. Yet it is — I shall argue, a necessary condition. The argument will be in two stages:

STAGE I

If a person were not taken to be the authority as to his own thoughts or wants, many of the social relationships and social activities we engage in could not continue. But they do continue; so a person must in fact possess this authority.

STAGE II

The existence of a criterion of what a man thought, or wanted, which was logically independent of what he said, would be incompatible with the existence of this type of authority, so there can be no such criterion and saying that p must be a necessary condition of thinking that p.

STAGE I

A great part of social life consists in revealing what one thinks and thought, what one wants and wanted by saying that p, or advocating x, or by reports of such sayings and advocacy. We do this on the one hand to explain and justify our actions to others by reference to the thoughts and purposes guiding them; and we plan and choose our actions with the sense that we must be ready to explain and justify ourselves in mind. On the other hand, we do it in deliberating with others about what to do and think, in planning concerted actions and in agreeing on attitudes.

Such revelations of thoughts and wants may take one of several forms

(1) I did x because it is, or was, the case that p.

(2) I did x because, as I said, it is, or was, the case that p.
(3) I did x because I think, or thought, that p.

They may be explicit claims to think or have thought, or to say, or have said something. But they may be simply statements or proposals for action. [The distinctive force of the reference to thoughts is to make explicit the role which statements and reference to statements have in explanation or initiation of behaviour — viz. that they did then and may now play a part in reasoning, whether true or not.] But, as we shall see, these distinctions do not affect the argument.

Few things can be more humiliating than having the question what one thinks or wants answered for one, by others. To say 'I did x to get a and because b', or 'I did x because I wanted a and thought that b' and be told one is quite wrong, in fact one thought that c and wanted d. To say 'Let's do x to get y because p' and be told that in fact one neither thinks that p nor wants to get y. To have our action, as *we* would say, misinterpreted, and thoughts or desires ascribed to us which we do not admit, or acknowledge, is something we find shocking and belittling. Humiliation results in such cases from the sense of being treated as a thing to be talked about and pronounced upon but not worthy of talking, or pronouncement. One cannot, with dignity, treat such occasions simply as cases of mistake because the possibility that one has made a mistake about one's thoughts, or wants, is ruled out by this very assumption of dignity, i.e. by the assumption that one is the authority in these matters; one may be deceitful but not in error. It follows that to be corrected in such a case cannot be *just* to have the facts put right for one. To be treated in that way involves of necessity a change of status, a demotion, a descent from authority to subjection.

We can see what it means to take what a man says seriously if we imagine the alternative, and quite different, situation in which what we now find humiliating is normal; where, *in contrast to our present position*, in which we are held to know what we think — the question is whether we have revealed it, — there is no presumption at all that *we* know what we think and want.

How, in such a situation, could I engage in any discussion, expecting others to take account of what I said, if what I thought was held to be unrelated to what I said. I could not even *set out* to express, or reveal, my thoughts since I should very likely be told that I didn't know what they were. Indeed *I* should have no reason to suppose that what I said *did* express my thoughts.

It might be objected that it is a gross exaggeration to claim that a person would be reduced to the status of an object, or be incapable of entering any form of discussion, if he were not the authority as to his thoughts and wants. After all, it might be said, his only loss would be authority as to the truth of a small class of statements — those of the form 'I think that p' and 'I want that q'. Loss of authority *here*, it would be said, hardly amounts to *total* exclusion from the whole range of activities which we engage in by saying that p, or advocating x. If one can't talk about one's thoughts, one can still talk about a great many other things. *But to argue in this way is to miss the point*. If a man is not the authority on his thoughts and wants, all his statements and proposals are affected. For if others can tell better than he can what he thinks and wants, why should *anything* he says on *any* subject be attended to.

He might say 'Let's do x since its the case that p'. But if, when he has said that p and advocated doing x, the question what he thinks, or wants is still *entirely open* and quite independent of what he has just said, how can one possibly treat his remarks with any seriousness. For theoretically we should still be utterly in the dark as to his thoughts and wants. Indeed on investigation his thoughts and wants might turn out to be utterly unrelated to what he has said. After all he is no authority on this matter.

All the sayings which would normally be called expressions of thoughts or wants are affected by the supposition that men are not the authorities on their own thoughts and desires. For if there existed a general method of knowing what a man thought and wanted on any subject, which was *independent of what he said* on these subjects, there would be no reason to be interested in what he said on any subject.

It might seem that a hypothesis which implied that it was impossible to take what anyone said on any subject seriously must be self-inconsistent. But the present claim is narrower. It is that such a hypothesis would imply that the social and linguistic practices of deliberation and discussion about actions and beliefs were impossible — the activities simply could not occur — and for this reason the hypothesis must be false. For any hypothesis which implies a falsehood must be false. But the hypothesis that we are not authorities as to what we think and want would imply that we could not deliberate and discuss future and past actions, or questions of truth — by saying that p, or advocating x — *and this is false*. The hypothesis, therefore, is false.

STAGE II

It follows from the previous argument that any hypothesis which *implies* the false hypothesis that we are not the authorities as to what we think and want, is false also. But the hypothesis that there exist criteria by which a man's thoughts and desires may be determined, independently of what he says, is such an hypothesis. For if there were such a criterion it would be possible, logically, that it was the sole criterion. But in that case it would be possible that we were not authorities in the sense specified above and this is not possible.

It follows that there can be no criterion, or sufficient condition, of thoughts, or wants, independent of what a man says; in other words that it is a necessary condition of a man's being held to think that p, or want x, that he has said that p, or proposed the getting of x.

So far I have argued that the event, *saying that p*, and the state, *thinking that p*, are connected; in that, first, the one implies the other, subject to certain provisos (deceit, change of mind) and second, the one is a necessary condition of the other. This has been to support the theory that mental states such as thinking that p, wanting an x and intending to do y are constructions out of linguistic events on the one hand and social practices with associated privileges, obligations, rewards and sanctions on the other.

But how is the state of thinking that p to be constructed from particular sayings? How can a *state* be constructed logically out of an *event* or events and what is this system of privileges and duties?

It is possible to construct a state from an event trivially as follows:

(1) *A has said that p* implies *A is in the state of having said that p.*

A similar but more complex example results in a state one might wish to identify with *thinking that p.*

(2) *A has said that p and has*)   (*A is in the state of having*
    not said that -p sub-) implies (*said that p but not having*
    sequently   (*said that -p subsequently.*

In this example the relation between the sentences superficially resembles the relation, *A has got on and not got off the fence*, bears to *A is on the fence*. But there is a difference. It is that *being on the fence* is a state independent of getting on and off, and independently identifiable. The state of *having said that p and not said that -p* is not like this. It is, as I suggested earlier, much more like being a debtor, i.e. having borrowed and not paid back. Being a debtor consists in *no more* than the occurrence of one event, borrowing, and the *non*-occurrence of another, repayment.

Now although being a debtor is trivially constructed out of these two events, the state is far from trivial. For borrowing has consequences.

The same is true of saying. *Here also is an event of continuing significance.* By saying that *p* a man puts himself in changed circumstances. For example, the fact that he has said that p will be referred to by others, either to explain, or to challenge his subsequent actions and statements. Here is an example:

A: Why is Fred leaving his wife?
B: He said that she was deceiving him.

[*Note the absurdity of continuing as follows:*
A: But he said that yesterday.
This only makes sense if associated with hypothesis of change of mind.]

Here a past event viz. 'A saying that p' is regarded as having, and treated as having, continuing relevance to the explanation and, consequently, the assessment and evaluation of whatever A subsequently says or does — hence to the assessment of A himself. *In general*, a person's actions and remarks are assessed and classified by others as consistent, or inconsistent, with what he has previously said. Where they appear inconsistent an explanation is required and reproach follows if it is not deemed satisfactory. Having said that p, then, a man is required either to act and speak consistently with what he has said, or to explain, defend and justify himself if he does not, e.g. by pleading change of mind. This necessity to defend oneself indicates the existence of a prima facie *obligation* to act consistently with what one has said.

But to plead change of mind is not easy. People who say one thing and then another and so on are called dilly, or vacillating. They risk having what they say disregarded. Consequently one who says that -p, having previously said that p, is liable to this kind of criticism unless the grounds on which he bases -p are better than those which led him to say that p. Clearly, then, there must be limits to the possibilities of changing one's mind without the risk of criticism.

The fact that A has said that p has, then, a continuing currency, or force, in this sense; it restricts what A can easily say, or do, subsequently without fear of criticism. In effect it imposes on him obligations which are difficult to avoid.

But there are also benefits to be gained from saying that p, or that q. For the fact that he has said that p may be referred to later by A in explanation, or justification of his own actions. Thus in a real sense, a person may choose now, to the extent that he chooses what he says, the grounds on which he will defend and justify his later actions. And even if we hesitate to speak of choosing what one says here, it will still be true that a person may insist that the explanations which are given of his behaviour are as much his as the behaviour. That one's own words should determine the range of possible explanations of one's actions surely constitutes a very great freedom and privilege. It means that one may determine the light in which one's actions are seen.

It is these privileges and obligations with all their attendant social sanctions which play the role for thinking that p that the laws of property and contract have in relation to being in debt. Their existence makes clear why entry into the state, with its potential of reward and punishment, should inevitably be a matter both of necessary conditions and of decisions the determining conditions for which are not specifiable. We shall wish on occasions to claim that although we *uttered 'p'* we did not *say that p*, or that though we did say that p, we did not mean it (thought it only for a moment), or did not intend to say it (thought it but meant to conceal it), or that we were lying, or have changed our minds. Correspondingly others will wish from time to time to disallow our claims to have said that p, holding it to have been a mere utterance or, allowing that we said that p, to enforce a judgement that it was said deceitfully. Thus while we may set down necessary conditions and specify the headings under which pleas may be entered or judgements made, we shall never discover a set of sufficient conditions for states like wanting an x, thinking that p, or intending to do y.

This account of certain mental states clearly requires a great deal more in the way of defence. We need in particular to give an explanation of deceitful and candid sayings which does not render the account circular. It would not do to propose that to assert that A thought that p was, substantially, to say that A had said that p candidly, if saying p candidly simply means saying that p and thinking that p.

A full treatment of the nature of deceit would take too long. I shall argue only two points. First that there *must* exist conditions of candidness which do not render the proposition 'A says that p candidly entails A thinks that p' trivially true and, second, that there is at least one case in which it is possible to specify a sufficient condition of candidness without any circular reference to thoughts.

First: The argument that there must *be a non circular condition of candidness.*

Let us suppose that saying that p without deceit is simply and irreducibly *saying that p and thinking that p*. [Saying p deceitfully – does appear to be saying that p and not thinking that p.]
I call this the *trivial condition of absence of deceit.*

Now if we take the proposition to which I attribute some importance as proving a link between saying that p and thinking that p.

A says that p without deceit implies that A thinks that p,
and insert the trivial condition of absence of deceit, we get:

A says that p and A thinks that p implies that A thinks that p.
This proposition is of the form:

$$(p.q) \rightarrow q.$$

which is, I think, equivalent to:

$$p \rightarrow (q \vee \text{-}q)$$

In other words:

A says that p implies either that A thinks that p or that he does not.
Clearly if this is what the original proposition means it is utterly *trivial*. And this *is* what it means if what I call the trivial condition of absence of deceit is the *only* possible one.

Conversely, if the original proposition is not or cannot be trivial, a non-trivial condition of absence of deceit must be possible.

In fact the proposition that:

A says that p without deceit $\rightarrow$ *A thinks that p.*

cannot be trivial. It cannot be simply equivalent to

A says that p implies either that A thinks that p or that he doesn't.

For unless there were a stronger connexion between what **A** says and what he thinks than that between p and q in $p \rightarrow qv\text{-}q$, there could be no deceit. Deceit depends on taking what a person says to represent what he thinks. What A says must, therefore, provide better reason for an opinion as to what he thinks than the proposition '*Either A thinks that p or he doesn't*', provides. It is difficult to imagine that anyone could be deceived as to my thoughts by my saying that p, if this implied only that either I thought that p, or I did not.

It follows that a non trivial condition of absence of deceit must exist. But what is it? What is *absence of deceit* if it is not just

saying that p and thinking that p?

Second: A non circular sufficient condition of candidness.
There is one case in which absence of deceit can be specified without triviality, or circularity. For deceit is saying that p while thinking that it is not the case that p. Now being said to think that -p implies, on the present theory, being said to have said that -p. If this implication is false, deceit is ruled out. It follows that in the case where A has said that p and has said nothing else, A has said that p without deceit, and may be held to have thought that p. This is to make it the essence of deceit to say conflicting things — but that I think is quite a natural view to take. The question which of the two conflicting things said is said sincerely will be a matter of judgement.

I began by arguing that a satisfactory empirical theory of the Mind must have two characteristics.
(1) In so far as it deals with objects, events and processes, these should be observable in an uncomplicated sense.
(2) Patent characteristics of the mental should not be ignored. In particular the two facts that mental states and events are in some sense private, and that a person is typically the authority as to the nature of his own mental states and events.

The present theory accounts for both these facts. It implies that a man has special authority in relation to his thoughts and wants. For no one can know what a man thinks or wants except as a result of knowing what he has said, or now says. Ryle was right, I think, to hold that no person has privileged knowledge of any matter of fact. Nevertheless each of us has a peculiar authority in relation to some events and states, among them thinking and wanting. For the difference between myself and others with respect to my thoughts is not that I have access to events to which they do not. It is that I am the person who says what I say. Until I say what I say no one knows or is in a position to say what I think (including me). And no one can say what I say for me.

A person's authority then rests, according to the present theory, on the following.
(1) His saying that p is a necessary condition of his being held to think that p.
(2) He cannot properly be *held to think* or *supposed to think* that p unless he is held or supposed to have said that p.
(3) He must be held to have thought that p, having been held to have said that p, unless he is accused of deceit.

There is nothing spooky about this authority. Nor is there about privacy. For me to know what I think is for me to have concluded, or said, that p ('to have decided that p' only *sounds* more natural), i.e. to have done something. But for me to know what another thinks is not to have done something, it is to have noticed something. I know what I think (when I do) in the sense that I have made it the case that I think p. This is not so when I know what others think. This is the force of the remark that the way in which I know what I think is different from the way in which others know it. For others to know what I think in the sense in which I know it would be for them to have made up my mind. (The situation is different when we speak of knowing *that* one or another thinks that p, but there is not time for that now.)

Finally, on the present theory, the only events referred to in speaking about thinking that p, or wanting something, are linguistic utterances, either public, or (contingently) private. To that extent Empiricism is satisfied. Now does there seem anything offensive to Empiricism in the remaining element of the theory — the idea of a social practice and its sanctions.

5

THE STATUS OF SENSE DATA

D. J. O'Connor

In the present state of philosophy in the English-speaking world, to choose to talk about sense data may seem perverse. What could be more boring for one's audience than to attempt variations on so threadbare a theme? And worse, what could be more unfashionable in the aftermath of Wittgenstein and Austin? My reasons for selecting this unpromising topic are twofold. First, the general theme of this series of lectures is empiricism. And whatever meanings we put upon that ambiguous word, it is clear that as a matter of history the problems of perception have been important problems for nearly all those philosophers who would consider themselves to be empiricists. And however unsatisfactory sense datum theories of perception may now be held to be, such theories have been central to the empiricist tradition. Secondly, it is important not to be too much impressed by the fact that a particular philosophical opinion is fashionable or unfashionable. The former certainly does not guarantee its truth nor the latter its falsity. It has often been remarked that philosophical opinions are very rarely refuted. Instead they fall out of vogue only to return some years later in another guise. It is perhaps time to take another look at the notion of sense data. The most ingenious and persistent attacks on analyses of perception in terms of sense data have been at best indecisive, as Professor Ayer showed in his reply to Austin's *Sense and Sensibilia*[1].

It must be admitted right away that many empiricists who have adopted some version of a sense datum theory of perception have damaged their case by making claims that are both indefensible and irrelevant. But this double mistake is a fortunate conjunction of errors. For the fact that a particular claim can be shown to be irrelevant to one's thesis draws the sting from the arguments that show it to be indefensible. What I have in

[1]   'Has Austin refuted the sense-datum theory?', in *Metaphysics and Common-sense* (London, 1969) pp. 126–48.

mind here are claims such as the following: sense data are the atoms or building blocks of our sense experiences; they are known directly and immediately in contrast to physical objects which are hypothetical and problematic. Sometimes such claims are linked, as they are in some of Russell's writings, with a method of philosophical analysis. Analysis yields hard, clear and certain units of cognition which, once found, can be reconstructed to justify some at least of our claims to knowledge.

None of these assumptions are anything but an embarrassment to a theory of perception which uses the concept of sense data. Even if there were no good philosophical arguments against an atomistic basis for knowledge, there is ample empirical evidence from experimental psychology to show that such a belief is groundless. Nor is the case for describing sense data as certain or indubitable (in contrast with percepts of physical objects which are doubtful or fallible) either defensible or helpful to the sense datum theory. The word 'certain' and its cognates and derivatives applies primarily to states of mind. It is a psychological predicate. 'I am certain that P' describes my degree of conviction about the truth of P where P is some proposition. And sense data are not propositions. It is true indeed that the proposition 'I am now seeing something yellow' is less corrigible than 'I am now looking at a lemon'. And there is *prima facie* a case for saying that corrigibility in a proposition is inversely correlated with the degree of certainty appropriate to the state of mind of one who is entertaining it. But this is to raise the third of the false claims about sense data, namely, that they are in some sense the premisses or evidence from which we infer or the basis on which we induce or assume the existence of the allegedly corresponding material object. Many of the philosophers who have adopted the terminology of sense data in their theories of perception have used language which suggests, if indeed they are to be taken literally, that they endorse such claims. For example, at one time even Professor Ayer was willing to compare the transition that we make from our immediate sensory data to belief in physical objects as a form of reasoning analogous to inductive reasoning.[1] But all talk of 'inference' in this context is clearly artificial. There are indeed rare situations where we do consciously make inferences about the nature of objects that we are presented with. For example, in identifying objects by touch in a dark room we may well make deliberate hypotheses as to the nature of the object based on our tactual and kinaesthetic sensations. And the same may happen when we make conjectures about the objects in our vicinity in conditions of bad visibility. Such conjectures are genuine forms of inference but they are fortunately untypical episodes in perceptual experience.

Nor can we say baldly that sense data are directly known to us while

---

[1]   *Foundations of Empirical Knowledge* (London, 1940) pp. 39 f.

physical objects are known only indirectly in being necessarily introduced to us through their good offices. To this the reply is often made that if I am looking at, let us say, the garden before me in a good light and with unimpaired eyesight, I am seeing the trees, grass and flowers as directly as I ever see anything. The standard cases of indirect vision are surely those of seeing things in mirrors, through microscopes, inverting lenses, on television screens and so on. This point must surely be well taken. However, the claim that awareness of sense data is in some defensible sense more direct than awareness of physical objects can be sustained. My point will be that the claim is badly expressed rather than simply false. If it is phrased more judiciously, there is something to it. But before we can see what substance the thesis has, it will be necessary to make explicit exactly what the sense datum thesis does assert and how it is to be established.

II

So far I have been dismissing statements often made about sense data on the ground that they are irrelevant to the thesis that there are such things as well as being indefensible in themselves. But I now have first to explain what I mean by saying that there are sense data and then to justify the statement. In one of the most recent (as well as one of the best) treatments of the problems of perception,[1] Professor George Pitcher introduces the subject with a long chapter entitled 'Sense Data and How to Avoid Them'. He starts by distinguishing two groups of philosophers who accept the existence of sense data. One group, of whom Hume is the chief representative, simply take it for granted that sense data, or in Hume's language 'impressions', are self-evidently given to us in sense perception. The other group, of whom Berkeley is the leader, believe that sense data are real but unobvious features of experience which require arguments to demonstrate their existence. Pitcher rejects the intuitions of the first group and sets himself to refute the arguments of the second. I shall accept his rejection of Hume's position and do my best to show that not all of the arguments for sense data are unsuccessful.

There is a second distinction among the supporters of sense-data that calls for comment. Professor Ayer, at one stage of his thinking about perception[2] suggested that to accept the theory of sense-data 'involves nothing more than a decision to use a technical language'. To believe in sense data does not, in other words, commit us to accepting a new range of entities over and above the ordinary inhabitants of the world; it commits us merely to using a terminology in our talk about perceiving that is philosophically less troublesome than more ordinary ways of talking. This

---

[1]   *A Theory of Perception* (Princeton, N.J., 1971) pp. 3–63.
[2]   Op. cit., p. 57.

approach to the problem has been elaborated by other writers in various ways. For example, Mr. Hampshire and Professor White have claimed that to describe the contents of one's immediate sensory experience and to claim to perceive physical objects is to use language in two quite distinct ways. Compare, for example, 'I see something yellow' with 'I see a lemon'. The first uses the descriptive and the second the identifying function of language and these are quite different.

I wish to reject this and other linguistic interpretations of the sense datum theory. My reasons for doing so will, I think, be obvious from my reasons for adopting the contrasting view. But we have only to ask: What am I describing? when I use language in this descriptive way. It can always be said that in using the identifying mode of language I am identifying (or at least purporting to identify) a part of the physical world. But what I am describing may often be something which is patently not an item of the material world at all — an after-image, a dream, the content of an hallucination, or some other demonstrably maverick inhabitant of a sensory field.

The alternative to a linguistic interpretation of the sense datum theory is that sense data are genuine items of experience. But if they really are such, it may be asked, why is there any need of argument to establish their existence? The answer to this question is that we need argument not to show that there really are such things but to show that certain recognisable features of our experience have properties which require these features to be emphasised as philosophically important. There are two stages to the argument. First, I have to show that there are features of experience that everyone admits to be genuine; secondly, it must be shown that these features of our sensory experience are so different in nature from the objects of the material world that they cannot be identified with them. What then do I mean by the term 'sense datum'? Simply that a sense datum is a part of a sensory field. A visual sense datum is a part of a visual field, a tactual datum part of a tactual field; and so on. Now no one presumably will deny that he has a visual field and that it has distinguishable parts in that it is extended and diversified. Thus no one, other than the totally blind, can deny that he has visual sense data on this definition. And a similar argument, if that word is justified, can establish the existence of sense data in all the other sensory modalities.

But so far nothing of any interest has been established. The only advantage in putting the matter in this way is to enable us to avoid a number of pointless questions about the nature of sense data: do they have properties that they do not appear to have; how long do they last? How many are there at a given moment? To all such questions we can reply that sense data have just those properties which parts of our sensory fields are found to have — and no more. What these properties are is an empirical question. However, sense data, so identified are left with the characteristic features which have given point to the theory which requires them and have excited the criticisms of opponents of the theory. These features are (1) that sense data are, in Pitcher's phrase, 'ontologically distinct' from material objects or from their surfaces; (2) that they are private to the individual who has them as part of his sensory field; and (3) that they are *immediately* or *directly* present to consciousness. These three features seem to be no more than a consequence of the fact that we define sense data as being parts of a sensory field, though some argument is required in respect of points (1) and (2).

The third point, that sense data are immediately or directly present to consciousness calls for explanation rather than argument. I said previously that it makes perfectly good sense to talk of being directly aware of the material things in the world about us if we are looking at them in good light with normal eyesight. So that if we are to insist that the visual field is presented to us more directly or immediately than the visual world, we must be using these terms in misleading senses. But it is surely obvious on reflection what this claim amounts to, however maladroitly it may often have been expressed. The visual field is more primitive than the visual world. It is its basic unconceptualised raw material. New born infants and patients blind from birth recovering from surgery to restore their sight are doubtless the only human creatures with unconceptualised visual fields. We no longer remember what it was like to have one. Professor Bruner has remarked how 'it is curiously difficult to recapture preconceptual innocence'.[1] This is true of someone trying to remember, for example, what written language looked like before he learned to read or what a foreign language sounded like before he learned to understand it. Certainly we cannot hope to divest ourselves of the complex conceptual network woven into our sensory field that gives our sense experience meaning and intelligibility. We can perhaps occasionally approach that state of 'preconceptual innocence' in artfully contrived situations in the psychological laboratory or in delirium or, momentarily, in awakening from sleep or coming round from an anaesthetic in unfamiliar surroundings. But for us, such situations are now disturbing and unpleasant. However, as infants, we all had such raw unconceptualised sensory fields. They were given to us prior to the world of material things; and they were the material necessary for our gradually learned concepts to mould into the familiar sensory world.

For simplicity, I shall talk chiefly in terms of the visual field. But analogous arguments can be put forward for other sensory modalities. Our visual fields as now given to us are so conceptually saturated, so moulded by learning the structure of the visual world that it is almost impossible for

[1]   *Beyond the Information Given* (New York, 1972) p. 162.

us to prescind from the conceptual load that gives meaning to what is presented to us. Certainly any expression in language of a visual experience, however primitive and ill-defined, is already conceptually tainted. (Even, for example, 'I see yellow'.) For language is pre-eminently a device for the storage and retrieval of structures of ideas. But with special training and care it is sometimes possible to see the world, for short periods, as a patchwork of colour, light and shade instead of a world of material objects and their environment. Artists and some experimental psychologists have this skill; and all of us can achieve the experience at times. We are then gazing at or contemplating the visual field instead of perceiving, or looking at or attending to the visual world.

The distinction in perceptual attitudes towards items of the visual field and those of the visual world is important. If we attend to it we can see what is wrong with Professor Ryle's well known argument against sense data. Ryle argued that 'this whole theory rests upon a logical howler, the howler, namely, of assimilating the concept of sensation to the concept of observation.'[1] If indeed our perceptual attitude to things observed were the same as that towards sense data, Ryle would be right in claiming that we would be involved in an infinite regress. Observing something would involve having sensations which in turn would involve having further sensations; and so on. But if we distinguish the unconceptualised visual field and the conceptualised visual world we can see that the visual stance appropriate to one is quite different from that appropriate to the other. It is therefore untrue that we assimilate sensing to observing. Nor do the success verbs suitable for the description of our perceivings and observings apply to crude sensations. But when we perceive something or purport to perceive it, we clothe a portion of our visual field with concepts. And perceiving or misperceiving depends on choosing the right set of concepts to clothe the raw data. Learning soon makes this process of selection completely automatic (though not therefore infallible).

This is one way to justify the often mis-stated claim that sense data are known to us more directly or immediately than are material objects. Visual sense data, that is, the contents of our visual fields, are indeed historically or developmentally prior to our having a visual world. For this has to be developed slowly, as the cases recorded by von Senden show,[2] over a long period of time. It is in this sense that sense data are known more directly or immediately than physical objects. This point is of some consequence for the intentional nature of perceiving, as we shall see.

But what good arguments can be brought forward to show that sense data, defined in this way, have the two properties of being private to the perceiving individual and 'ontologically distinct' from material objects or

---

1   *The Concept of Mind* (London, 1949) p. 213.
2   *Space and Sight*, trans. P. L. Heath (London, 1960).

their surfaces? Many arguments have been used in the history of the dispute about the nature of perception purporting to establish and to refute these claims. The necessity for economy in the limited compass of a lecture makes it advisable to select the arguments for these positions that can be stated briefly, are admitted by those who reject them to be prima facie strong arguments and which have not been decisively refuted.

To establish the point that visual sense data, that is parts of the visual field, are not identical with the surfaces of material things I shall consider the familiar but difficult case of double vision. Suppose that I look at the pencil on the table in front of me and then squint or press an eyeball with my finger. That part of the visual field that I take to be the pencil is distorted so that I now seem to see two pencils instead of one. There are certainly two appearances of the pencil existing side by side. And they cannot both be identical with the visible surface as part of the pencil because one is sharp edged and the other, because my right eye is short-sighted, very blurred. So there is a something or other which is a part of my visual field and which is clearly not to be identified with the visual surface of the material object to which its appearance would lead me to refer it. This something or other is a sense datum with the required property of being, in Pitcher's phrase, 'ontologically distinct' from the physical object with which it is no doubt in some complex way causally connected. In the case that we are considering, the phenomenon is produced artificially; but there are plenty of cases where some disorder of the eye or the nervous system brings about the same effect.

Professor Pitcher answers this argument by saying that 'in double vision a person does not see two somethings (e.g., two pencilish sense data); he sees one thing (e.g. a pencil) twice, once with the left eye and once with the right.'[1] But this reply whatever it may be worth for binocular double vision certainly does nothing to cope with the more serious cases of double vision where only one eye is involved. In certain pathological conditions, two or more appearances of the same object may occur in the visual field of a single eye.[2] And these cases can certainly not be dealt with by Pitcher's reply. For the patient with monocular double vision is aware of two somethings in his visual field which have only one correlate in the physical world. Thus at least part of the visual field in such cases is ontologically distinct from that material object. And so, at least in some cases, visual sense data as I have defined them, are not to be identified with the surfaces or parts of the surfaces of material objects.

The argument from double vision is a special case of the argument from illusion which Pitcher sees as being based on a premiss which he calls

[1] Op. cit., p. 41.
[2] W. S. Duke-Elder, *A Textbook of Opthalmology*, IV (London, 1950) p. 3866.

Assumption A. It can be phrased as follows: If something, X, appears to have a visual quality Q to a percipient P where X does not in fact have Q, then something else, Y, distinct from X really does have Q. And this something is a sense datum. Pitcher rejects this assumption on the basis of arguments which do not seem to me to be satisfactory but which I have no space to examine here. In any case, Assumption A is hardly in question when we are discussing the argument from double vision. As Professor Price pointed out long ago[1] being double is not a quality. To say that something is double is just to say that there are in fact two of whatever we are talking about. Cases recorded in textbooks of ophthalmology and neurology yield more bizarre and spectacular instances of double vision. For example, there is a form of visual perseveration (called paliopsia)[2] where the patient sees the same incident recur in his visual field which he has observed to occur in reality a few seconds previously. This seems more dramatic because of the time interval replacing the spatial dislocation. But it simply serves to reinforce the lesson that we should learn from everyday cases of double vision.

There is another argument which establishes the same conclusion. It is well known to experimental psychologists that the sensitivity of sense organs does not match, point for point, the variety of the stimuli to which they respond. Let us consider, from a large number of possible examples, the following; We have several instances of a shade of colour which vary gradually from C_1 to C_n. It often happens that C_1 is not distinguishable to a normal eye from C_2; nor is C_2 from C_3; nor is C_3 from C_4. However, C_1 *is* distinguishable from C_4. Thus there must be variations in the qualities of the physical object that are not matched by variations in the visual field. (And this conclusion can, of course, be reinforced by evidence from physics.) Thus sense data, in such instances cannot be identical with parts of the physical world; for the physical world in question differs qualitatively from one part to another and the 'corresponding' sense data do not. Such an argument shows that sense data can *lack* properties that the physical world possesses. And of course we may argue from the phi-phenomenon and the cinematograph and the like for the converse conclusion that there are properties that the visual field has which the corresponding features of the physical world do not have. Either way the argument goes to show that sense data and the physical world are, in Pitcher's sense, 'ontologically distinct'.

These arguments prove no more than that *some* visual sense data, that is, some parts of the visual field are sometimes distinct from the material objects of which commonsense unreflectingly supposes them to be a part. It does not show that *all* visual sense data have this property. A

---

[1] *Perception* (London, 1933) p. 57.
[2] Macdonald Critchley, *The Parietal Lobes* (London, 1953) p. 304.

hard-shelled realist might grudgingly admit that sense data, so identified, are occasional rare phenomena which, like clairvoyance or telekinesis, need not disturb our intellectual complacency. But having admitted that some segments of the visual field do sometimes show this defining property of being distinct from the physical world that we look for in sense data, how can we prevent sense data from taking over the whole of the visual field? Certainly there are few properties of the field itself which declare some pieces of it to be distinct from and others to be parts of the material objects of the visual world. Still the realist would want to insist that the arguments so far considered show no more than that a few parts of the field show this untypical aberrancy. We have not shown that most parts of our fields are not safely and respectably married to physical objects.

The usual way of dealing with this problem is to emphasise the continuity of normal with abnormal sensory presentations and the impossibility of saying where one gives way to the other. But this approach which relies on the imperceptible transition of aberrant appearances into normal ones is clearly not available to anyone who relies on the argument from double vision. For that is based upon observed *discontinuities.* So I shall depend on the next argument not only to establish that sense data, in the sense defined, are private to a conscious individual but also that they constitute the whole of the visual field and not just the demonstrably 'wild' parts of it.

This argument depends on the scientific account of the process of sensory stimulation – the physics and physiology of the sense organs and the nervous system. There is no need to rehearse the details of this machinery which is sufficiently well-known to anyone with an interest in sense perception. The common principle is that various forms of energy emitted by or reflected from the objects of the material world are coded by sensory receptors into electrical impulses in the afferent nerves and then de-coded by brain mechanisms into our sensory fields. The metaphor of coding and de-coding is, of course, question begging in so far as it suggests that the sensory world is a replica of the physical world by which we are being currently stimulated. But it is not possible to find a neutral and informative description for what is a unique process. At least we know it to be true that the information that comes to us through the senses comes to us packaged in successively different forms – physical energy, neural energy and, finally, a sense field.

It is this knowledge that lends support to the sense datum account of perception. I said earlier that the belief that our sensory information about the material world is direct and immediate is, in one sense of those words, obviously justified in normal perception. But the scientific picture does raise serious doubts about saying that normal sense perception is direct and immediate in an unqualified sense of the phrase. For to say that such events or processes are direct and immediate is surely to imply that there are no other hidden events and processes that are necessary intermediate stages between, say, opening my eyes and seeing what is before me. But what the scientific picture shows us is just that there are very complex and detailed intermediaries of this sort. So that we may claim that it is well established that in an accepted sense of the words our perception of the external world is far from direct and immediate. But this consideration gives no ground for distinguishing between the visual field and the visual world in this respect. Sense data are, in this sense of the phrase, no more directly and immediately given than are the objects of the visual world.

But the scientific account of sense perception has further consequences. The first is that electrical processes in the nervous system are necessary conditions for any sensory experience. Without them, we would not have experiences of this sort at all. Moreover, in certain states, such processes are also sufficient conditions for the sensory experience. Our consciousness of a vivid dream or of the phenomena of a drug-induced hallucination require no external stimulation of sense organs but only the internal activation of nervous mechanisms. No one doubts that such states, for which nervous activity is both necessary and sufficient, present us with sensory fields which are both totally distinct from the objects of the external world and at the same time private to the observer. But, it may be said, they are both untypical and parasitic on our normal sensory transactions with the world of material objects. Without the normal states, we could hardly have the abnormal ones.

Let us concede this point in order to get to more important ones. In ordinary sense experience, nervous activity is necessary but not sufficient to produce a sense field. If we list the conditions that are individually necessary and jointly sufficient to produce a visual field, we must include electromagnetic radiation of certain restricted wavelengths reflected into the eye, a transparent medium, an eye of normal efficiency, an intact optic nerve and so on. All of these are integrated into a causal process whose end product is the visual field. This end product is the final effect of the series of causes that are its necessary and sufficient conditions. If we accept this conclusion, it is clear that visual sense data satisfy the two conditions of privacy and non-identity with the object that have traditionally been accorded to them. The fact that the latter stages of the process are events in the percipient's brain guarantees their privacy. And it also guarantees the second condition. For the occurrence of a visual field mediated by events in my brain and having every detail of its constituent data controlled by those events can hardly be anything but 'ontologically distinct' from the surface of the physical object from which the necessary light rays were reflected. We have traced the path from object to percipient which is the relevant causal process.

To this argument there is a well-known objection. Professor Mundle writes that it 'confuses the *mechanism* on which the perception is dependent with the *objects* that are perceived.'[1] And Mr. Don Locke adds: 'The theory is that stimulation of the retina, etc., produces a visual percept in our minds, but quite obviously what these processes produce is not what we see but the perception itself. The end result of these causal processes is perception — what we perceive is the thing, whatever it is, that comes at the beginning, the thing that reflects the light waves on to our retina.'[2] It is not easy to see just what this objection amounts to if it is intended to make more than the trivial verbal point that what we perceive is a physical object and not either sensory processes or sense fields.

Certainly we do not sense, still less perceive or even necessarily know about the various physical and neural processes on which our perceptual knowledge depends. And it is true that the objects of perception are material things which are public and independent of any observer. But we can only be aware of these public objects through information given to us in our sensory fields. Moreover, the properties of those fields, both general and specific, are controlled by the processes that produce them to a degree unusual and perhaps unparalleled in other causal procedures.

In most causal processes we can distinguish clearly between process and object, between those features of the final product which are the outcome of the process and those which are independent of it. For example, motor cars, aspirin tablets and chicken's eggs are identifiable objects in which we can distinguish between those features which are the outcome of the causes which produce them and those which are, so to speak, native to the materials out of which they are made. For it is easy or at least practicable to identify separately the original ingredients out of which the final product is made. (The steel, glass, rubber, etc., of the car or the calcium, aminoacids, DNA molecules, etc., of the egg.) But this is not the case with the process of perception. The various kinds of energy which assault our sense organs are completely changed into other forms in their passage through the nervous system. And the original nature, structure and source of this energy can only be conjectured on the basis of complex and hazardous arguments. (This is one of the reasons why representative accounts of perception are so much more difficult to make plausible than causal accounts.)

We must therefore distinguish the intentional objects of our perceptual experience from its sensory objects. The former are the public inhabitants of the physical world that we believe ourselves (though sometimes mistakenly) to be perceiving. The latter are the fragments of our sense fields which are the basis for conceptual interpretations that we project into the public and intentional world of material things. These sense fields

---

[1] 'Commonsense versus Mr. Hirst's theory of perception', *Proceedings of the Aristotelian Society* (1959–60).
[2] *Perception and Our Knowledge of the External World* (London, 1967) p. 116.

are at once causally created end products of the physical and neural processes that are their necessary conditions and the only evidence available to us of the nature of the external world. Sensing becomes perceiving when sense fields are interpreted as conceptually organised and intentionally distanced. The difference is the familiar one between seeing (or otherwise sensing) and 'seeing as...'

III

I have tried to present the sensory world as given to us in two layers. There is the primary basic unconceptualised sensory field given to us at birth which is gradually moulded by concept formation into our familiar material everyday world. I have argued that the primordial sensory field has the three characteristics traditionally accorded to sense data; it is, in one sense, direct and immediate; it is distinct from, that is, not at any point identical with the material world; and it is private to the sensing individual. However, I am certainly not claiming that, in still another sense of the phrase, we do not see and touch the objects of the material world directly and immediately. Our visual *fields* are private and distinct from the external physical world. But we do really see the inhabitants of the public visual world and not some private projection of them. This is because what we see and touch are conceptually structured items of sensory awareness. And concepts are, of course, the very stuff of the public communicable world of our common shared experience. (This truism is just an expression of an obvious empirical fact of human existence. It is a contingent feature of the way we have to live that language and other conceptual codings are public institutions. This is the truth (and the only truth) at the bottom of the false though fashionable doctrine of the logical impossibility of a private language.) Concepts not only give structure to our sense data. By endowing them with publicly recognised meanings they translate them from the sensible to the observable level, give them the requisite epistemic distance and independence that their status as objects of knowledge requires.

This brings me to the last point that I want to make. Two of the most important (and the most difficult) of recent papers on sense perception have been Professor Anscombe's Howison lecture[1] and Professor Hintikka's 'On the Logic of Perception'.[2] Both of these emphasise the role of the concept of intentionality for the proper understanding of the nature of sense perception. I want to say something about this point in connexion

---

[1]   'The Intentionality of Sensation', in *Analytical Philosophy*, 2nd series, ed. R. J. Butler (Oxford, 1956).
[2]   In *Models for Modalities* (Dordrecht, 1969), pp. 151–83.

with what I have said so far. (I shall not try to fit what I have to say into the context of the Anscombe or the Hintikka theories. Indeed, I am not sure that I fully understand them.) Intentionality is a difficult and disputed subject; but a traditional and widely accepted way of explaining what we mean by intentional objects is that they are characteristically objects of mental attitudes – fear, hate, hope, desire, belief or perceptual acceptance. (It is the last with which I am immediately concerned.) I can feed or photograph a lion only if it is there to be fed or photographed. But I can fear, dislike, doubt the existence of, wish for or believe in something that does not exist. So too, I can see something that is not really there in the sense that I can see an X as a Y, a snake as a piece of stick or vice versa or a bush as a man. We could conveniently but loosely define intentional objects as those that we can be mistaken about.

In other words, it is not sense data, the raw unconceptualised elements of our sensory fields, that are intentional objects. It is rather the objects of perception that are intentional. Raw sensory fields are ambiguous in that they may be clothed with a variety of conceptual apparel. But until they are structured in this way, the possibility of error does not arise. Thus it is not sense data but rather physical objects, real or putative, that are intentional. Moreover, the heavier the conceptual load with which we interpret our sense fields, the greater the risk of mistake and so, in a sense, the greater degree of intentionality. Consider, for example, the following series of assertions:

(A) I see something yellow.
(B) I see a yellow flower.
(C) I see a buttercup.
(D) I see a specimen of *Ranunculus acris*.

As we go from (A) to (D), the conceptual load is increased at each stage and so too the degree of corrigibility. And as corrigibility increases, so does the risk that the object that we are affirming to be under observation does not really exist. In such cases, conceptual load is positively correlated with intentionality.

In this lecture I have tried to do three things, one principal and two subsidiary. First, I have attempted to do something towards reinstating the notion of sense data as an explanatory concept in the philosophical theory of perception. Secondly, I have suggested, very sketchily, the way to a causal account of perception which will avoid the subjectivist traps in which such theories have usually been entangled. Any development of this suggestion requires a psychological account of concept formation and a philosophical theory of concepts. These are large issues which can only be mentioned here; but they are fundamental to an adequate theory of sense perception. And lastly, I have tried to show that the element of intentionality that several philosophers have diagnosed in the phenomena of perception can be recognised in the physical objects, putative or real, that we perceive rather than in the sense data which are the medium through which we sense them.

If anyone wishes to reject the main conclusion about sense data, he must either deny that he has a visual field or show that, consonant with our knowledge of sensory physics and physiology, it does not have the properties of privacy and separateness from the material world that have been claimed for it. The arguments that I have offered for this conclusion are, of course, of respectable antiquity but as long as they have not been conclusively refuted, none the worse for that. However there is a final point that deserves some emphasis. Those features of the material world that incline us to stress its publicity, independence, order and stability are not native to our sensory fields but rather are built into them through concept formation. No doubt most of our empirical concepts do reflect features of the physical world: but they are not innate properties of sensory experience for all that. It is by familiarity from early childhood that we come to regard them as integral to the sensory backcloth into which they are woven. And so we come to attribute to our private neurologically dependent sense fields qualities that they do not possess. These facts make it psychologically very difficult to appreciate the force of some of the arguments for sense data. But of course they are irrelevant to whatever logical force those arguments may possess.

6

WITTGENSTEIN ON SEEING AND INTERPRETING

P. B. Lewis

In those twenty or so pages of section xi of Part Two of the *Philosophical Investigations* in which Wittgenstein discusses the concept of noticing an aspect and its place among the concepts of experience, there are three passages which are explicitly concerned with the relations between seeing and interpreting in the experience of noticing an aspect.

The first passage occurs on the very first page of the discussion (*P.I.*, p.193) : in it Wittgenstein seems to object to the claim that, when we see a figure in different ways, we interpret the figure and see it in the way in which we interpret it.

The second passage occurs on page 200. Here Wittgenstein appears to defend the idea that it is possible to see an object according to an interpretation.

The third passage occurs on page 212: in it Wittgenstein expresses his inclination to say that when we notice now one aspect, now another aspect of a figure, we really see something different each time, rather than to say that we only interpret what we see in a different way.

In this paper, I intend to look at these passages in some detail and, in particular, to consider how they are related to one another.

I shall begin with the third passage. The context in which it occurs does not make it clear whether Wittgenstein is referring to a specific example of noticing an aspect or whether what he says is intended to apply to any example of such an experience. However, the particular sentences I have already mentioned are also to be found in section 208 of that collection of slips known as *Zettel*; and there they occur in conjunction with a specific example. So, as much for convenience as anything, I shall begin by considering those sentences in their context in *Zettel*.

The passage is as follows:

Let us consider what is said about a phenomenon like this: Seeing the figure ∓ [Fig. 6.1] [1] now as an F, now as the mirror image of an F.

I want to ask what constitutes seeing the figure now like this, now another way? – [The sentences which follow also occur in the *Investigations*[2]] Do I really see something different every time? Or do I merely *interpret* what I see in a different way? – I am inclined to say the first. *But why?* . . . [3]

I want to draw attention here to a peculiarity in both the question, and in Wittgenstein's handling of the question, 'Do I really see something different each time or do I merely interpret what I see in a different way?'

Wittgenstein seems to treat the alternatives presented in this question as though they are exclusive of one another, for he justifies his inclination to assert that I see something different by ruling out that I interpret what I see in a different way. The assumption seems to be that if I am seeing something different each time, then I am not interpreting what I see in a different way: and, conversely, if I am interpreting what I see in a different way, then I am not seeing something different each time. But this assumption is not self-evidently true. Why could it not be the case both that I see something different each time and that I interpret what I see in a different way? If it made sense to say this, one might account for the fact that I see something different each time by referring to the fact that I interpret what I see in a different way. But however that may be, the possibility that the alternatives are not mutually exclusive seems on the face of it to be acknowledged by Wittgenstein himself in the second of the passages on seeing and interpreting which I have already mentioned. For in it Wittgenstein maintains that there need be no friction, no difficulty in talking of seeing according to an interpretation.

As well as Wittgenstein's handling of the question, I want to suggest that, at least at first, the question itself is puzzling. The situation is this : I say that I am seeing the figure now in this way, that is, as an F, and now in that way, that is, as the mirror image of an F. Someone might ask here whether I *see* the figure in different ways. This could be expressed as the question, 'When it is said that I see the figure in different ways, is this really a case of *seeing*?' And this can be expressed as the question 'When it is said that I see the figure in different ways, do I really have a new or a different visual impression each time?' Put in this form, it is reasonable, if not necessary, to regard the question, 'Or do I merely interpret what I see in different ways?', as expressing an exclusive alternative. For the question now

---

[1]   I shall refer to this figure as 'the double-F figure'.
[2]   Although, with the exceptions of punctuation and emphases, the German is identical in the *Investigations* and in *Zettel*, the English translations are slightly, but not significantly, different.
[3]   The answer given to this 'But why?' in *Zettel* is similar in certain respects to the answer in the *Investigations*. I shall consider them later.

reads, 'Do I have a different visual impression each time or do I have only one visual impression on the basis of which I make different interpretations?' But the question Wittgenstein asks is not, 'Do I really *see* the figure differently each time or do I merely *interpret* what I see in a different way?'; rather, the question Wittgenstein asks is, 'Do I really see something different each time or do I merely interpret what I see in a different way?'

If one maintains, as Wittgenstein does, that I see something different when I see the figure as an F from what I see when I see the figure as a mirror image of an F, one could scarcely deny that I see the figure differently each time. That I see the figure differently is a weaker claim than the claim that I see something different each time. It is possible to maintain the former and deny the latter. There is not in ordinary speech any straightforward inference from 'I am seeing it differently now' to 'I am seeing something different now'. But given this, what follows, if anything does, from ruling out that I interpret what I see in a different way, is that I see the figure differently and not that I see something different. Since Wittgenstein provides no further argument to establish the stronger conclusion, either in the passage as it appears in *Zettel* or as it appears in the *Investigations*, I find it puzzling that the question he raises should be of the form, 'Do I really see something different each time or do I merely interpret what I see in a different way?' rather than of the form, 'Do I really see the figure differently each time or do I merely interpret what I see in a different way?' For this reason, I shall understand the question Wittgenstein asks in its latter, weaker, form, and return to the former, stronger, version towards the end of the paper.

To a certain extent, the difficulties I have raised about the question Wittgenstein asks in the third passage on seeing and interpreting can be clarified by considering the first passage on seeing and interpreting.

You could imagine the illustration[1]

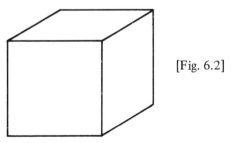

[Fig. 6.2]

appearing in several places in a book, a text-book, for instance. In the relevant text something different is in question every time: here a glass

---

[1]   I shall refer to this figure as 'the schematic cube figure'.

cube, there an inverted open box, there a wire frame of that shape, there three boards forming a solid angle. Each time the text supplies the interpretation of the illustration.

But we can also *see* the illustration now as one thing now as another. So we interpret it, and *see* it as we *interpret* it. (*P.I.*, p. 193)

The final sentence of this passage might appear to be a remark of Wittgenstein's; but the first sentence of the next paragraph indicates that this is not so. 'Here perhaps we should like to reply...', Wittgenstein says; which suggests that the sentence, 'So we interpret it, and *see* it as we *interpret* it', is possibly an interjection from an imaginary interlocutor. To appreciate the point of the interjection, we need to examine some of the features of the passage.

Wittgenstein has, it seems, contrasted the text supplying different interpretations of the figure, on the one hand, with seeing the figure now as one thing, now as another, on the other hand. As it stands, this is not a contrast between interpreting the figure in different ways and seeing the figure in different ways. We can distinguish knowing that on this page the figure represents a box and interpreting the figure as a representation of a box. Wittgenstein's point is that we can also — that is, in addition to just knowing that it is or interpreting it as — we can also *see* it as a representation of a box. It is on this claim that the interlocutor's interjection impinges: for he responds, 'So we *interpret* it, and *see* it as we interpret it', or, as the German might be translated,[1] 'We interpret it so, and *see* it in the way that we interpret it'. The force of this interjection is to threaten the contrast Wittgenstein has drawn by claiming that seeing the figure as a representation of a so-and-so is itself consequent upon interpreting it as a representation of a so-and-so.

It is worth noting that the interlocutor's claim apparently corresponds to what I suggested is missing from Wittgenstein's treatment of the question, 'Do I see something different each time or do I merely interpret what I see in a different way?', and that is the possibility that I interpret what I see *and* that I see something different or see the figure differently. With this in mind, it would be tempting to argue that the reason why Wittgenstein does not consider this possibility in the later passage is that he considers and rejects it in the earlier passage. To argue in this way, though tempting, would be to neglect the intervening passage in which Wittgenstein apparently defends the idea of seeing according to an interpretation. Before concluding that Wittgenstein rejects on page 193 what he defends on page 200, we should look more closely at the interlocutor's position. Wittgenstein's reply throws some light on it.

The description of the immediate experience (or 'what is got

---

[1]   ' — Wir deuten sie also, und *sehen* sie, wie wir sie *deuten*.'

immediately', as Miss Anscombe translates the German[1]), that is, the description of the visual experience as 'seeing the figure as (a representation of) a box' is, Wittgenstein states, an indirect description, for it is a description 'by means of an interpretation'. According to the interlocutor, what the statement, 'I see the figure as a box', means (or what I mean when I say, 'I see the figure as a box') is that 'I have a particular visual experience which I have found that I always have when I interpret the figure as a box or when I look at a box'. Now, Wittgenstein argues, if this is what I mean, then I ought to know it. Furthermore, I ought to be able to refer to or to describe the visual experience directly 'and not only indirectly. (As I can speak of red without calling it the colour of blood)'. (*P.I.*, p. 193–4.)

What I want to attend to in this reply is the interlocutor's position as it is presented by Wittgenstein. When I say, 'I see this figure as a representation of a box', or when I say, 'I see this figure as a representation of a glass cube' or 'I see this figure as three boards forming a solid angle', I am, on the interlocutor's position, providing different indirect descriptions of my visual experience. They are *indirect* descriptions, because they are descriptions by means of or in terms of interpretations; and they are *different* descriptions, because there are different interpretations. The implication is that the direct descriptions of the visual experience would be the same in each case, descriptions which as it happens I am not ordinarily aware of.

This account of the interlocutor's position seems to me to bear a strong likeness to some of the things Locke says about perception.[2] Locke, you will remember, holds that in perception, 'the ideas we receive by sensation are often in grown people altered by the judgment . . .' (*II*,9.8), the act of judgment being 'performed so constantly and so quick, that we take that for the perception of our sensation which is an *idea* formed by our judgment; so that one, viz., that of sensation, serves only to excite the other, and is scarce taken notice of itself. . .' (*II*,9,9); the idea received by sensation 'being only a plane variously coloured, as is evident in painting'. (*II*,9,8). In terms of Locke's account, noticing the aspects of the schematic cube figure [Fig. 6.2] would consist in receiving an idea of a plane figure which, as a result of previous experiences of seeing boxes, glass cubes, etc., and seeing representations of boxes, glass cubes, etc., excites the judgment to frame the idea of a three-dimensional object such as a box or a glass cube, etc.; but, since we are not usually aware of either the original idea received in sensation or the procedure of judging, we say that we see the figure as a representation of a box, as a representation of a glass cube, etc.

---

1 '. . . Die Beschreibung der unmittelbaren Erfahrung . . .'
2 J. Locke, *An Essay Concerning Human Understanding*, Bk II, ch. 9. All references are to the 5th ed. as edited by J. W. Yolton for Everyman's Library, 1961.

I do not wish to claim that Wittgenstein had Locke's account of perception in mind when writing about seeing and interpreting. I do, however, wish to claim that Locke's account does imply a position similar to that of Wittgenstein's interlocutor, and that it was against the background of some such conception of perception as is expressed by Locke that Wittgenstein developed his discussion of noticing an aspect. The central feature of that conception of perception is the belief that it is possible in any perceptual situation to make a clear distinction between what is given through or presented to the senses and what is contributed by the workings of the intellect. This belief is often manifested in the propositions (1) that that which is given through or presented to the senses is essentially private; (2) that that which is given through or presented to the senses constitutes the visual impression in any perceptual situation; (3) that the description of that which is given through or presented to the senses on any occasion is the description of what is really seen; (4) that any further description of what is seen is the result of judgment, inference, or interpretation — in short, the workings of the intellect. All these propositions are subscribed to by Locke, and they are all, to a greater or lesser extent, examined in Wittgenstein's discussion of noticing an aspect.

Understanding the interlocutor's position in terms of Locke's account of perception exposes a previously unnoticed implication: that, according to the interlocutor, I do not really *see* the schematic cube figure differently — when I say I see it now as this, now as that, I have only one visual impression on the basis of which I make different interpretations. Understood in this way, the interlocutor still threatens Wittgenstein's contrast between knowing what the figure represents or interpreting it as a representation of a so-and-so and seeing it as a representation of a so-and-so. For the interlocutor, in effect, denies that such a contrast can be made : he would claim that I say I see the figure as a representation of a so-and-so, instead of saying that I interpret it as a representation of a so-and-so, only because I am not aware of having made an act of judgment.

In response to such a position, it is natural to want to ask, 'When I say I see the figure now as this, now as that, do I really *see* the figure differently or do I merely *interpret* what I see in a different way?' This is the weaker version of the question Wittgenstein asks in the third passage on seeing and interpreting. Wittgenstein asks this question, I suggest, because of the threat from the interlocutor. This explains why Wittgenstein justifies his inclination to say that I *see* the figure differently by simply ruling out that I am *interpreting* what I see in a different way. It also explains why the possibility that I interpret what I see *and* that I see the figure differently is not considered. It is not considered because it is not regarded as a genuine possibility by the interlocutor. For on the interlocutor's position, the suggestion that I see something in the way that I interpret it entails that I do not really *see* it in that way. And this explains why Wittgenstein defends the idea that I can see something according to an interpretation in the second passage on seeing and interpreting: he defends it against the interlocutor's attack.

The source of the interlocutor's claim that what we call seeing the figure differently is really interpreting the figure differently is that, in noticing different aspects of a figure, the visual impression is unchanged. To appreciate Wittgenstein's response to the interlocutor, we need to have before us an outline of his views about visual impressions.

For Wittgenstein, the criterion of the visual experience or visual impression is the representation of 'what is seen', where by 'representation' is meant both pictorial representation and verbal description.[1] (*P.I.*, p. 198). This reflects Wittgenstein's rejection of the view that inner or personal experiences are essentially private and his acceptance of the view that descriptions of how things look to me are logically secondary to descriptions of things. Given that as a rule you agree with our descriptions of things, your answer to the question, 'What do you see?', provides us with a criterion of how what you see looks to you, a criterion of your visual experience or impression. Your answer need not consist of a verbal description: you could produce a picture or point to one of a number of pictures. If on a particular occasion, you describe something which is green as red and produce or point to a picture of something red, this provides us with a reason for saying that this green thing looks red to you. The representation of what is seen, whether in words or in pictures, is the criterion of the visual impression because in normal conditions things are as they look to us; and in abnormal conditions, we can retreat from saying 'I see this', where 'this' is followed by a description or picture, to saying 'What I see looks to me like this', where 'this' can be followed by the same description or picture. At least one qualification needs to be made here, for in certain circumstances I might, for example, describe as blue something which *is* blue even though it looks green to me: I would do this perhaps because I am aware that I am looking at the object in yellow light. Following Vesey,[2] we can identify how the object looks to me by reference to how I would describe the object had I no reason to think otherwise.

Now, as Wittgenstein points out (*P.I.*, pp. 194—5), you might, on looking at the duck-rabbit figure,

[Fig. 6.3]

---

[1] The German translated by 'representation' in 'the representation of "what is seen" ' is 'Darstellung'. Later, Wittgenstein speaks of '. . . two-dimensional representation whether in drawing or in words'. *PI.*, p. 198.

[2] G. N. A. Vesey, 'Seeing and Seeing As', *P.A.S.* (1955—6).

not realise that it is ambiguous and, at one time, describe what you see as a representation of a duck and, at another time, describe what you see as a representation of a rabbit. On Wittgenstein's criterion, we would have reason for saying that at first the figure looked to you like a representation of a duck and that later the same figure looked to you like a representation of a rabbit. Similar points could be made with respect to the double-F figure [Fig. 6.1] and the schematic cube figure [Fig. 6.2]. Usually, of course, we are aware of the ambiguity of such figures, but it will not do simply to conclude, as Vesey does at one point,[1] that in experiencing a change of aspects there is a change in how the figure looks to me even though I believe truly that there is no change in the appearance of the object. This neglects the fact that I obtain that belief by *seeing* that the figure remains the same and not by being told or inferring it from my knowledge of the conditions of observation (which might be the case when I look at an object before and after an hallucinatory drug takes effect). This point can be brought out by considering that, although the description I would give of what I see had I no reason for thinking otherwise would be different before and after experiencing a change of aspect and before and after the drug takes effect, the copy I would make (or point to) of what I see before and after experiencing the change of aspect would be the same, but the copy I make (or point to) before the drug takes effect would be different from the copy I make (or point to) after it takes effect.

Since a copy of what is seen is just one kind of representation of what is seen, we have, on Wittgenstein's criterion, a reason for saying that in experiencing a change of aspect the visual impression is unchanged, for the copy is unchanged, and for saying that the visual impression is different, for the description is different. This indicates that it would be a mistake to maintain that in experiencing a change of aspect one has a new or different visual impression. The most that could be maintained, following Wittgenstein's criterion, is that the sense in which the visual impression is different before and after experiencing a change of aspect is not the same as the sense in which the visual impression can be said to be different in perceptual situations where either the object seen or the conditions of observation change.

One way of understanding the interlocutor's position at this point is to think of him as holding that the copy of what is seen is the sole criterion of the visual impression: the copy is the criterion of what is presented to the senses. Following this criterion, he is led to maintain that the visual impression remains the same throughout an experience of a change of aspects. The change in description of what is seen is then regarded as a

---

[1] See Vesey's postscript to his remarks as chairman of a discussion between R. L. Gregory and G. E. M. Anscombe on the topic 'Perceptions as Hypotheses', in *Philosophy of Psychology*, ed. S. C. Brown (London, 1974).

consequence of a change in interpretation. Whatever the merits or demerits of the interlocutor's criterion of the visual impression, his position here shows that the fact that one describes what one sees differently before and after noticing an aspect cannot be a sufficient reason for claiming that the visual impression is in some sense different, for this is compatible with saying that one makes different interpretations on the basis of a single visual impression. What is required here is an investigation into the criteria for the application of the expressions 'seeing' and 'interpreting'; or, in Wittgenstein's words, 'how to tell whether something is to be called a case of interpreting or of seeing'. (*Z.*, section 212). This brings us back to the third passage on seeing and interpreting, and to Wittgenstein's justification of his inclination to say that we see something different or that we see something differently.

Interpreting and seeing are for Wittgenstein categorially different. 'Seeing is not an action, but a state' (*Z.*, section 208; cf. *P.I.*, p. 212), he says; whereas 'interpreting is a procedure' (*Z.*, section 208): it is 'to think, to do something' (*P.I.*., p. 212). These remarks suggest the possibility of a grammatical exercise of the kind made familiar by Ryle; but Wittgenstein takes a different line.

In the *Investigations*, he says that 'it is easy to recognize cases in which we are *interpreting*. When we interpret we form hypotheses, which may prove false'. (*P.I.*, p. 212). What kind of hypotheses Wittgenstein means can by seen from the corresponding passage in *Zettel*. There he says that interpreting the double-F figure [Fig. 6.1] might "consist in somebody's saying 'That is *supposed* to be an F'; or not saying it, but replacing the sign with an F in copying; or again considering: 'What can that be? It'll be an F that the writer did not hit off' . . . I should call it 'interpretation' ", Wittgenstein writes, "if I were to say, 'That is certainly supposed to be an F; the writer does all his F's like that'." (*Z.*, section 208).

The figure might in fact be a 'T' with the writer's personal embellishment, thus $\mp$. I would therefore be wrong in supposing that the figure is an F, and replacing it with an F in copying would be a mistake. Hence, to interpret the figure as an F would be to form an hypothesis which might be, and in this case is, false. The hypothesis, the interpretation, is an hypothesis about the identity of what is seen, produced in a situation where the identity is not known, and for which evidence can be found — evidence which may be either for (e.g. 'He does all his F's like that') or against (e.g. 'The author informs us that it is a "T" ') the hypothesis. With respect to the schematic cube figure [Fig. 6.2], we could interpret it as, or hypothesise that it is, a representation of a box, rather than of a cube, etc. And in Wittgenstein's example (*P.I.*, p. 193) we could verify or confirm the interpretation or hypothesis by reading the text, which would tell us what it is a representation of on this particular page.

In the *Investigations*, Wittgenstein contrasts interpreting in this sense with seeing in the following way:

> Now it is easy to recognize cases in which we are *interpreting*. When we interpret we form hypotheses, which may prove false. – 'I am seeing this as a . . .' can be verified as little as (or in the same sense as) 'I am seeing bright red' . . . (*P.I.*, p. 212).

It is not easy to discern Wittgenstein's thought in this passage. At first it seems as though there is a confusion between verifying the hypothesis or interpretation I have formed and verifying that I am forming an hypothesis or an interpretation; for what Wittgenstein is supposed to be contrasting with 'I am seeing it as a . . .' is surely 'I am interpreting it as a . . .'. The purpose of drawing this contrast is to bring out that interpreting is a procedure, whereas seeing is a state. This suggests that, in considering the similarity of 'I am seeing this as a . . .' to 'I am seeing bright red', what needs to be emphasised in the latter statement is the word 'seeing' rather than the words 'bright red'. That is, what is significant about 'I am seeing bright red' is that it is an example of *seeing* rather than which example of seeing it is. Nevertheless, as we shall see, there is something to be gained from considering the specific nature of the example.

It makes sense to ask, 'Why are you or what are your reasons for (meaning: what justifies you in) interpreting the figure as a representation of a box?', whereas it is absurd to ask, 'Why are you or what are your reasons for (meaning: what justifies you in) seeing bright red?' It is part of the concept of action that there should be reasons which justify what we do and so make what we do intelligible; but there are no reasons which justify our seeing bright red, for seeing is a state, not something we do. Similarly, it seems absurd to ask, 'Why are you or what are your reasons for (meaning: what justifies you in) seeing this figure as a representation of a box?' There are no reasons which justify our being in particular sensory states (though there are no doubt explanations in a causal sense). If it were discovered that the figure is not a representation of a box, this would not in any way affect my statement, 'I am seeing this as a representation of a box', but this discovery would force me to give up my interpretation or hypothesis that the figure is a representation of a box, just as realising the inadequacy of my reasons for interpreting the figure as a representation of a box would force me either to abandon or modify my interpretation.

The question, 'What are your reasons for interpreting the figure as a representation of a box?', is equivalent to the question, 'What makes you think, or what reasons have you got for hypothesising, that the figure is a representation of a box?'; and it might be argued that a question of the same form could be asked of someone who says he is seeing bright red – that is, 'What makes you think or what reasons have you got for saying that what you see is bright red?' The answer to this question, as Wittgenstein makes clear in the *Brown Book* is, ' "Nothing *makes* me call it red; that is, *no reason* . . .".' (*BB.*, p. 148). My calling what I see red is a manifestation of my knowledge of the meaning of the word 'red' (*P.I.*, section 382), but to say, 'I call it red because I know what 'red' means or what red looks like', is not to state evidence by reference to which I justify calling what I see red. Similarly, to the question, 'What makes you think or what reasons have you got for saying that you are seeing the figure as a representation of a box or that it is a representation of a box you are seeing the figure as?', it would be an answer to say, 'Nothing makes me say this; that is, no reason' or 'I know what a box is; I know what representations of boxes are like'. In this respect, 'I am seeing this figure as a . . .' is similar to 'I am having an image of a . . .' (cf. *P.I.*, p. 213): making the utterance presupposes knowledge of the criteria for the application of the relevant concept, but is not made as a consequence of employing those criteria.

The implications of this investigation of the grammar of the expressions 'seeing' and 'interpreting' are twofold. It shows, first of all, that the interlocutor is mistaken in maintaining that what I mean by the statement, 'I see this figure as a . . .', can be elucidated in terms of the statement, 'I am interpreting this figure as a . . .'. Rather, as Wittgenstein might have put it, the statements occupy different places in logical grammar. Secondly, Wittgenstein's remarks suggest the nature of the criteria by means of which we tell whether someone is seeing, rather than interpreting, a figure as a representation of a so-and-so. Since interpreting is forming hypotheses, someone who interprets a figure as a representation of a so-and-so will as a rule be prepared to consider this as one among a number of possibilities, will consider reasons for, and against, his interpretation; interpreting will, then, as a rule, involve pausing, reflecting, deliberating. In the absence of such criteria, where the response to the figure is unhesitating, spontaneous, we have reason for saying that he sees the figure in a certain way. As Wittgenstein writes in *Zettel*, in connection with the double-F Figure [Fig. 6.1], '. . . if I have never read the figure as anything but an F or considered what it might be, we shall say that I *see* it as F; if that is, we know that it can be seen differently . . .'. (*Z*, section 208). In general, our grounds for saying that someone sees the figure in a particular way, as opposed to saying that he interprets it in a particular way, are his reactions to the figure, where his reactions include what he does and what he is prepared to do as well as what he says and what he is prepared to say. The differences are revealed in what Wittgenstein calls 'fine shades of behaviour' (*P.I.*, pp. 203, 204, 207), which include gestures indicating familiarity with the figure and the tone of voice expressing surprise and recognition.

It is useful to compare these views with what Wittgenstein has to say about seeing emotions and consciousness in people's faces.

'Look into someone else's face', Wittgenstein suggests, 'and see the consciousness in it, and a particular *shade* of consciousness. You see on it, in it, joy, indifference, interest, excitement, torpor and so on'. (Z., section 220).

This is indeed how we ordinarily speak. What gives us reason for saying that we *see* emotion or consciousness is the fact that 'we describe a face immediately as sad, radiant, bored, even when we are unable to give any other description of the features'. (Z., section 225). Here an interlocutor might wish to claim that, when we say we see sadness in someone else's face, what we really mean is that we interpret what we see as expressing sadness; to which Wittgenstein's reply is that we ought to be able to refer to our visual experience directly and not only indirectly, by means of an interpretation. That is, if we are interpreting what we see, we ought to be able to describe what we see prior to providing an interpretation. And the point is that, frequently, we cannot do this; we find it difficult to describe 'facial contortions', that is, to describe faces without using psychological concepts. These are the terms in which we naturally, spontaneously, describe what we see.

Similarly, we find it difficult to describe conventional pictorial representations as just flat patches of colour. It is characteristic of our reactions to conventional pictures to describe and reidentify them by means of concepts of the things they are representations of, and in this respect they can be compared with those kinds of puzzle-pictures which we can at first only describe as configurations of colour and shape. It is against this background of our ordinary talk of pictures that we can understand why Wittgenstein's question in the third passage on seeing and interpreting is of the form, 'Do I really see something different each time or do I merely interpret what I see in a different way?', rather than of the form, 'Do I really see the figure differently or do I merely interpret what I see in a different way?'. In this context we talk of seeing things (which are represented) *in* pictures. Figures such as the duck-rabbit figure and the schematic cube figure are distinguished by the fact that the different things which can be seen in them cannot be seen simultaneously. Thus, the typical expressions of the experience of a change of aspect, the exclamations, 'Now it's a duck!' or 'Now it's a cube projecting out of the page!', not only give us reason for saying that one sees the figures differently, but also give us reason for saying that one sees something different each time.[1] As Wittgenstein puts it, 'The expression in one's voice

---

[1]   The case of the double-F figure [Fig. 6.1] is different: we do not see different things represented in the figure, we do not see it now as the representation of F, now as the representation of a mirror image of an F. To justify saying that we see something different when we see the figure differently, one might fall back on the claim that, when we see the figure as an F, we would describe what we see as an F had we no reason to think otherwise; and, when we see the figure as a mirror image of an F, we would describe what we see as a mirror image of an F had we no reason to think otherwise.

and gestures is the same as if the object had altered and had ended by *becoming* this or that'. (*P.I.*, p. 206).

Now if we acknowledge that there are criteria for saying that there are cases of seeing a figure in different ways which do not involve interpreting, then there should be no objection *a priori* to the suggestion that there might be cases which satisfy criteria for saying that both seeing and interpreting occur. We might think here, for instance, of the familiar fact that it is easier to find the solution of some puzzle-pictures than it is to find the solution of others. Of cases where the aspect dawns after a period of trying out various possibilities — 'it's a representation of a house, a face, or a horse' — or where, knowing that it is a representation of a face, we try to find the face in the picture, we might wish to say that they are cases of seeing the pictures as a result of, or according to, an interpretation.

In the second passage about seeing and interpreting (*P.I.*, p. 200) which I mentioned at the beginning of this paper, Wittgenstein refers to the bare triangular figure:

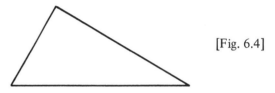

[Fig. 6.4]

He indicates that we can think of it now as a representation of a triangular hole, now as a representation of a solid, and then see it now as a representation of a triangular hole, now as a representation of a solid; or, again, we can think of the figure now as a representation of a mountain, now as a representation of an overturned object, and then see it now as a representation of a mountain, now as a representation of an overturned object. These remarks are followed by the question, 'But how is it possible to *see* an object according to an *interpretation*?', to which Wittgenstein responds, 'The question represents it as a queer fact, as if something were being forced into a form it did not really fit. But no squeezing, no forcing took place here.' (*P.I.*, p. 200).

Wittgenstein is here evidently defending the possibility of seeing an object according to an interpretation. The defence is raised, I suggest (and as I have already suggested), against the interlocutor who appears in the first passage on seeing and interpreting. According to the interlocutor's position as I have elaborated it, it makes no sense to talk of seeing according to an interpretation, for seeing is determined by what is given, what is presented to the senses. Hence, for the interlocutor, talk of *seeing* differently as a consequence of *interpreting* differently is going to seem as though something — viz., the workings of the intellect — is being forced into a form — viz., seeing — which it does not really fit. But this appearance of squeezing or forcing results from neglecting the ordinary criteria for saying that someone is seeing as opposed to interpreting. It results, in fact, from accepting only one kind of representation of what is seen — a copy or description in two-dimensional terms — as the only genuine kind of representation of what is seen. This is not to imply that a copy is an incomplete description of one's visual experience, for, as Wittgenstein says, 'the circumstances decide whether, and what, more detailed specifications are necessary. — It *may* be an incomplete description, if there is still something to ask'. (*P.I.*, p. 199). The point is that in cases of noticing an aspect of something, a copy is always an incomplete description of the visual experience because there is always something further to ask.

I should like to end this paper by making two comments on Wittgenstein's example of seeing an object according to an interpretation.

Wittgenstein indicates that we can think of the bare triangular figure as a representation of a mountain and then see it as a representation of a mountain. But if thinking of the figure as a representation of a mountain is to count as interpreting the figure in a particular way, this does not seem to be the same sense of 'interpreting' which I considered earlier. For when I think of the figure as a representation of a mountain and see it in that way, I am not forming the hypothesis that the figure is a representation of a mountain. I know that it is not what I am seeing it as: it is just a bare triangular figure. To think of it as a representation of a mountain is not to think *that* it is a representation of a mountain.

At one point in his discussion of noticing an aspect, Wittgenstein suggests that '. . . What a figure could also be . . . is what it can be seen as . . .' (*P.I.*, p. 206). The bare triangular figure could also be a representation of a mountain, and this, among other things, is what it can be seen as. Perhaps the idea of interpreting as forming hypotheses can be linked with the idea of thinking of the figure now as this, now as that, by means of the notion of what a figure could also be. For to think of the figure as a representation of a mountain involves thinking that it could also be a representation of a mountain; it would make no sense for someone to claim that one can think of the figure as a representation of a mountain and at the same time to deny that the figure could also be a representation of a mountain. But to think of what else the figure could be a representation of is logically akin to forming various hypotheses about its identity as a representation: for that involves considering what the figure could be a representation of. To think that the figure could also be a representation of a mountain is not to think that the hypothesis, 'It is a representation of a mountain', is or might be true; but it is to think that it is an hypothesis which could be made concerning the identity of the figure if its identity were not already known. Possibly, then, it could be said that the difference between thinking of the figure as a representation of a mountain and interpreting it as a representation of a mountain amounts to the difference between entertaining and asserting an hypothesis.

My second comment concerns Wittgenstein's idea that thinking of a figure now as this, now as that, and then seeing it now as this, now as that, is a case of seeing an object according to an interpretation. One might understand the phrase 'seeing an object according to an interpretation' differently — along the lines indicated by Wittgenstein's remark in the first passage on seeing and interpreting, that 'the text supplies the interpretation of the illustration'. (*P.I.*, p. 193).

We could imagine the bare triangular figure [Fig. 6.4] being used to represent different things on different pages of a textbook: as I turn the pages, I see the figure as a representation of whatever it is that it represents on each particular page. Although I do not think of the figure now as this, now as that; although I do not interpret the figure in different ways, I might still be said to be seeing the figure according to different interpretations.[1] 'The figure as a representation of a mountain' and 'the figure as a representation of an overturned object' are different interpretations in the sense that these are descriptions of different ways of seeing the same figure. Thus, we might say that another interpretation of the figure would be to see it as a representation of a wedge.

It might now be claimed that this way of speaking implies that all seeing of pictorial representations, even conventional representations, is seeing according to an interpretation. For, as we learn from Wittgenstein's later work, all representations are susceptible to different interpretations. (cf. *Philosophical Grammar*, section 100; *Z*. section 236). Consider, for instance, an example from early on in the *Investigations* (*P.I.*, p. 54): a pictorial representation which we describe as a picture of an old man walking up a steep path leaning on a stick might be described by a Martian as a picture of an old man sliding downhill in that position. So, it might be claimed, *we* see the representation according to one interpretation, the Martian sees the representation according to another interpretation.

This, I think, neglects the important point made by Wittgenstein in the course of his discussion of following a rule:

> . . . there is a way of grasping a rule which is *not* an *interpretation*, but which is exhibited in what we call 'obeying the rule' and 'going against it' in actual cases. (*P.I.* section 201).

Applying this to pictorial representations, we could say that there is a way

---

[1] In other words, 'seeing an object according to an interpretation', need not entail 'seeing an object according to an act of interpreting'. Cf. *Z*., section 217. I am grateful to Vesey for emphasising this point in the course of the discussion following the presentation of the paper.

of reacting to pictures which is not an interpretation, but which is exhibited in what we call 'seeing something in a picture' and 'failing to see something in a picture' in actual cases. Seeing an old man walking uphill in the picture is not seeing according to an interpretation: this is what we call a case of seeing something in a conventional picture. The fact that there might possibly be different ways of seeing it does not enter into our reactions to it. This is just where conventional pictures are distinguished from what we call ambiguous pictures: for the fact that the latter pictures can be and are seen in different ways by us is involved, to a greater or lesser extent, in our reactions to them.

7

NEW PHENOMENALISM AS AN ACCOUNT OF PERCEPTUAL KNOWLEDGE

Alan Hobbs

To be an Empiricist with respect to knowledge of the natural world, is to insist that all knowledge of that world is rooted in perceptual experience. All claims which go beyond the deliverances of the senses must, in the end, be justified by, and understood in terms of, relations holding between those claims and sensory data. Crucial to the Empiricist case, therefore, is an account of how perception can be a source of knowledge. How can sensory experiences provide, for the owner of those experiences, information about objects and events which exist independently of the experiences themselves?

The following essay scavenges in contemporary sources to arrive at a fresh Empiricist account of perceptual knowledge. There are sufficient parallels with earlier doctrines to call the outcome 'New Phenomenalism', but the label is not important. The materials for the thesis have been gathered (and probably twisted) from several current writers, most notably P.F. Strawson and Jonathan Bennett,[1] but no one of these writers is a proponent of the expounded thesis as a whole. As with a composite photograph, no face completely fits.

Empiricism has, in a long tradition, oscillated between the unsatisfactory alternatives of Idealism and the Causal Theory of Perception. This oscillation has been generated by two apparently conflicting thoughts. The first is that sensory states are independent of, and caused by, the objects about which they provide knowledge. The second is that our claims about the world can be understood and justified only in terms of remarks exclusively about our sensory states. The former thought draws the Empiricist towards a causal theory of perception; the latter pushes him

---

[1] J. Bennett, *Locke, Berkely, Hume* (Clarendon Press, 1971) chs II, III, VI, XIII; and his *Kant's Analytic* (Cambridge University Press, 1966) esp. Chs 2, 3, 8, 9, 13–15. P. F. Strawson, *Individuals* (Methuen, 1959) Pt I; and his *The Bounds of Sense* (Methuen, 1966) Pts 1, 2, 4.

into the arms of Idealism. The thesis here dubbed 'New Phenomenalism' attempts to embrace both thoughts at once.

The central claim of new phenomenalism can be (obscurely) expressed thus:

> There is some general conceptual connection between statements about our sensory states and our possession of knowledge about a world of objects existing independently of the sensory states themselves.

To lessen the obscurity of this central claim, we are given a sketch of perceptual knowledge which runs something like this:

> A man divides his sensory states into (roughly) two piles: those which can be construed as perceptual experiences of an independent world, and those which cannot be thus construed. This twofold classification cannot be understood if one concentrates only on the presented characteristics of each sensory state in isolation. Macbeth will never know whether he is having an hallucination of a dagger, rather than perceiving one, unless he begins to relate sensory states one to another over time. If he picks a long enough temporal sequence of such states, then it will become clear to him that a sub-class of these states can be construed as perceptions according to the following principle:
>
> 'These sensory states are just those, and in just that order, that I would expect if there were an orderly independent world of objects of which I had fragmentary perceptions from a point of view within that world.'

Selections from this 'original sketch' will be quoted and examined in later sections of the paper. To understand it, three questions must be answered.

(1) What are sensory states? How are they given to consciousness, and in what form are they reported?

(2) We are told that a man 'construes' certain of his sensory states as perceptual experiences of an independent world. What is the nature of this construing exercise? Is it reductive (as in Idealism and in Linguistic Phenomenalism), or does it take the form of a non-deductive inference from effect to cause (as in the Causal and Representative Theories)?

(3) New Phenomenalism portrays sensory states as independent of the experienced objects which cause those sensory states. How is this independence to be reconciled with the claim that the senses provide us with knowledge? How is the sceptic to be answered?

The answers given to these questions will illuminate what we have called 'the central claim', and thereby reconcile the two conflicting strands of Empiricist theories of perceptual knowledge. We take the questions in turn during the next three sections.

I

Here is a basic truth about sensory states: anyone who perceives a changing public world undergoes changes in sensory state which vary systematically with changes in the public world. It is through these changes in sensory state, related to a point of view, that he gets to know of public changes. To state his case, the new phenomenalist needs to make statements about these sensory states (let us, nostalgically, call them 'sense-datum statements'); statements in terms of which he can clarify the nature of perceptual knowledge. The form of such sense-datum statements can best be given by drawing on the work of J.M. Hinton.[1] Hinton suggests, broadly, that the only illuminating linguistic form available to us, in specifying the content of sensory states, is an exclusive disjunction, one of whose disjuncts is a perceptual claim. Thus, Macbeth, whether ignorant or not about the specific nature of his state, could informatively say 'Either I am seeing a dagger, or I am visually hallucinating a dagger, or . . .', and so on for the other sensory categories.[2] The importance of using this disjunctive form lies in four factors.

First and most obviously, such disjunctions meet the prime condition that no sense-datum statement should imply the truth of any claim to perceptual knowledge. The disjunction as a whole will be true if any one of its disjuncts is true, but the disjunction itself gives no hint as to which disjunct has that privilege.

Secondly, the disjunctive form enables the new phenomenalist to stress the necessary interconnections between the concepts of perception and hallucination. Although it is perfectly correct to talk of sensory states by saying things like 'It is with me as though I were perceiving an orange', it is philosophically misleading. It appears to give the concept of perception some sort of priority. The new phenomenalist wishes to insist that it would be just as correct to specify one's sensory state by saying 'It is with me as though I were hallucinating an orange'. In other words, the disjunctive form allows us to make it explicit that we do not face something called 'The problem of perception'; our task is to solve the problem of perception-hallucination-illusion-etc. To give an account of any one of these concepts is necessarily to give an account of them all.

The third benefit is that such statements clearly avoid the reification of

---

[1]   J. M. Hinton, *Experiences* (Clarendon Press, 1973) esp. IIb.

[2]   For convenience, we shall speak of these disjunctions as if they were between perception and hallucination only.

sense-data. They tell us what *states* the man may be in, but they do not insist that he is aware of any object. Such a stand is much more significant than a crude swipe with Occam's Razor. The objection to reified sense-data is not that an account of perceptual knowledge finds them merely unnecessary; it is that the sense of their postulation is problematic, and that the help they appear to offer is illusory. As to the sense of their postulation, an account is required of the sort of thing they are. A sort of thing is given by a list of predicable properties. The only adjectives available for predication are ones which are literally applicable only to ordinary public objects: 'red', 'round', 'solid' etc. To admit that these adjectives apply to sense-data only in some metaphorical sense, is to admit that the status of sense-data is no more specified by these adjectives than the status of a passage is specified by calling it 'purple', or the status of an argument by calling it 'solid'. But even if one could ignore the problem of their status as a sort of thing, one could not overcome the philosophical redundancy of their postulation. To admit non-physical objects of awareness, is to admit additional claims to perceptual knowledge into an exercise which was designed to clarify the notion of perceptual knowledge itself. One does not gain an understanding of 'Smith perceives a public apple' by being told that it implies a statement of the form 'Smith perceives a private quasi-apple'. If sense-datum statements are construed as statements about the man's sensory state, then these problems do not arise. To say 'It is with Smith such that either he is seeing a red apple, or he is hallucinating a red apple, or ...' is not to imply that there is something red. The disjunction makes it quite clear that the adjective 'red' qualifies the noun 'apple'. Nothing red is in the offing unless the disjunction is made true by the truth of the perception disjunct.

The last advantage of a disjunctive account is vitally important to an understanding of new phenomenalism. Since each sense-datum statement will contain a perception statement as one of its disjuncts, it is impossible to use sense-datum statements in any exercise which could be dubbed 'An analysis of perception statements'. One cannot have, as part of the analysans, the very statement that constitutes the analysandum. Traditionally, sense-datum statements have been taken as marking the characteristics of something common to perception, hallucination, illusion. This common element is then used in the analysis of perception statements. The disjunctive account cannot be thus used. To say 'It's either a cow or a horse' is not to commit oneself to a precise statement of some underlying characteristic shared by cows and horses; it is to make a statement about the different types of animal which might be present. We must, therefore, see the new phenomenalist as engaged in the task of clarifying a move from a set of disjunctive sense-datum statements to a set of non-disjunctive perception, illusion and hallucination claims. The move to be understood is not a move from statements about one kind of thing (sense-data) to statements about another kind (external objects); it is a move from disjunctions to particular disjuncts of those disjunctions. It follows from this that the new phenomenalist is interested in sensory states only in so far as those states are regarded as epistemic.[1] The central contention is that there are non-empirical connections between the general notion of conceptualised (epistemic) experience and our possession of justified beliefs about an objective world. Put more fully (in a way to be clarified in later sections), the new phenomenalist holds that we cannot understand how sensory states could be a source of knowledge unless we come to see that our manner of knowing these sensory states presupposes that we credit ourselves with knowledge of an objective world obtained through them. Our sensory states cannot be known at all unless they are known under the concepts employed in disjunctive sense-datum statements; and those concepts cannot be employed without crediting ourselves with perceptual knowledge of an objective world.

In conducting the investigation in terms of relations between epistemic states, the new phenomenalist also avoids commitment to a problematic feature of traditional Empiricist theories of meaning and epistemology. Locke, Berkeley and Hume, to different degrees and with varying emphasis, all contend that meaningful utterances and empirical beliefs must be traced back to simple sensory impressions. These sensory impressions are held to provide an exit from word-word expositions of meaning, and an escape from the regress of belief-belief justifications. At the ground-level of meaning and of belief, the subject simply confronts his sensory impressions and thereby acquires both basic meanings and basic beliefs. Crucial to these theories is the notion of a sense-impression as an unconceptualised, non-epistemic particular. Without such a notion, the distinctive character of these analyses of meaning and of basic belief would collapse. The hybrid of phenomenalism which this paper sets out ignores these traditional doctrines. The connections which it claims to trace are between one type of belief-reporting statement and another; not, as with traditional Empiricism, between a type of belief-reporting statement and some non-epistemic state.

In summary, the answer to our first question is this. For our new phenomenalist, sensory states are epistemic. The beliefs involved in these sensory states are expressed by disjunctions of (roughly) perception and hallucination claims. No such sense-datum statement implies the truth of any straightforward claim to perceptual knowledge, nor is any reification

---

[1] For the debate about seeing as epistemic, see G. J. Warnock, 'Seeing', and G.N.A. Vesey, 'Seeing and Seeing As', both in R. J. Swartz, (ed.) *Perceiving, Sensing and Knowing* (Doubleday, 1965); F. I. Dretske, *Seeing and Knowing* (Routledge and Kegan Paul, 1969) esp. ch. 2; G. Pitcher, *Perception* (Princeton University Press, 1971).

HUNT LIBRARY
CARNEGIE-MELLON UNIVERSITY
PITTSBURGH, PENNSYLVANIA 15213

of sense-data involved. The new phenomenalist faces the task of explaining the nature of the move from sense-datum statements to perceptual knowledge. The resultant explanation can be expected to clarify the status of perceptual knowledge,[1] but it cannot (because of the form given to sense-datum statements) constitute what has been traditionally called 'an analysis of perception'.

II

Our second question concerns the nature of the move from sense-datum statements to perceptual knowledge. We are told that each perceiver comes to 'construe' some of his sensory states as perceptual experiences of objects which are independent of those sensory states. Is this 'construing' to be regarded as some form of reductionism, or is it a species of non-deductive inference from effect to cause?

Obviously, new phenomenalism is not a form of Idealism. For an Idealist, material objects are nothing more than collections of sensory states. An Idealist is, therefore, committed to the view that there can be no material objects without the existence of sensory states; the link between existential material object statements and existential sense-datum statements, is one of logical implication. Since the new phenomenalist insists that perceived objects have an existence independent of sensory states, Idealist reductions are not available to him. As to the sense of 'reduction' in old linguistic phenomenalism, a verdict is more difficult. By dropping the model of a collection, and adopting the more formal instrument of logical construction, the linguistic phenomenalist is able to abandon the existential implication embraced by Idealists. Since material object statements are held to be logically equivalent to long conjunctions of *hypothetical* sense-datum statements, an existential material object claim implies no existential sense-datum claim. To say that if certain conditions obtain, then certain sense-data are to be had, is not to say that either clause of that hypothetical is currently true by itself. But the minimal sense of 'independence' emerging from this analysis is not strong enough for the new phenomenalist. In particular, he wishes to insist that material objects stand, as causes, to (some) sensory states as effects. This does not seem to be an intelligible claim under old phenomenalism. As I understand it, an (old phenomenalist) material object could no more cause sense-data than the average postman could affect individual postmen. In the absence of any other clear offers to characterise the reductive relation,

---

[1] Or, equally, 'the status of hallucinatory knowledge'. As we said earlier, one cannot elucidate the job done by the concept of perception without, at the same time, spelling out the role of the concept of hallucination.

we must conclude that the new phenomenalist's construing exercise is not a variety of reductionism.[1]

So we seem to be left with some form of non-deductive inference. Looking back to our original sketch of the construing process, it is clear that the move made is not that of a Causal or Representative theory. Our subject is not pictured as moving, by inference, from premises about what he is aware of (his sensory states) to conclusions about things (public objects) of which he is not aware. The correct gloss is that he finds himself in various sensory states and comes, over time, to understand that, on certain of these occasions, he is aware of public objects and that, on other occasions, he is merely hallucinating. We are concerned, not with inferences from items of one category to items of another, but with our way of determining the status of our sensory state.[2] To be aware of something is, under this thesis, to bring some categorial concepts to bear on one's sensory states.

But we are not yet clear about the import of the phrase 'bring some categorial concepts to bear on one's sensory states'. Nor have we been given any adequate characterisation of the epistemology of this exercise. Our only lead lies in the concluding sentences of the original sketch:

> If he picks a long enough temporal sequence of such states, then it will become clear to him that a sub-class of these states can be construed as perceptions according to the following principle:
> 'These sensory states are just those, and in just that order, that I would expect if there were an orderly independent world of objects of which I had fragmentary perceptions from a point of view within that world.' ,

These instructions drift us towards the idea that our sensory states come to be categorised as 'perceptual', 'hallucinatory' etc. only through the postulation of an ordered world which somehow serves to *explain* the temporal sequence of our sensory states. We have already said that the new phenomenalist rejects the move made by the traditional causal theory; namely, that of treating sensory states as clues to (and produced by) objects which lie beyond consciousness. But what other notion of explanation is available?

It is tempting, but finally wrong, to employ the following model. Suppose yourself seated behind an apparatus which restricts your range of

---

[1] It would be foolish to think that enough has been said here. One of the prime sources for our construction of new phenomenalism, Jonathan Bennett, still cleaves to the vocabulary of logical construction. See, for example, *Locke, Berkely, Hume*, pp. 133–9, 352–3.

[2] F. N. Sibley has some useful remarks about 'status concepts' in his 'Analysing Seeing', in *Perception*, ed. Sibley (Methuen, 1971) pp. 122–3.

vision. Not only are you constrained to view the world through a small hole; the hole also has a shutter which periodically blocks out all of the scenery. In front of the apparatus the experimenter produces a sequence of changes involving several objects, and you, as victim, are asked to say, on the basis of the fragmentary glimpses allowed by the apparatus, what you take to be going on in front of the hole. Faced with such a situation, it is clearly correct to say that your statements about the sequence of changes going on in front of the hole constitute an explanatory hypothesis with respect to the fragments of scenery that you were permitted to glimpse. You take yourself to have seen bits of a jig-saw puzzle, and the task is to guess at the missing pieces. The guessing will be done by making certain assumptions about continuity of change, identity of objects glimpsed at different times, and so on. This model, despite its undoubted attractions, must be rejected by the new phenomenalist. Instead of expounding the explanatory role of the concept of a-world-perceived in relation to our sensory states, this model has illustrated the explanatory role of a complete world in relation to a sequence of perceptual glimpses. In other words, it has presupposed that the concept of a perceived-world is already in operation. The explanandum in the model is a sequence of perceptions, and the explanans is a complete world (including the apparatus). In new phenomenalism, by contrast, the explanandum is a sequence of sensory states, and the explanans is the concept of a-world-perceived; the concept of perception itself must be part of the explanation.[1]

But the model did help. It drew our attention to the fact that there can be empirically grounded explanations which do not fit the restricted pattern of inferences from observed effects to hidden causes. Let us follow this up by returning to another remark made in the original sketch:

> . . . one cannot understand this twofold classification (into perceptions and non-perceptions) unless one concentrates on the temporal sequence of sensory states.

Consider the following line of reasoning:

> We distinguish[2] between perceptual and non-perceptual states. The only way of making that distinction must be grounded in our sensory states. (Empiricist Creed)

[1]   A similar objection applies to certain attempts to solve the Other Minds problem. Many putative solutions start from a model which presupposes that the concept of mind is already in operation. Behaviour is described in a vocabulary which could not be used unless the concept of mind was *already* playing its explanatory role.
[2]   If a factual premise seems out of place, then there are Kantian arguments in Strawson and Bennett which seek to show that we *must* make this distinction.

But (as Hume[1] saw) the character of our sensory states alone does not generate that distinction.

The distinction can be generated only if we recognise the role played by our concept of an ordered world in making that distinction.

The role played is that of allowing us to construe certain of our sensory states as giving (fragmentary) perceptual knowledge of an ordered world.

Hence, there is a conceptual connection between making the distinction, and our possession of knowledge of an independent world; unless we credit ourselves with such (perceptual) knowledge, the distinction cannot be drawn.

As with the original sketch, the line of argument is crude. Detailed versions would undoubtedly insist on increasing the variety of basic distinctions grounded in our knowledge of an objective world, and on linking them together by subsidiary arguments. This procedure again has its paradigms in the work of Strawson and Bennett. But the central claim stands out: only by crediting ourselves with knowledge of a world, independent of our sensory states, can we understand the general distinction between perceptual and non-perceptual experience. We now see that it is not the postulation of an external world that constitutes the crucial explanatory move. It is that the temporal sequence of sensory states is explained by the hypothesis that the sensory states permit of being ordered under the concepts of perception, hallucination etc. The concept of an ordered, independent world is brought in as part and parcel of the concept of perception; not as a postulate which explains (already identified) perceptual states. Hence, the new phenomenalist's central claim, set out at the beginning of this paper. The general conceptual connection between statements about our sensory states, and our possession of knowledge about an independent world, is mediated by the concept of perception (and its bedfellows). Sensory states can provide no knowledge at all until they are brought under concepts. As soon as they are specified by the disjunctive statements described in section I, one is operating with a set of concepts including that of perception. But (by Empiricist doctrine) all concepts, if they are to be concepts at all, must have some specifiable work to do in relation to experience. Hence, the sequence of sensory states must be construed as providing adequate justification for perception (and hallucination) claims. And this means that we cannot employ the concepts used in sense-datum statements unless we sometimes credit ourselves with (perceptual) knowledge of an independent world.

[1] 'But 'tis evident, that whenever we infer the cont'd existence of the objects of sense from their coherence, and the frequency of their union, 'tis in order to bestow on the objects a greater regularity than what is observ'd in our mere perceptions.' *Treatise*, I.iv.2. (Selby-Bigge, p. 197).

III

Despite our progress in the last section, we may still be uncertain about the epistemological placement of new phenomenalism. This final task can be tackled by examining some characteristic remarks of Strawson and Bennett on the topic of scepticism. We shall take the liberty of reading these remarks as a statement of consequences following from an acceptance of new phenomenalism. (This is a liberty because, as we said at the outset, new phenomenalism is a rag-bag construction from a number of contemporary philosophers). Both Strawson and Bennett reject a species of sceptical question roughly marked by this formulation: 'Do objects really exist independently of our sensory states?'

> Consider now the question 'Is anything in the objective realm in any way as it appears to be?' – which turns into the question 'Is there really any objective realm at all?' We cannot tackle this question, all in a lump, by any of the methods we ordinarily use to check on the evidence of our senses; for those methods involve assessing some bits of sensory evidence by trusting others, whereas our present question forbids us to trust our senses at all until after the question has been answered... So someone who conjectures that perhaps there is really no objective world 'out there' is either misusing the ordinary distinction between what really is the case and what (going by what we see, feel, etc.) appears to be the case, or else he is employing some unordinary distinction which could be expressed in the same words. In the latter case, of course, he owes us an explanation of what unordinary distinction he has in mind. (J. Bennett, *Locke, Berkeley, Hume,* pp. 64–5).

> What is needed is a distinction between the import of the question, 'Do bodies exist independently of perceptions?', as raised within the conceptual scheme to which we are committed in experience, and the import of that question, as raised within the context of the entire (Kantian) critical philosophy. So long as our questions and replies are raised and given within the framework of the scheme of ideas to which we are necessarily committed in experience, the answer to our question must be affirmative – and a trivial enough affirmative at that ... We can have no extraneous standard or scheme in terms of which we can give an esoteric sense to the question whether such objects *really* exist, as we must empirically conceive of them as existing, independently of our perceptions. The question can be understood only in the sense of the scheme itself to which we are committed and in that sense it admits of but one commonplace answer. (P.F. Strawson, *The Bounds of Sense,* pp. 259, 262).

In terms of section II, the impossibility of raising sceptical doubt amounts to this. Anyone raising that doubt must express it thus: 'Are those sensory states which I call 'perceptual experiences' really perceptual experiences at all?' The trouble with this question is that it makes use of a distinction (between perceptual and non-perceptual experiences) which, if the argument of the preceding section is cogent, cannot be made without the questioner automatically crediting himself with perceptual knowledge. His understanding of what would count as a perceptual experience consists in his understanding of how the notion of a fragmentarily perceived, independent world allows him to organise his sensory states.

Unfortunately, this dismissal of scepticism does not get to the heart of the new phenomenalist thesis. The sceptic will be worried, quite rightly, by the refusal to concentrate on the hypothesis which stands behind all the small-scale justifications of particular perceptual claims. His complaint will be that no sufficient justification has been given for the implicit move from

In employing these concepts of perception, hallucination etc., we must credit ourselves with knowledge of an objective world

to

We have knowledge of an objective world.

In particular, he sees some disparity between the new phenomenalist's insistence that independent, public objects are the causes of those sensory states dubbed 'perceptual', and the apparent denial that a fallible causal hypothesis underpins our general belief in the existence of an independent world.

In order to do justice to both parties, we must come to understand the distinction between

An hypothesis presupposed in order to get particular justifications of perceptual claims started

and

An hypothesis employed in justifying particular perceptual claims.

New phenomenalism can, quite consistently, accept that the cross-checking described by Bennett and Strawson, *employs* no general causal hypothesis, and that such a general hypothesis is *presupposed* by all such piecemeal cross-checkings. An hypothesis presupposed is not an hypothesis employed. And it is the former that the sceptic wants to know about.

Maybe we can clarify this by thinking again about the epistemic nature of sensory states (section I). We often remark that a man who is asked to describe his experiences replies by giving descriptions of those public objects which he would take to be confronting him, if his experiences were to be construed as perceptions. Even if he is convinced that the objects of his experience are illusory or hallucinatory, he still reports their content in public object terminology. Let us say that the descriptions given are always of the sort that would be employed if the belief concerned were a perceptual belief. More richly, the focus of our consciousness (given by the type of description employed in specifying our sensory experiences) is always on the public world, and never on any intrinsic properties of our internal states. When a full-blooded perceiver is asked to describe his experiences, he describes (other things being granted) what he would take to be the public objects of those experiences. If the new phenomenalist is right, he describes (part of) the cause of his sensory states. Since the focus of our consciousness is on public objects, and not on any intrinsic features of our sensory states, it is impossible for us to arrive at perception claims by treating our sensory states as analogous to clues about the external world. A man faced with a clue can characterize the clue without begging any questions about the sort of (absent) thing which is liable to produce it. As we have seen, the conscious subject in the new phenomenalist story is not in this sort of position. Sensory states are presented to consciousness under descriptions befitting the independent objects of perception which cause (many of) those states. In effect, this means that the distinction to be drawn between perceptions and non-perceptions requires us to treat all sensory states as *claims to perceptual knowledge* of an independent world. The sub-class of allowable claims is that sub-class which can be coherently construed as glimpses, over time, of an ordered independent world in which the subject himself has a place and a point of view; the sub-class of rejected claims being that sub-class which cannot be thus construed. The new phenomenalist rightly insists that this process of sorting out admissable from inadmissible perceptual claims uses no empirical inferences from effects to hidden causes. The appearance/reality distinction is drawn *within* experience. The construing is analogous to the sort of task facing a man who is asked the question, 'Which sub-class of these particular claims about the world can be true together, if the world is described in the following way?' The only difference is that the description of the world must itself be generated by extrpolation from the finally accepted sub-class of particular claims; chicken and egg must produce each other. The crucial contrast with the traditional Causal Theory is that, in new phenomenalism, all the beliefs have, as their object, the public world. Hence, no inferences are required from queer mental items to everyday tomatoes.

So the situation is this. In using the concepts of perception-hallucination, we commit ourselves to the truth of an overall hypothesis concerning the existence of an ordered, objective world which stands in certain causal relations to our sensory states. Assuming the truth of this hypothesis, we can then go on to sort out the acceptability of particular perceptual claims. This latter exercise is not itself a species of causal inference.[1]

What, then, of our sceptic? The new phenomenalist must admit that the hypothesis of a-world-perceived *is* an hypothesis, and not a necessary truth. Whether we count it as known a priori or as known empirically, is largely a verbal matter. One might wish to call it 'a priori' because all particular justifications presuppose and start with it. Also because no other hypothesis of comparable power, or fertility of detail, has been constructed.[2] On the other hand, an empiricist might well wish to remind us that the hypothesis is rooted in facts about the sequence and content of our sensory states. It may well be that any creature capable of crediting itself with knowledge of an objective world, necessarily undergoes sensory states that admit of conceptualisation in the way the new phenomenalism describes. But that, even if established, does not show that sensory states, conceptualised in this way, necessarily generate knowledge (rather than justified belief). The sceptic (as usual) is right in his claim that what we call 'knowledge' is a bootstraps operation; there is no possibility of closing all gaps, between justified belief and knowledge, by further investigation or argument. The only epistemologists likely to lose any sleep over this conclusion are those who mistakenly believe that in order to have knowledge, we must be able to prove that we have knowledge.

---

[1] We should not deny that, on special occasions, particular perceptual claims may be established by appeal to known causal regularities. Such claims, however, arise within the context of other perception claims which are not so established. H. P. Grice, 'The Causal Theory of Perception', in R. J. Swartz (ed), op. cit., is particularly instructive on this point.

[2] On the notion of an hypothesis without rivals, see H. Putnam's 'Other Minds', in *Logic and Art* ed. R. Rudner and I. Scheffler (Bobbs-Merril, 1972) pp. 80–2.

8

HUME'S IMPRESSIONS

R. J. Butler

It is a pleasure to read Hume, and to watch him explore recalcitrant problems with agility of mind and grace of style. Ironically these twin abilities have worked against each other from the beginning, in the first place because in the matter of writing Hume was an innovator – nobody before him had so successfully albeit unwittingly adapted French syntax to the writing of English-and-Scottish – and in the second place because on the grace of his style subtleties of thought flow past his readers, who then accuse him of obscurity. So abstruse were his writings to his contemporaries that he failed to achieve the literary recognition for which he craved; and even today, long after the elegance of his style has been received, it is said by Passmore that Hume in contrast to Berkeley 'was a philosophical puppy-dog, picking up and worrying one problem after another, always leaving his teeth-marks in it, but casting it aside when it threatened to become wearisome.'[1] Similarly Selby-Bigge says in his introduction to the *Enquiries*:

His pages, especially those of the Treatise, are so full of matter, he says so many things in so many different ways and different connexions, and with so much indifference to what he has said before, that it is very hard to say positively that he taught, or did not teach, this or that particular doctrine. He applies the same principles to such a great variety of subjects that it is not surprising that many verbal, and some real inconsistencies can be found in his statements. He is ambitious rather than shy of saying the same thing in different ways, and at the same time he is often slovenly and indifferent about his words and

---

[1] J. A. Passmore, *Hume's Intentions* (Cambridge, 1952) pp. 87–8.

formulae. This makes it easy to find all philosophies in Hume, or, by setting up one statement against another, none at all.[1]

It is my contention, in contrast, that when Hume's words are weighed clause by clause, his care in deploying terms becomes apparent, and alleged inconsistencies and obscurities and irrelevancies by and large disappear. Not that Hume never makes mistakes, but rather that he tends to make them consistently, and further his mistakes are such that the ferreting of them makes the chase worth while. They are, to my mind, a thoroughly different bevy from those habitually chased by Hume-hunters.

For Hume the begin-all of philosophy lay in the analysis of perceptions, which in the opening sentence of Book I he divides exhaustively into impressions and ideas. No question is more urgent upon coming to his system than to find out precisely what he means by a perception. In the Thomas Reid–T.H. Green–J.A. Passmore tradition it has become customary to treat impressions as sense-data now being received, and ideas as sense-data now being remembered or imagined or reflected upon, so that all perceptions are construed in one way or another as sense-data. All of the notable sense-datum theorists – Russell,[2] Moore,[3] Broad,[4] and Price[5] – read Hume in this way, the most extreme being Price. 'I think', he wrote in *Perception*, 'that all past theories have in fact started with sense-data. The Ancients and the Schoolmen called them *sensible species*. Locke and Berkeley called them *ideas of sensation*, Hume *impressions*, Kant *Vorstellungen*. In the nineteenth century they were usually spoken of as sensations, and people spoke of visual and auditory sensations when they meant colour-patches and noises . . .'[6] More recently Price has reconstructed the section 'Of scepticism with regard to the senses' as a close but slightly inaccurate anticipation of his own theory. Hume's successive perceptions become sense-data which contain gaps, and the idea of continued existence is explained by the mind's having filled in the gaps in those sense-data we have.[7]

Doubtless this interpretation of perceptions as sense-data is reinforced by Hume's random references to images of the mind, by his notion that ideas are copies of impressions, and by his use of words which may be

---

[1] References to Hume's *A Treatise of Human Nature* and *An Enquiry Concerning Human Understanding* are referred to in the text by abbreviations 'T' for *Hume's Treatise of Human Nature*, ed. L. A. Selby-Bigge (Oxford, 1888); 'E' for *Hume's Enquiries*, ed. L. A. Selby-Bigge, 2nd ed. (Oxford, 1901).

[2] B. Russell, *The Problems of Philosophy* (London, 1912) pp. 95–6.

[3] G. E. Moore, *Some Main Problems of Philosophy* (London, 1953) pp. 104–6.

[4] C. D. Broad, *The Mind and Its Place in Nature* (London, 1923) pp. 233–4.

[5] H. H. Price, *Hume's Theory of the External World*, (Oxford, 1940) pp. 15 ff.

[6] H. H. Price, *Perception* (London, 1934) p. 19.

[7] H. H. Price, *Hume's Theory of the External World*, loc. cit., pp. 21–2 et passim

construed pictorially, such as 'correspond', 'represent' and 'resemble'. Yet close scrutiny of the words which Hume introduces technically — 'perception', 'impression' and 'idea' — and of the word 'image', which is never introduced technically and has in the text more non-pictorial than pictorial uses, cannot but raise difficulties in foisting upon Hume a sense-datum theory. Such an interpretation is alien to the spirit of Hume. For whatever sense-data *are*, and this is a question which to this day remains unanswered, they are *not* beliefs. Yet Hume says all over the place that beliefs are ideas: the peculiar characteristic of such ideas is that their force and vivacity may very nearly approach that of impressions (T 97n).

Precisely the same remarks apply to the view which T.H. Green took over from Thomas Reid, that perceptions are sensations. For whatever sensations are, they are not beliefs; yet it is quite possible that beliefs are accompanied by tweaks and twitches and twinges and even by picture-images. In challenging the received interpretation of Hume's theory of perceptions, that by perceptions he means either sensations or sense-data, I do not wish to deny that Hume's perceptions may be accompanied by such sensations. What is denied is that Hume regards such sensations as inseparable from or identical to perceptions *per se*. Even when Hume says that 'belief super-adds nothing to the idea, but only changes our manner of conceiving it' (T 101) and further says *'that belief is more properly an act of the sensitive, than of the cogitative part of our natures*' (T 183), adding in the Appendix *'that belief is nothing but a peculiar feeling, different from the simple conception*' (T 624), he is not saying that the perception believed is a sensation or a sense-datum.

Hume's theory of perceptions is part of his 'science of man', which encompasses 'the extent and force of human understanding': it seeks to explain 'the nature of the ideas we employ, and the operations we perform in our reasonings'. On this Hume was emphatic. 'The sole end of logic,' he writes, 'is to explain the principles and operations of our reasoning faculty and the nature of our ideas' (T 19). Perhaps Hume's greatest contribution to philosophical analysis is his keen awareness of the distinction between the *and* of separability, as when one compiles a grocery list, and the *and* of inseparability, as in 'The globe of white marble is both figured and coloured.' When Hume speaks of the principles and operations of our reasoning faculty *and* the nature of our ideas, is he using the *and* of separability or the *and* of inseparability or both? This is a matter which can only be settled by examining each of Hume's principles and operations of the mind in turn. Here it is enough to advance very tentatively the thesis that Hume may on occasion regard a principle or operation of the mind as inseparable from a perception, and the somewhat stronger but equally tentative thesis, that it may be the case with all perceptions that they are inseparable from some principles or operations of the mind.

'All the perceptions of the human mind resolve themselves into two distinct kinds, which I shall call IMPRESSIONS and IDEAS' (T 1). With these words Hume begins one of the most puzzling paragraphs of the *Treatise*. Since he announces in the next sentence that the difference is merely one of degree, Hume has been accused of confusing a difference of kind with a difference of degree in introducing his basic distinction.[1] As it happens only one use of 'kind' coincides with Aristotelian species, viz. the Aristotelian use: in other settings it quite often marks a difference in degree. 'There are two kinds of sound, loud and soft.' 'There are two kinds of light, bright and dim.' 'There are two kinds of pain, sharp and dull.' Hume's tendency to rebel against accepted terminology is quite de-liberately echoed in the parallel passage in the first *Enquiry*, where he says 'we may divide all the perceptions of the human mind into two classes or species, which are distinguished by their different degrees of force and vivacity' (E 18). He never wavers in insisting that the *only* difference between impressions and ideas concerns their degree of force and vivacity. That is to say, perceptions are on a continuum, with impressions at one end and ideas at the other.

In the tradition of Humean criticism which runs from Thomas Reid through T.H. Green to J.A. Passmore, 'degrees of force and liveliness' are taken to refer to the intensity of the datum and its clarity of outline. Doubtless the words introducing the distinction between impressions and ideas have reinforced this interpretation: 'The difference betwixt these consists in the degrees of force and liveliness with which they strike upon the mind, and make their way into our thought and consciousness'. Perceptions striking upon the mind was as unfortunate a choice of metaphor for Hume as was the *tabula rasa* for Locke, in that for the casual reader both metaphors suggest a passive mind receiving and recording data. Far from being a positive metaphor about a passive mind, perceptions-striking-upon-the-mind is intended to be neutral. In amplifying his use of the word 'impression' in the footnote to this paragraph, Hume says 'I would not be understood to express the manner, in which our lively perceptions are produced in the soul, but merely the perceptions themselves' (T 2n). Perceptions-striking-upon-the-mind contrasts with what causes them to strike: this contrast between a perception and its cause is never overlooked by Hume, even when the cause is unknowable. Thus of impressions of sensation he says 'their ultimate cause is, in my opinion, perfectly inexplicable by human reason, and 'twill always be impossible to decide with certainty, whether they arise immediately from the object, or are produc'd by the creative power of the mind, or are deriv'd from the author of our being' (T 84). Causes of impressions are therefore under no circumstances to be assimilated to perceptions-striking-upon-the-mind, and in talking about perceptions-striking-upon-the-mind

---

[1] N. Kemp Smith, *The Philosophy of David Hume* (Oxford, 1941) p. 209.

Hume is not suggesting that the mind is passively imprinted by something from without.

The Reid-Green-Passmore interpretation is further fortified by Hume's reference to ideas as 'faint images' of impressions:

> Those perceptions, which enter with most force and violence, we may name *impressions*; and under this name I comprehend all our sensations, passions and emotions, as they make their first appearance in the soul. By *ideas* I mean the faint images of these in thinking and reasoning; such as, for instance, are all the perceptions excited by the present discourse, excepting only, those which arise from the sight and touch, and excepting the immediate pleasure or uneasiness it may occasion (T 1).

And then the fatal words:

> I believe it will not be very necessary to employ many words in explaining this distinction. Every one of himself will readily perceive the difference betwixt feeling and thinking (T 1–2).

Since the difference is merely one of degree borderline cases will probably arise, and so Hume immediately draws attention to the existence of such cases:

> The common degrees of these are easily distinguished; tho' it is not impossible but in particular instances they may very nearly approach to each other. Thus in sleep, in a fever, in madness, or in any very violent emotions of soul, our ideas may approach to our impressions: As on the other hand it sometimes happens, that our impressions are so faint and low, that we cannot distinguish them from our ideas (T 2).

To this Kemp Smith raises the following objection:

> What makes it impossible to interpret Hume ... as asserting the difference to be merely one of degree in force and liveliness is precisely his argument that impressions can be so faint as to be *confounded* with ideas, and ideas so vivid as to be *mistaken* for impressions. Were a difference of liveliness what really *constituted* the difference, the mistaking of images for impressions and *vice versa*, owing to variations of liveliness, could not occur. The difference being then *identified* with difference in liveliness, the lively would *as such* be impressions, and the less lively would *as such* be ideas.[1]

_____
[1]   Ibid., p. 210.

Hume would doubtless reply that whenever he compares an impression with its subsequent idea, the only respect in which they differ is in the degree of force and liveliness. But not all impressions have the same degree of force and liveliness, and hence they cannot be identified by their degree of force and liveliness except in relation to the subsequent idea. Sometimes ideas very nearly approach impressions in force and liveliness, and at other times impressions are as faint and low as ideas usually are. The causal relation which Hume here postulates on the basis of observation and experience is analogous to that between the first vibration of a plucked string and its subsequent vibrations. We cannot identify first vibrations by their loudness except in relation to the subsequent vibrations.

There would seem to be no doubt that in Hume's theory of perceptions the only discernable difference between impressions and ideas is a difference in the degree of force and liveliness. Half a dozen paragraphs on, however, Hume presents in the manner of Newton the first of his principles of the mind: *'That all our simple ideas in their first appearance are deriv'd from simple impressions, which are correspondent to them, and which they exactly represent'* (T 4). But how can an idea which differs from its antecedent impression in force and liveliness exactly represent that impression. Clearly it cannot exactly represent its force and liveliness, whatever those words may mean.

The dominant tradition of Humean criticism cannot accommodate Hume's initial statement that impressions and ideas differ only in degree side by side with his first principle. Furthermore, by treating a perception as a static datum presented to a passive mind, representatives of this tradition have left themselves no option but to align the contrast between feeling and thinking with that between impressions and ideas.[1] But what could possibly be meant by saying that all our simple thoughts are exact copies of simple feelings? Kemp Smith is so influenced by the dominant tradition at this point that he would have us substitute 'sensing' for 'feeling':[2] but the question which I have just posed remains undiscussed. Nor on the traditional interpretation can any adequate account be given of how we form the idea of a shade of blue which we have not previously seen, although Hume clearly saw this as a singular but not serious objection to his theory. 'That idea of red, which we form in the dark, and that impression, which strikes our eyes in sun-shine, differ only in degree, not in nature' (T 3): this statement, on the traditional account of picture-images and sense-data, makes sense only if an idea is a remembered impression — a thesis which for Hume would wreak havoc with his theories

---

[1]   J. Bennett, *Locke, Berkeley, Hume* (Oxford, 1971) p. 224.
[2]   Op. Cit., pp. 209–10.

of memory, of the imagination, and of sympathy. And what, on the traditional interpretation, are we to make of the following statement from this same opening section of the *Treatise*: 'Our ideas upon their appearance produce not their correspondent impressions, nor do we perceive any colour, or feel any sensation merely upon thinking of them' (T 5)?

In constructing a metaphysical system it is not unusual for a piece of machinery to be put into service before being given its warrant of fitness. There is nothing wrong with this: one cannot be expected to explain everything all at once. This is precisely what is happening in the first section of the *Treatise*. Hume's distinction of reason, his *and* of inseparability, is already being pressed into service, but it is not explained until the end of the essay on abstract ideas. There Hume raises the question how we are able to form the abstract ideas of figure and colour, when we never experience the one without the other. His answer is that we are able to observe and compare contrasting comparisons. We are able to compare a globe of white marble with a globe of black and a cube of white, and 'find two separate resemblances, in what formerly seem'd and really is, inseparable' (T 25). By comparing the contrasting comparisons we are able to form two separate classes, annexing 'figure' to the one and 'colour' to the other. It is an important aspect of Hume's philosophy, present whenever he uses a distinction of reason, that whatever is thus distinguished is really 'the same and undistinguishable' (T 25). Having drawn attention to the two separate resemblances he writes: 'After a little more practice of this kind, we begin to distinguish the figure from the colour by a *distinction of reason*; that is, we consider the figure and colour together, since they are in effect the same and undistinguishable; but still view them in different aspects, according to the resemblances, of which they are susceptible.' Meinong regards this as a contradiction. If figure and colour are the same and undistinguishable, 'then it remains a riddle how colour comes to be distinguished at all, be it through the most complicated mental operation'.[1] Hume's point, however, is that what is distinguishable in a merely relative way by contrasting comparisons with other perceptions cannot be counted separately, and is in reality not distinguishable: the globe in the next room is not distinguishable from the white marble object in the next room.

Earlier we asked how can an idea which differs from its antecedent impression in force and liveliness exactly represent that impression, and there seemed no way of answering. Now we are able to say that just as figure and colour are different aspects of the globe, so every perception

[1] K. F. Barber, 'Meinong's *Hume Studies*: Translation and Commentary', Ph.D. thesis (University of Iowa, 1966; reproduced by University Microfilms, 1967) p. 170.

has *its* different aspects. To begin with, there is the aspect denoted by those words 'force and liveliness'; let us call this the *feeling-tone*. There is also the respect in which an idea exactly resembles its antecedent impression: let us call this the *conceptual content*. We are able to compare perceptions having the same conceptual content but varying in feeling-tone with perceptions having the same degree of feeling-tone but different conceptual contents, and thereby form a distinction of reason. In calling ideas *faint* images of impressions, Hume is underscoring his initial point, that the difference consists only in the force and liveliness with which they strike upon the mind: it is purely a matter of degree. And in calling ideas faint *images* of impressions, no loss of content is implied: if there is loss of content an image is not faint but imperfect.

There are, then, two aspects of perceptions, the one concerned with thinking, the other with feeling. Besides the conceptual content and the feeling-tone there is also the object of the perception, the *ideatum*, that towards which the mind directs itself, or that which the perception is about: let us call this the *intentional object*. A perception of x, whatever x may be, and whether or not x exists, has x as its intentional object. Although there is a *distinctio rationis* between the conceptual content and the feeling-tone of a perception, there is no such distinction between the conceptual content and its intentional object, since the conceptual content refers one to the intentional object. There is, however, only a distinction of reason between a perception and its intentional object, which enables Hume to speak of the impression of a shoe and the shoe as if these were one and the same thing (T 202). Within Hume's system, they *are* the same thing. More precisely, there is merely a distinction of reason between a perception considered as a member of a succession of perceptions in the mind and its object, to which *we* may ascribe different relations, connections and durations (T 68). The activities of the mind by which we move from the intentional object to physical object are described by Hume with considerable psychological insight.

Other aspects of perceptions may come to light, for one never knows what hidden features await discovery upon comparing comparisons hitherto uncompared. Besides the *distinctio rationis*, Hume notes but seldom uses Locke's analytical weapon, the division of perceptions into complex and simple; but notice how Hume, in the second paragraph of the opening section, defines simplicity: 'Simple perceptions or impressions and ideas are such as admit of no distinction nor separation' (T 2). That is to say, a perception is simple if all its parts or aspects are inseparable from each other, no matter how many parts or aspects there may be.

Quite the most important question which arises in considering these aspects is the precise nature of the conceptual content, because on this aspect turn questions about the conceptual identity of perceptions. Those who think of Hume's perceptions as picture-images or sense-data invariably link perceptions with terms rather than propositions, but there are very good reasons for believing that Hume thought of perceptions propositionally. Not that whenever one has a perception one has a proposition in mind, but rather that if one were to say what one had in mind when one has a perception one would use a proposition rather than a term. In the first place Hume speaks of perceptions as thoughts (T 234), and as thoughts they may be either true or false. In the second place, his remarks on existence suggest that every object is conceived of as existing: '... in that proposition, *God is*, or indeed any other, which regards existence, the idea of existence is no distinct idea, which we unite with that of the object ...' (T 96n). That is to say, the idea of God is the same as the idea that God is: the perception of x is the same as the perception that x is. 'Whatever we conceive, we conceive to be existent' (T 67). A perception is to be explicated at the very least by an existential proposition, which however may be false:

> But let us consider, that no two ideas are in themselves contrary, except those of existence and non-existence, which are plainly resembling, as implying both of them an idea of the object; tho' the latter excludes the object from all times and places, in which it is supposed not to exist (T 15).

In the third place a perception may be an object of belief. The difference between a simple conception and a belief lies solely in the *manner* in which we conceive an idea: '... the only remarkable difference, which occurs on this occasion, is, when we join belief to the conception, and are persuaded of the truth of what we conceive' (T 97n). For these three reasons it seems indisputable that if one were to express what one has in mind in having a perception, one would do so by means of a proposition.

The problem of the missing shade of blue is insuperable if one demands a picture-image, but if what is required is a conceptual content the problem evaporates, except for Hume's 'contradictory phenomenon' that here we have an idea which lacks an antecedent impression. All of the shades of blue except the missing one have been previously observed. They are arranged in serial order form from the deepest to the lightest.

> ...'tis plain, that he will perceive a blank, where that shade is wanting, and will be sensible, that there is a greater distance in that place betwixt the contiguous colours, than in any other (T 6).

The conceptual content of any shade other than the missing shade might be expressed by saying that there is a shade of blue observed at t_1 which is adjacent both to the shade observed at t_2 and that observed at t_3, t_2 being darker than t_3. The conceptual content of the missing shade is of precisely the same form except that in expressing it the phrase 'observed at t₁' is omitted, a minor matter since the entire colour-range apart from this shade is firmly anchored by previous observations. What is important about the missing shade of blue is that it is the first of several cases Hume gives of ideas which the mind, working on precedent perceptions, is able to form by its own activity.

Although perceptions are to be expressed propositionally there is always the possibility that the proposition is not in its final form because of distinctions of reason awaiting discovery. Before distinguishing colour from figure, Hume says, we consider them together, 'since they are in effect the same and undistinguishable.' After making the distinction of reason we are able to view them either together or in different aspects (T 25). It is the same with every distinction of reason. This entails paradoxically that the conceptual content of a perception is not subject to change, since we view all the aspects together; but the proposition by which it is expressed may change, since after making the distinction of reason we have words for, say, figure and colour. Is it not the case that we sometimes *know* we have an idea which defies expression? Often the reason why we cannot express it adequately is because we do not know how to make distinctions of reason which desperately need making: we are unable to compare our idea with other ideas which will bring out contrasting comparisons.

This is well illustrated by Hume's difficulties in elucidating what he means by the 'force and liveliness' of a perception. It should immediately be said in Hume's defence that he was grappling ahead of his time with an idea which had no touchstones in contemporary philosophy or that of his predecessors. Hume's reticence in discussing the feeling-tone of perceptions, having mentioned that perceptions are associated with both thinking and feeling, is deliberate: 'I believe it will not be necessary to employ many words in explaining this distinction. Every one of himself will readily perceive the difference betwixt feeling and thinking'. And indeed this is the only kind of appeal which is possible in initially making the distinction, since anything which Hume could say about the feeling-tone of a perception would be said in terms of the conceptual content of another perception which has its *own* feeling-tone. This regress, fortunately, is not vicious: it is not unlike the regress in Frege, that any expression naming the *Sinn* of another expression has its own *Sinn* and *Bedeutung*. But whereas in Frege it is logically impossible to state what is meant by *Sinn* in Hume there is no such impossibility: we can state precisely what he means by the force and vivacity of a perception.

Hume uses the same family of words to characterise three important distinctions. Members of this family include 'force', 'liveliness', 'vivacity', 'vigour', 'firmness', 'strength', 'solidity', 'steadiness', 'intensity', 'vividness' and their correlatives 'faintness' and 'weakness'. The distinctions made in terms of this family are

(1) that between impressions and ideas;
(2) that between a belief and a simple comception; and
(3) that between ideas of the memory and ideas of the imagination.

Now, it might be said that of these the first is basic, since a belief is 'a lively idea related to or associated with a present impression' (T 96), and a memory is an idea of an impression which was present and is now past. Nevertheless, Hume's use of the same characteristics in discussing memory and belief throws light upon impressions differing from ideas in their degrees of force and liveliness.

Hume seldom uses two words where one will do. Usually when he uses a phrase like 'experience and observation' he means one thing by 'experience' and quite another by 'observation'. The present case is an exception, for in talking about 'force and liveliness' he uses a whole battery of words to refer to a single quality *of the mind* in having a perception. Thus he says an idea which is believed is able to bestow on the impression from which it is derived, if it has been forgotten, 'the same quality, call it *firmness* or *solidity* or *force* or *vivacity*, with which the mind reflects upon it, and is assured of its present existence' (T 105–6). After he had finished the *Treatise* Hume wrote an Appendix which contains a confession of his difficulty in explaining precisely what he meant by saying that belief, as contrasted with simple conception, is 'a particular manner of forming an idea' (T 97). The confession continues:

> An idea assented to *feels* different from a fictitious idea, that the fancy alone presents to us: And this different feeling I endeavour to explain by calling it a superior *force*, or *vivacity*, or *solidity*, or *firmness*, or *steadiness*. This variety of terms, which may seem so unphilosophical, is intended only to express that act of the mind, which renders realities more present to us than fictions, causes them to weigh more in the thought, and gives them a superior influence on the passions and imagination (T 629).

This remarkable passage ends with the statement that belief gives ideas 'more force and influence; makes them appear of greater importance; infixes them in the mind; and renders them the governing principles of all our actions.'

The first thing to be noticed is that the feeling-tone of a perception, its force and vivacity, is an act of the mind. This is not a slip of the pen: here we have Hume's considered opinion. It fits in well with his doctrine that belief is 'an idea conceived in a peculiar manner' (T 96–7). Since every perception has its feeling-tone we may take this as support for the stronger thesis tentatively advanced above, that it may be the case with all perceptions that they are inseparable from some principles or operations of the mind.

The second point to be emphasised is that whatever Hume means by force and vivacity, the feeling-tone of a perception is closely linked with its influence. In his prolix discussion of causation Hume links belief in the causal connection with the transference of the force and liveliness of an impression to a related idea. He says that given the impression we *anticipate* the idea. That is to say, the impression influences us to behave in a certain way. One might say that the resulting belief in the causal connection *is* our ability to anticipate. But this leaves out an important feature of Hume's account of the belief, our immediate awareness of the act of anticipating. It is this immediate awareness that constitutes the feeling-tone of the impression. Furthermore, our awareness of the *manner* in which we will connect this perception with other perceptions determines the influence which it has on our actions.

In this connection, consider the section entitled 'Of the influence of belief.' Here Hume says that the effect of belief

> is to raise up a simple idea to an equality with our impressions, and bestow on it a like influence on the passions. This effect it can only have by making an idea approach an impression in its force and vivacity (T 119).

He adds, significantly, that 'whenever we can make an idea approach the impressions in its force and vivacity it will likewise imitate them in its influence upon the mind, and *vice versa* . . .' Or consider the passage in which Hume is comparing the force and vivacity of the different degrees of evidence, 'which have an influence on the passions and imagination, proportion'd to that degree of force and vivacity which they communicate to the ideas' (T 153). The greatest of these degrees is the memory; but, as he remarks elsewhere, 'an idea of the memory, by losing its force and vivacity, may degenerate to such a degree as to be taken for an idea of the imagination' and 'an idea of the imagination may acquire such a force and vivacity, as to pass for an idea of the memory, and counterfeit its effects on the belief and judgment' (T86).

What emerges is that ideas having the force and liveliness which comes with conviction and assurance have a dominance which other ideas lack.

> They strike upon us with more force; they are more present to us; the mind has a firmer hold of them, and is more actuated and mov'd by them. It acquiesces in them; and, in a manner, fixes and reposes itself on them (T 624).

This dominance is felt rather than conceived.

When any object is presented, the idea of its usual attendant immediately strikes us, as something real and solid. 'Tis *felt*, rather than conceiv'd, and approaches the impression, from which it is deriv'd, in its force and influence (T 627).

It might be said that the quality which Hume refers to by force, liveliness, etc., is our immediate awareness of the extent to which the perception dominates by virtue of our proneness to associate it with other perceptions. Impressions are the stronger in this respect on account of the multiplicity of connections which are open to them when they first appear. In becoming ideas many of these connections cease to be possible, and the perception's dominance wanes accordingly. It may well be that there is a pattern in the way perceptions wane, for example that impressions are characterised by a multiplicity of 'spontaneous' connections whereas ideas are characterised more by the 'rule-governed' connections appropriate to a language. If there were such a pattern this would not entail a difference of kind between impressions and ideas: it would still be the case that impressions merely fade and become ideas. It is important that both ideas of the memory and beliefs approach impressions in force and liveliness precisely because we are aware of their influence, of the extent to which they govern our actions. They govern our actions because of our tendency to connect them with other perceptions. We are immediately aware of a perception's connectibility-for-us, and it is this awareness of possible connections which Hume denotes by such words as 'force' and 'vivacity'. Hume observes that there is 'no particular name either in *English* or any other language, that I know of' which denotes precisely what he means by the term 'impression' (T 2n; cp. E 18). Nevertheless he has chosen the closest word in the language, for the force of an impression lies in the extent to which it impresses us.

Consider the following example. I am sitting by the fire. Suddenly there is a deafening clap of thunder. I rush outside to see if the house has been hit, and to my relief all is well. The impression wanes with the elimination of the most obvious connections, and more are eliminated with the passage of time, until as an idea there are decidably fewer connections which we are prone to make than it had as an impression.

In contrast to this dramatic example consider the casual glance at the salvias in the garden. One might compare them to last year's salvias, or think that next year one will plant marigolds. One might let the eye wander to the lawn beyond. The point is that in so far as the salvias are in focus, in so far as they are objects of attention, one is aware of a range of possible connections: when one ceases to be aware of their connectibility, one ceases to notice the salvias.

This interpretation is supported by what Hume has to say in amplifying his remark in the opening paragraph of Book I that 'in sleep, in a fever, in madness, or in any very violent emotions of soul, our ideas may approach our impressions'. In 'Of the influence of belief' Hume writes

> When the imagination, from any extraordinary ferment of the blood and spirits, acquires such a vivacity as disorders all its powers and faculties, there is no means of distinguishing betwixt truth and falsehood; but every loose fiction or idea, having the same influence as the impressions of the memory, or the conclusions of the judgment, is receiv'd on the same footing, and operates with equal force on the passions (T 123).

That is to say, if the discriminating activities of the mind are suspended, all possible connections of a perception with other perceptions remain open, and any perception at all has the force of an impression on its first appearance. When distinguishing figure from colour we are remarking two aspects of a perception so intimately related that they may be viewed together, and this intimacy is a feature of all distinctions of reason. In the case of figure and colour we can readily understand this intimacy, because the figure is the boundary of the colour. In the case of other distinctions of reason it is not always so easy to describe this intimacy, but nevertheless such a description is demanded by a correct and thorough-going analysis. How then is the feeling-tone of a perception related to the conceptual content? The answer is that our immediate awareness of the dominance of a perception, whether it is an impression or an idea of the memory or a belief, is nothing but our realisation of the importance for us of its conceptual content. If this is so, how can the feeling-tone fade while the conceptual content remains precisely the same? The answer to this question is that the conceptual content may become less relevant with the passage of time: the fading of feeling-tone *is* our realisation that the conceptual content has become less relevant. If the perception loses all its feeling-tone and we cease to be aware of any possible connections we are no longer cognizant of its conceptual content: we no longer have the perception. Thus the conceptual content and the feeling-tone are inseparable from each other: like figure and colour they may be viewed together, and like figure and colour neither can be experienced without the other.

In distinguishing impressions from ideas Hume wrote initially 'I believe it will not be necessary to employ many words in explaining this distinction. Every one of himself will readily perceive the difference betwixt feeling and thinking.' Was Hume aligning feeling with impressions and thinking with ideas? This is the way he has generally been understood; but the very absurdity of the resulting doctrine, that a thought is a faint feeling, throws light on what has gone wrong. There is a sense of 'feeling' for which one can substitute, as Kemp Smith did, the word 'sensing'; and there is quite another sense of 'feeling' which one uses when one says 'I would not say that for fear of hurting his feelings'. The one use, read into Hume by sensationalists and sense-datum theorists, is derived from 'feel' with a sensation as direct object, e.g. 'I feel a tickle in my throat', or from 'feel' with something other than a sensation as direct object, but where sensations are clearly alluded to, e.g. 'I feel a spider crawling up my leg' or 'I feel rain in my bones'. The other use, which Hume's theory requires, derives from 'feel' followed by a noun-clause, 'I feel that ...' The all-important contrast is not between feeling a sensation and thinking, but between feeling *that* and thinking *that*, where in feeling *that* we are focussing upon an immediate awareness, a realisation of the importance to us of something. There is no textual evidence that Hume was aware of this contrast between two uses of 'feeling': nor is there any textual evidence against it. He found great difficulty in expressing precisely what he meant in this context, but nevertheless he used the right word: our realisation of the importance of the conceptual content of a perception is, briefly, the way we feel.

9

WHAT IS THE VERIFIABILITY CRITERION A CRITERION OF?

Stuart Brown

As my title implies, I think the verifiability criterion is indeed a criterion of something. I do not intend, therefore, merely to commemorate it. On the other hand I am not sure that those who put it forward in its more liberal forms as a criterion of 'factual significance' or 'literal meaningfulness' were right in what they identified as the consequence of a sentence's failing to satisfy it. What I want to argue for, in a somewhat reductionist spirit, is a resurrected version of the 'weak' verifiability criterion. My resurrected version will certainly appear more rarefied, in so far as it is independent of (and does not therefore require to be embodied in) empiricism. It will, I hope, also be purified of some of the mortal blemishes from which the criterion, as construed by members of the Vienna Circle, seems not to have recovered.

I

I have already implied that the verifiability criterion should not be considered as inseparably linked to empiricism. I should therefore want to distinguish those objections to Logical Positivism which are objections to the verifiability criterion from those which are objections to empiricism. It is indeed confusing not to do this since the question as to how, if at all, verifiability is connected with meaning can as well arise *within* empiricism. It is worth remembering that Russell rejected the verifiability criterion and therefore Logical Positivism. It is worth remembering, since Logical Positivism is hostile not only to metaphysics but to the radical scepticism which is often a prolegomenon to it. There is a strand of empiricism, of which Russell was a notable representative, which takes the scepticism seriously, if not the metaphysics. For example, given that the only conscious states of which I have experience are my own, might I not be mistaken in ascribing conscious states to anything else? Again, even if there were other conscious beings than myself, given that the words I use only acquire meaning for me because of the way they relate to my experiences, how do I know that others, in using the same words, are talking about similar experiences? These are two sorts of sceptical problem which arise on common empiricist premises. A common empiricist answer would be to say that while it is logically possible that there are no conscious beings other than oneself or, even if there were, that their experience of what they call 'green' might be quite different from mine, neither of these hypotheses is at all probable. What is admitted as logically possible, however, is admitted as having a truth-value and as therefore meaningful. But, at least on the terms on which such possibilities are contemplated, nothing would count as an empirical ground for deciding for or against them. So contemplated, such 'hypotheses' are to be dismissed as 'meaningless', according to Positivists.[1]

Logical Positivism, with its tendency towards behaviourism, is at odds with that other strand of empiricism which readily leads to scepticism about other minds. And the dispute is over meaning. Contrary to what is implied in some of the literature,[2] what is called '*the* verification criterion' is not identical with any criterion — since there is no *single* one — which can be referred to as '*the* empiricist criterion of meaning'. In concerning myself with this internal dispute, however, I shall not be offering a defence of empiricism. Rather I shall be assuming, for the sake of argument, what is common ground between the differing parties. Part of my purpose in doing this is to emphasise the independence of the issues from questions about the adequacy of empiricism. These issues can be represented in terms of differing answers to the question which I posed as the title of this lecture. That question can be re-expressed in the following way:

If there are no considerations which count as tending to determine the truth (or falsity) of an hypothesis (H) as opposed to that of any apparently competing hypothesis, then . . .

Different criteria are put forward by different ways of filling the blank. My attention will be confined to three:

(a) . . . there is no reason to believe H.
(b) . . . 'H' is devoid of 'cognitive meaning'.
(c) . . . no assertion put forward as an independent judgment about H

---

[1] And were so dismissed, respectively, by A. J. Ayer (see *Language, Truth and Logic*, 2nd ed. (Gollancz, 1946) pp. 128 ff.) and Moritz Schlick (see his paper, 'Positivism and Realism', Pt 3, trans. D. Rynin, in *Logical Positivism*, ed. Ayer (Free Press of Glencoe, 1959) pp. 92 f.). Both Ayer and Schlick, in the passages referred to, offer behaviouristic accounts of statements ascribing experiences to others.
[2] For example, in C. G. Hempel's paper, 'Problems and Changes in the Empiricist Criterion of Meaning', *Revue Internationale de Philosophie* (1950).

can be an expression of belief or doubt as to H's truth or falsity.

What is generally referred to as 'the verifiability criterion' is the criterion formed by filling in the blank with (b) and by specifying empiricist criteria which set limits on what is to be accepted as a 'consideration' tending to settle the apparent dispute between those who advocate H and those who advocate some competing hypothesis. Broadly, following Hume, acceptable considerations are those which fall into one of two classes. Either they have to do with 'relations of ideas', in which case they rest on the principle of contradiction; or else they have to do with 'matters of fact', in which case the final court of appeal is the evidence of sense-experience. Considerations put forward which do not conform to these standards of rationality are not recognisable to empiricists as tending to settle the issue between H and any competing hypothesis. They are to be committed to the flames.

These standards of rationality, determining what is to count as a reason for supposing H true or false, are common ground as between empiricists. But they may equally be accepted by those who, like Russell, seem committed to favour filling in the blank with (a). Not only have empiricists the option, so to speak, of any of these three answers, but one can – as I do in favouring (c) – accept any of these answers and retain the option of rejecting empiricism. Thus separation of the verifiability criterion from the standards of rationality needed to give it teeth has the advantage, I believe, of focussing our attention on the question about the connection between verification and meaning without our assuming that such a connection, if it existed, could only be expressed in empiricist terms.

II

I have implied that the verifiability criterion, in the more liberal forms in which Ayer and Schlick, for example, were advocating it in 1936, is not a criterion of meaningfulness at all. In this section of the paper I shall try to explain how the criterion, so articulated, is severed from the theory of meaning. In Ayer's case, I shall argue, this connection is severed at the very point where he makes a necessary modification to the criterion to avoid being committed to regarding scientific hypotheses of unrestricted generality as meaningless. The unmodified criterion is indeed a criterion of meaningfulness, if – at least for the reasons which led Ayer to modify it – an untenable one. So it will throw light on how Ayer's criterion fails to be a criterion of meaning to begin with some remarks about the unmodified or strong version which at least succeeds in this respect.

It is now generally accepted that Wittgenstein's *Tractatus Logico-Philosophicus* does not espouse a verificationist theory of meaning. It

seems, however, to have been the largest single influence on the way
members of the Vienna Circle formulated the criterion as a criterion of
meaning. There are many affinities between the *Tractatus* and doctrines
subscribed to independently by the Circle. It is not surprising, therefore,
that they should have taken a keen interest in it. But some, at least, went
further, interpreting the *Tractatus* as the 'decisive turning point in
philosophy'[1] which paved the way for their developments. Wittgenstein
had written that 'in order to be able to say, ' "p" is true (or false)', I must
have determined in what circumstances I call 'p' true, and in so doing I
determine the sense of the proposition'. (*Tractatus*, 4.063) That remark is
a general statement of a view expressed earlier in the same sentence, that
'in order to be able to say that a point is black or white, I must first know
when a point is called black, and when white'. It looks as if Wittgenstein is
here endorsing the view that to understand a proposition one must know
how to tell whether it is true or not, know its method of verification. Yet
Wittgenstein's actual statement of what it is to understand a proposition is
quite different. In *Tractatus*, 4.024 he had written: 'To understand a
proposition means to know what is the case if it is true.' This implies,
where the meaning of the proposition can be stated, that it will be given in
terms of its *truth* conditions, which is another matter altogether. However,
if Wittgenstein's 'elementary propositions' are *construed as* 'observation
statements', in something like the manner of Russell's 'atomic
propositions', the confusion of verification conditions with truth
conditions may not be critical. For, it seems reasonable to believe, the
only way I can know what red is and therefore understand statements of
the form 'x is red' is by being acquainted with red things. This empiricists
will insist on not only for 'red' but for any other term that can occur in an
atomic proposition. But, if I know what red is, when I see it, smoothness
when I feel it, etc. it surely follows that it is logically possible for me
conclusively to verify any such atomic proposition.

Now Wittgenstein also held that every proposition, and therefore
anything which could be said or had sense, was a truth-function of
elementary propositions. (*Tractatus*, 5.3) Thus, 'If all true elementary
propositions are given, the result is a complete description of the world.'
(*Tractatus*, 4.26) The Positivists at one time shared this view. The claim
that conclusive verifiability in principle by sense experience is a necessary
and sufficient condition of a sentence being 'cognitively meaningful'
follows from this view, together with a particular doctrine of atomic
propositions. There is no evidence that Wittgenstein envisaged such an
empiricist interpretation of his account of elementary propositions. But,

---

[1]   Thus Schlick, in the introductory piece he wrote for the first volume of the
Circle's journal, *Erkenntnis* (1930–1), quoted from David Rynin's translation in
Logical Positivism, ed. Ayer, p. 54.

rightly or wrongly, he was interpreted in this way. Hence arose the verifiability criterion in its strongest and consequently most drastic form.

One consequence of the view shared by Wittgenstein and several members of the Vienna Circle, that no sentence made sense which was not a truth-function of elementary propositions, is that unrestrictedly general hypotheses are meaningless. No finite number of observation statements could entail the truth of the claim 'There are no abominable snowmen' or 'All men are mortal'. Not unrelatedly, perhaps, assertions of causal relation, e.g. 'The cause of the First World War was the assassination of Archduke Ferdinand', appear to assert a causal nexus between two events, the earlier being put forward in explanation of why the later event occurred. The whole assertion appears, therefore, not to be a truth-function of its constituents. It does not follow, that is to say, from its being at one time true to say, 'Archduke Ferdinand will be assassinated' and, additionally, also true to say 'War will break out', that it is true to say 'If Archduke Ferdinand is assassinated, war will break out'. Something *more* appears to be involved.

Wittgenstein, in a passage strikingly reminiscent of Hume,[1] roundly denies that there is a 'causal nexus' to justify the inference from one elementary proposition to another. (*Tractatus*, 5.136) It seems clear, too, that the *Tractatus* cannot allow as having sense any universal sentence which is not analysable into conjunctions or disjunctions of elementary propositions.[2] This seems to be a reason for Wittgenstein's inclusion of his singular discussion of the status of the laws of mechanics. (*Tractatus*, 6.3 ff.) It is interesting to note that earlier philosophers in the positivist tradition (e.g. Mach) had found themselves confronted with similar problems. These acquired, thanks to Wittgenstein's logic, a new precision. But the Logical Positivists inherited the same dilemma: for a statement to be a statement of natural law it seems as if it must be of unrestricted generality, in which case it cannot be analysed in terms of a finite set of elementary propositions: if, on the other hand, it can be so analysed it cannot be a statement of natural law. Carnap, in his *Der logische Aufbau der Welt* (1928), grasped this dilemma by its second horn and attempted to reduce statements of natural law to finite sets of observation statements. Schlick and Waismann, on the other hand, held firmly to the

---

[1] In his remarks in this passage Wittgenstein shows an indebtedness to Hertz and, perhaps through Hertz, to Mach. Mach himself acknowledged that his point of view was 'close to' that of Hume. So, while the connection between Wittgenstein and Hume is probably at several removes, in their views on the 'causal nexus', the resemblance is no coincidence.

[2] This is conceded in the *Philosophische Bemerkungen* (Blackwell, 1961) pp. 66 ff., 200 ff. F. P. Ramsey, in his posthumously published *The Foundations of Mathematics* (1931), had argued that if a universal sentence is not a conjunction 'it is not a proposition at all' (p. 238).

view that statements of natural law must be of unrestricted generality and accepted the consequence that these strings of words are, in a way, nonsense.[1]

I cannot here enter into the question whether *strong* verificationism is credible on these terms. What I want to emphasise about it is that, as modelled on the *Tractatus*, it is quite clearly a view about how propositions have the sense they have, quite clearly therefore a view about meaning. One of the remarkable facts about our use and understanding of language, which seems to have impressed both Wittgenstein and Schlick,[2] is that we can immediately understand what is said by word-combinations which are quite new to us, without knowing whether or not they are true. That a particular new combination of words is going to be meaningful or meaningless, and what (if anything) it means, must in some way be secured *in advance* of its being used. This means that a theory of meaning concerned with demarcating meaningful from meaningless combinations of words cannot be confined to criteria which are *retrospective*, which only apply to sentences, once formed. It must involve a range of doctrines, both about how individual words acquire a currency and about syntax or grammar. The verifiability criterion, applied in a retrospective and one-by-one way to the utterances of metaphysicians, may be a means of spotting meaninglessness. But that consideration alone, in the absence of a theory as to the kinds of symbol that can enter in to elementary propositions and of how these relate to other propositions, will not serve to give substance to the allegation that metaphysical utterances are meaningless. This point is taken, at least implicitly, by Carnap, in his emphasis on building a logical syntax. As he admits: 'if our thesis that the statements of metaphysics are pseudo-statements is justifiable, then metaphysics could not even be expressed in a logically constructed language'.[3]

What I am suggesting is that strong verificationism, in spite of the considerable difficulties it may have, has at least the merit of being derived from a theory of meaning. Verificationism, however, is best known in Britain through the modified version of it presented in Ayer's *Language, Truth and Logic*. For reasons connected in part with the difficulties I have mentioned, Ayer rejected strong verificationism. In its place he advocated a more liberal criterion, which would avoid the 'heroic' course of Schlick — that of saying that statements of natural law are nonsense. He proposed

---

[1]   See Schlick's paper, 'Die Kausalität der gegenwärtigen Physik', *Naturwissenschaft*, XI (1931).

[2]   See Schlick's *Gesammelte Aufsätze*, p. 153 ff., relevant parts of which are quoted in translation by Waismann in his *The Principles of Linguistic Philosophy* (Macmillan, 1965) ch. XV.

[3]   In his paper, 'The Elimination of Metaphysics Through Logical Analysis of Language', *Logical Positivism*, ed. Ayer, p. 60.

to allow that a putative proposition is genuine if it is at least weakly verifiable, i.e. 'if it is possible for experience to render it probable'. (op. cit., p. 37) Now this, since it brings back scientific hypotheses into the domain of factually significant propositions, seems a step in the right direction. But, with this step, I believe, Ayer cuts his verifiability principle adrift from the kind of rationale which would justify regarding it as a criterion of *meaningfulness*.

That this is so may be made clearer if Ayer's position is contrasted with Russell's. For Russell, the question whether a sentence which is universal in its form is meaningful is already settled once it is established that the function in question is significant. *Generalization*, as he sometimes called it,[1] is one of the syntactically permissible operations whereby a significant sentence can be transformed into another significant sentence. For Russell, then, it is possible for there to be significant universal statements which are amenable to empirical verification or falsification. Russell regarded solipsism as a significant, because logically possible, hypothesis. 'There is no logical impossiility', he once wrote,[2] 'in the supposition that the whole of life is a dream, in which we ourselves create all the objects that come before us'. This hypothesis, though empirically indistinguishable from the hypothesis that there is an external world, has a quite different meaning, according to Russell.[3] According to Ayer's criterion, however, the Cartesian doubt about the existence of a material world cannot be meaningfully expressed. Indeed there is a range of metaphysical entities, including material substances, which Russell thinks might exist though there is no reason, to his mind, for believing that they do. His programme of substituting 'logical constructions' for 'inferred entities' is not a programme designed to expose the true meaning of talk about tables, classes, numbers, etc. It is rather a programme for avoiding commitment to such entities.[4] Ayer, in spite of his frequent adoption of Russellian terminology, is committed to regard expression of 'belief' in such metaphysical entities as meaningless. He offers a phenomenalist account of commonsense talk of material things and a behaviouristic account of commonsense talk of the mental states of others.

Ayer believed, in presenting his versions of the verifiability criterion,

[1] See, for example, the section of 'Syntax and Significance' in his *An Inquiry into Meaning and Truth* (Allen & Unwin, 1940) ch. 13(C).
[2] *The Problems of Philosophy* (1912) p. 22.
[3] Russell, in his paper 'Logical Positivism', implies, I think wrongly, that verificationists would say they had the *same* meaning. See *Logic and Knowledge*, ed. R. C. Marsh (Allen & Unwin, 1956) p. 376. But it is clear in this paper that Russell would have disagreed with anyone who thought solipsism meaningless.
[4] See, for example, *Mysticism and Logic*, p. 148.

that it accorded with how, in everyday and scientific contexts, one use of the meaningful/meaningless distinction is made. One difficulty I find in such a suggestion is that the distinction between genuine propositions, which *are* bearers of truth and falsity, and those which are not, is a distinction which seems to have no point except in the context of something like a philosophical discussion. It requires some initiation to see the point behind such questions as 'Are ethical judgements *true or false*?' or 'Do religious utterances *make sense*?' Failing there being any prospects of showing that such a weak verifiability criterion, construed as a criterion of meaningfulness, is *analytic* for some concept of meaning, the stock criticism that it fails to satisfy itself is one that cannot be taken lightly. For in the absence of a supporting theory of meaning, it becomes quite unclear that any case remains for construing the verifiability criterion as a criterion of meaningfulness at all.

It seems indeed that Ayer himself has come round to something like this view. In a broadcast and subsequently published discussion he has expressed the opinion that he would perhaps have been more 'prudent' to have put forward the verifiability criterion as a means of demarcating scientific from non-scientific statement, rather than as a 'criterion of meaning'.[1] His formulations, both in the First and in the Second Edition of *Language, Truth and Logic*, proved too liberal to exclude metaphysical utterances. I cannot, in the present compass, hope to review the developments these difficulties occasioned. There have been many refinements and alternatives proposed.[2] I am not aware, however, of any which attempts to restore for the criterion a firm basis in the theory of meaning. Many contributors to this discussion write as though they would happily settle for a criterion which adequately separated out the sentences of empirical science. That involves a programme which has its own interests. But, from a Positivist standpoint, it has the disadvantage of leaving up in the air the conviction that no other kinds of sentence can be the means of saying something 'true' or 'false' but not analytic. That answer to the question 'What is the verifiability criterion a criterion of?' seems to me, for this reason, too mild.

I return, therefore, to my doubt as to whether the verifiability criterion, in its more liberal and plausible forms, really is a criterion of meaning at all. This is not a doubt as to whether there is any connection between verification and meaning. For it seems that there is such a connection. There is, at any rate, a range of general terms which only exist in the language because there are accepted conventions for applying them,

1 *Modern British Philisophy*, ed. Bryan Magee (Secker & Warburg, 1971) p. 56.
2 There has been a series of papers by Hempel in which he offers a critical review of the literature. See his 'Empiricist Criteria of Cognitive Significance' and 'Postscript 1964' in *Conceptions of Cognitive Significance*.

i.e. conventions which make it possible for people to agree that certain applications are true and certain false. These conventions do also affect the joint application of two or more words. We do not have, for instance, conventions for the phrase 'unconscious pain', do not know, therefore, what would count as unconscious pain. We might, for some reason, come to have a use for such a phrase. But this would involve a change from what we presently count as a reason for (and therefore weakly verifying) 'He is in pain' or 'He is unconscious of his pain'. This would involve a change in what we mean either by 'pain' or 'unconscious' or, of course, both.

Positivists sometimes use this sort of example as though it were an argument for saying that the meaning of a proposition can be given only in terms of the rules for its verification. Schlick, for instance, considers a friend's request, 'Take me to a country where the sky is three times as blue as in England'. He goes on, quite rightly, to say:

> I should not know how to fulfil his wish; his phrase would appear nonsensical to me, because the word 'blue' is used in a way which is not provided for by the rules of our language. The combination of a numeral and the name of a colour does not occur in it; therefore my friend's sentence has no meaning, although its exterior linguistic form is that of a command or a wish.

Schlick goes on to comment that his friend might give his sentence meaning by indicating 'certain definite physical circumstances concerning the serenity of the sky which he wants his phrase to be a description of'. In this way his wish might become meaningful. So far, so good. But Schlick goes on immediately to conclude:[1]

> Thus, whenever we ask about a sentence, 'What does it mean?', what we expect is instruction as to the circumstances in which the sentence is to be used; we want a description of the conditions under which the sentence will form a *true* proposition, and of those which will make it *false*.

This conclusion does not follow. The argument seems to take something like the following form:

Verification conditions determine the meaning of (some) combinations of words;

A sentence is a combination of words;

Verification conditions determine the meaning of sentences.

[1] 'Meaning and Verification', *Philosophical Review* (1936) section 1.

At best the conclusion seems like a wild generalisation. By the time he wrote this paper Schlick, very much under the influence of Wittgenstein[1] apparently, had abandoned that basis for his verificationism which his interpretation of the *Tractatus* had provided. Yet, to derive such a conclusion, it would be necessary first to define a simple class of sentences to which he could apply the moral derived from his example. Then he would need, as he does not in this paper, to embark on a Carnapian type of programme which would provide him with some sort of rationale for extending that verificationist moral to all sentences. As things stand, it seems to me, there is a yawning gap between his reasons and the conclusion he puts forward as supported by them. Schlick himself, in the manifesto with which he introduced the first issue of *Erkenntnis* (1930), had declared quite firmly that the reason why unanswerable questions consist of 'empty sounds' was that 'they transgress the profound inner rules of logical syntax discovered by the new analysis'.[2] In the absence of a programme of logical analysis of Tractarian scope there ceases to be any ground advanced for the view that unverifiability in principle is a sure sign of meaninglessness.

On this dispute within empiricism, it will be apparent that I side with Russell. Like him, I am inclined to think that one can articulate logical possibilities which are quite unverifiable in principle but which are no less meaningful for that. I have in mind such possibilities as that the world might, as some once alleged, have been created in 4004 B.C. complete with fossils to try our faith, and so on. Russell once wrote of this suggestion:

> There is no logical impossibility about this view. And similarly there is no logical impossibility in the view that the world was created five minutes ago, complete with memories and records.[3]

It is possible, it seems to me, to frame such hypotheses so that it is logically impossible for them to be verified or falsified. For example, it is logically possible both that human beings are the only beings in the universe capable of verifying anything and that at some time it should suddenly and quite unexpectedly come about that there were no longer any human beings. This hypothesis is belted against any possibility of

---

[1] This paper acknowledges a great debt to conversations with Wittgenstein. But Professor Anscombe is surely quite mistaken in construing the paper, as she does in her *An Introduction to Wittgenstein's Tractatus*, pp. 152 ff., as though it was an interpretation of the *Tractatus*, or based upon one.

[2] See *Logical Positivism*, ed. Ayer, p. 56.

[3] *An Outline of Philosophy*, 1927 (Unwin Books, 1970) p. 7.

verification and, while the first part can be falsified, it can be amended so that the second part becomes a hypothesis, not about human beings, but about 'verifiers'. Thus amended it becomes proof even against the most liberal verificationism, which is broad-minded about what can count as a reason for believing a hypothesis true or false.

There is a last ditch defence of the verifiability criterion as a criterion of meaningfulness. It is to take the fact that we can think of such hypotheses as showing that verification and falsification are, after all, possible, if only from an 'angelic' point of view. This would not require believing in the existence of beings having such an 'external' point of view on the universe, only that it makes sense to suppose that there are such beings or that there is a vantage point from which it could be ascertained that the universe had come into being, had instantaneously doubled in size, or whatever. But this seems to lead to an unhappy regress. To suppose that 'H' is only meaningful if 'H is verifiable' is meaningful, i.e. if it makes sense to talk about such a vantage point outside the universe, is to raise questions about the verifiability of 'H is verifiable'. So not only would such a last ditch defence lead to none of the restrictions which the verifiability criterion was intended to impose, it introduces problems of its own. On these terms the option of insisting that all meaningful statements must be verifiable in principle is unlikely to prove inviting to anyone.

III

I believe that there is, none the less, something right in the Positivist's emphasis on the verifiability criterion. There is, I think, something wrong with hypotheses whose truth or falsity could only be recognised from an angelic point of view. What is wrong, however, is not that such apparent hypotheses fail, after all, to have a truth-value − fail, that is to say, to have any cognitive import. It is, rather, that we *cannot* form beliefs one way or the other with regard to them. It is not just that we *ought not* to hold beliefs one way or the other about such hypotheses as H. Nothing would count as *making up one's mind* that H is true or false where nothing counts as a consideration favouring H or its negation. That this is so emerges from an adequate account of such epistemic concepts as 'belief'.

It is tempting to construe questions of the form 'What makes *X* believe that *p*?' as psychological. So in a way they are. But they are not *straightforwardly causal*. No answer to a straightforwardly causal question is precluded in advance of experience. My wiggling my ear won't make the billiard ball go into the pocket. Indeed it cannot. But this is not something which we know *a priori*. The Humean dictum that anything can be the cause of anything is widely applicable. And I am calling 'straightforwardly causal' those cases to which it *is* applicable. It does seem applicable to some psychological cases. For instance there seems no restriction in advance of experience on what will do as an answer to the question 'What makes X *wish* that *p*?'. In this way it seems a straightforwardly psychological matter if a man *cannot* wish his opponents in a competitive game the best of luck. He may say the *words*, of course, as convention may require. But he may be *unable* to feel the sentiment his words express. What prevents someone from wishing that the best team will win, or whatever, is something we know about from experience alone. The 'cannot' in 'I cannot wish them well' is, in this sense, a straightforwardly psychological, straightforwardly causal, 'cannot'. (I do not mean that the causal 'cannot' is in all respects straightforward.)

There is at least one restriction which the *concept* 'wish' appears to place on the range of antecedents of what we count as *wishing* for something. If someone says that he wishes for something precisely because he has it already, we may attach some sense to what he says. But we would not call it 'wishing'. That means that the 'cannot' in 'You cannot wish for what you have already' is not a *causal* 'cannot'. It is, rather, a kinsman of the *logical* 'cannot'. But the restrictions, if any, on what can make people wish that *p* are discovered in experience. There is no absurdity in a man's wishing his enemies well or wishing that the world would come to an end because he is sublimely happy.

Believing that *p* is, however, by no means as unfettered as wishing that *p* in this respect. There are, it seems to me, specific restrictions on what antecedents there can be where a state of mind is one of belief. These restrictions arise from our epistemology, from what we count as a reason. For example, we should not accept, in answer to the question 'What makes him believe it will rain tomorrow?' such explanations as 'Because 2 + 2 = 4'. It is not that there cannot be people from whom, given the stimulus '2 + 2 = 4', we obtain the response 'Hence it will rain tomorrow'. Only, if we do come across such people, we will not know what to make of their response. It will not be recognisable as an expression of belief unless further clarification tends in the direction of answering the question 'What makes him believe that?' with something which is recognisable as a *reason* for believing it. By the phrase 'recognisable as a reason' I do not mean to imply that it should be a good reason. It might be that the person had attended a logic class where he had been taught that necessary truths are entailed by the truth of any proposition, only had got it muddled, misremembering what he had heard as 'The truth of any proposition is entailed by a necessary truth'. Thus, recognising '2 + 2 = 4' as a necessary proposition, he infers that it will rain tomorrow since the weather happened to be uppermost in his mind at that time. We must also suppose that he did not hear his logic teacher say things which would imply that any necessary truth is entailed not only by 'It will rain tomorrow' but also by 'It will not rain tomorrow'. In some such way, perhaps, we might be able to connect almost any proposition with almost any other proposition so as to make one recognisable as a reason, or part of a set of reasons, for believing the other. But we can only do this in certain ways and not in others, in accordance not with psychological laws but with epistemological norms.

It is such norms to which reference is being made when it is said that it is *impossible* to believe something, when one person says to another, 'You *can't* believe that. You *must* believe this.' Such modal expressions are, in common speech, often used with a rhetorical flavour. But I think they also have a strict use, in which it follows from 'He *cannot* believe p' that he *does not* believe p. Perhaps it can be said of a man who believes he is Jesus Christ or Napoleon that, since he *can't* believe that he *does not* believe it, but that rather these words express a different belief about himself. But such cases are difficult to discuss in the abstract and doubly difficult, no doubt, for a layman. There are, in any case, plausible examples which are not so far removed from the conditions under which beliefs are normally formed. Engels, for example, once wrote of Thomas Carlyle that he had for the past several years 'chiefly occupied himself with the social condition of England — he, the only educated man of his country to do that!'.[1] This remark might have been an exaggeration, something Engels did not really believe for a moment. But, if so, why did he write it? And then, how *could* he have believed it? Steven Marcus has suggested that Engels could not, surrounded as he was by official reports into the conditions of the poor and the effects of the Poor Laws, have really believed that Carlyle was the only educated man in England to be chiefly concerned with its social condition. The interpretation which Marcus offers of the situation implies that the clause in which Engels appears to express a belief about Carlyle in fact expresses a belief about himself. As Marcus puts it:[2] 'the truth of that clause is to be read in the statement that at the end of 1843 Friedrich Engels was the only educated man (known to himself) of his country who was chiefly occupied with such matters'.

Marcus goes on to offer an explanation of how Engels could have been so identified with Carlyle as to express a belief about himself in terms of a claim about Carlyle. It is not my purpose to endorse Marcus' explanation as historically correct any more than it is to ascribe to him my account of belief. My point is that the possibility of such an account being right shows that not everything that looks like a belief is one and not every belief is the belief it looks as if it is. Moreover we can and do make use of epistemological norms in assessing whether or not the antecedents are at all appropriate to the belief which is being professed, and, if not, to what belief they are appropriate.

These norms operate in two ways in cases where it is suggested that

---

[1]   In a review of Carlyle's *Past and Present*, written in 1843, *Werke* 1, 528.
[2]   *Engels, Manchester and the Working Class* (Weidenfeld and Nicolson, 1974) p.103.

someone *must* believe something *different* from what he professes or appears to believe. In the first place they are invoked to rule out what is professed as something that person *could not* have believed. Thus Marcus tacitly assumes − and rightly I suppose − that the evidence there was around Engels of educated Englishmen other than Carlyle being highly occupied with the country's social condition would have the same effect on Engels as upon us, namely, to preclude a contrary belief. In the second place such norms may point to an alternative belief. Marcus indicates that, so far as Engels was aware, there was no one of *his* country who was chiefly occupied with the social condition of England around that time. (Marx did not move to England until 1849.) The difficult part of Marcus' account, it seems to me, has not to do with belief so much but in explaining how Engels could have *written* what he did, how, in professing one belief he could, in effect, be evincing another.

Now in saying that it is legitimate to infer that X does *not* believe *p* from the impossibility of his believing it, I am clearly committed, by the principle of *Modus Tollens*, to accept also that if someone *does* believe *p* then it is not impossible for him to believe it. Certain considerations about Engel's behaviour, e.g. his frequent repetition of this claim about Carlyle, would incline us to accept that he did believe it and therefore to reject Marcus' interpretation. One possibility would be that what Engels means was that Carlyle was the only educated *Scotsman* to be chiefly occupied about the social condition of England. Perhaps it would be wrong to assume that Engels would have fallen victim to the imperialist propaganda which has promoted the use of the word 'England' for the whole of Britain. However that may be − and it is quite possible that we just cannot make out what Engels believed about Carlyle − some explanation of a belief is called for from anyone who attributes it to someone in circumstances where it seems impossible for such a belief to be held. My main concern is to argue that it cannot both be the case that X believes that *p* and that it is impossible for X to believe that *p*. Moreover, I want to claim, it is our being subject to epistemological norms rather than straightforwardly psychological laws which prevents our holding certain beliefs.

It should not be thought surprising that we do use such norms in deciding whether an assertion is really a profession of a belief. For believing that *p* is, at any rate in that sense of 'believing' I am presently concerned with, believing that *p is true*. Someone who was totally indifferent to truth − someone who cared nothing for just reasoning − would be someone to whom we could not ascribe beliefs at all. It is because an interest in the truth is the motive characteristic of someone who is trying to make up his mind on some matter that believing which is motivated in some other way, as in self-deception, is seen as a sort of perversion. Yet even in cases like these some semblance of rationality is preserved. If it were not preserved in those cases, they would cease to involve belief at all and collapse into some weaker state such as being determined to act as though something were true. There having to be an answer to the question 'What makes him believe that?' which accords with epistemological norms we are familiar with is a necessary condition of our being right in ascribing a particular belief. Failing such familiarity, of course, it might still *be* a belief, although we do not recognise it as such. And there are mistakes we can make in applying the norms we do apply. None the less there can be cases where, in the absence of antecedents which conform to norms as to what counts as a reason for believing something, we will be fully justified in refusing to accept a profession of belief as expressing a belief.

The clearest cases where this is so have perhaps an air of artificiality about them. Supposing, for example, it is known that one of two propositions is true and the other false, since they are contradictories, but that there is no reason whatever for regarding one as true and the other as false. Supposing further that someone, recognising that this is so — recognising that there is what I shall call an *"epistemic vacuum'* between the two propositions — nonetheless *plumps* for one. What I want to say is that, however we construe his plumping for one rather than the other, this is not a case of *belief*. Here *belief* seems quite different from *action*. The captain of a football team, when playing away, has to call 'Heads' or 'Tails' before the start of the game. He has to *plump* for one rather than the other. No doubt actual captains of football teams have all sorts of beliefs or half-beliefs about how the coin will fall in different situations. ('Heads' is lucky at Anfield, 'Tails' at Maine Road, etc.) But many others will recognise the 'epistemic vacuum' for what it is, will recognise, in other words, that the coin is no more likely to fall one way than the other, that there is no reason therefore to believe that the coin will fall 'Heads' rather than 'Tails'. None the less they must act, they must call 'Heads' or 'Tails'. They can act and, of course, do act in an 'epistemic vacuum'[1] although there can, for them, be no question of belief. Perhaps some scientific education is what has made such belief impossible for them. To say that it is *impossible* for them to believe it is not to make a covert reference to the operation of a psychological law but to note that they have learnt only to count certain considerations as reasons for believing and not others.

There are many problems which are raised by such an account. For instance, there is a cluster of problems about what I have referred to as 'epistemological norms' — whether they can be articulated in a systematic

---

[1] I do not intend to imply by saying this that no causal explanation can be given of the particular ways such a captain does call when the coin is tossed. Such explanations would obviously not refer to his beliefs about the outcome, though other beliefs about the situation, e.g. that it was for him to call, are likely to feature.

way, whether different language-groups may be subject, in forming their beliefs, to different norms, and so on. Again, such an account faces difficulties which are analogous to those relating to regresses in justification. If I excuse myself from coming to grips with these problems here, it is because they are not peculiar to my account.

IV

Let us return then to my original question. How are we to fill in the blank:

> If there are no considerations which count as tending to determine the truth (or falsity) of an hypothesis (H) as opposed to that of any apparently competing hypothesis, then . . .

I suggested in Section II that it does not follow that 'H' is meaningless in that sense which implies it has no truth-value. If what I have said in Section III is on the right lines, there appears to be an 'epistemic vacuum' with respect to H. Can we conclude that no assertion of H can be construed as an expression of belief that H? Such a conclusion would need to be qualified. For there is a distinction between the reasons why a particular person believes *p* and reasons which bear on the truth of *p*. Now this distinction is not of consequence in the present context where we are concerned with people making up their own minds. But there are a great many beliefs which people hold on the authority of others. Thus a scientific authority might, as a hoax, assert in a lecture, together with totally obscure and irrelevant reasoning, that the universe had in fact just instantaneously doubled in size. And it would, in such a circumstance, be quite intelligible that others will believe it. We can, in some such way, imagine some people believing almost anything. For being justified in believing something may involve having some further belief to the effect that certain sources are reliable sources of information. Such cases seem to presuppose beliefs which do involve the exercise of judgement, in this case as to reliability, perhaps, or some judgement from which *that* is inferred, such as the speaker being a Fellow of the Royal Society.

However that may be, my conclusion about the status of H needs to be expressed more weakly, perhaps as follows:

> . . . then no assertion purporting to be a judgement that H can express *belief* that H.

The reference to belief might be thought unnecessary here, since it may be thought implied in the use of the word 'judgement'. I retain it partly because some use 'judgement' as a synonym for 'decision'. A referee may have to make *decisions* in an epistemic vacuum. I am inclined to think that, in such a case, he is unable to *judge* the situation. However that may be, he is not able to form a *belief* about it, if, say, his view was obstructed and he could consult no one else, unless he is a very bad referee who is swayed by the claims of the players or some other consideration which referees are supposed to treat as irrelevant.

On the Logical Positivist's construal of the verifiability criterion, H will be neither true nor false. On my reconstruction I have only spoken so far of the impossibility of judging H to be true. It is, however, clear that the same considerations apply where it is asserted that H is false. My version of the verifiability criterion will therefore read as follows:

> If there are no considerations which count as tending to determine the truth or falsity of an hypothesis (H) as opposed to that of any apparently competing hypothesis, then no assertion put forward as an independent judgement about H can be an expression of *belief* or doubt as to the truth or falsity of H.

The acceptability of this criterion does not in any way turn on the acceptability of empiricism. Added to an empiricist epistemology, however, it has many of the consequences of the Positivists' criterion, except of course that, instead of saying metaphysical or religious utterances, because they fail to satisfy it, are meaningless, it will be said that they fail to express beliefs. Even so, not all the consequences will be analogous in this way. My criterion, while it is no less destructive of some forms of scepticism, permits agnosticism in both metaphysics and religion, even where there is nothing which counts as a reason for belief or disbelief, given empiricist standards. It is destructive of scepticism in those cases where scepticism involves belief, e.g. the belief that we do not really know that there are conscious states other than our own, i.e. that there are grounds for doubt. In this case the absence of such grounds ensures that there is nothing for doubt to feed on. And, if there is nothing for doubt to feed on, there is nothing to substantiate a claim to knowledge. The belief that one knows something seems to involve a belief that the doubts there can be in such cases are taken care of. If that is so, the fact that there could be no substance to such doubts deprives that belief of any substance. This in turn makes the dispute an empty one. The epistemic vacuum in the face of which doubt becomes impossible affects the dispute itself in so far as the opposed position must appear to be that just such doubts have been eliminated. Perhaps that is the substance of what is maintained by those who say that such disputes are 'meaningless'.

10

EMPIRICISM IN SCIENCE AND PHILOSOPHY

Errol E. Harris

The term 'Empiricism' has had at least two different, though not un-connected, applications in modern thought, one to scientific method and the other to philosophical theory. My intention in this lecture is to try to show that, while these two applications of the term have a common source, their actual referents are widely divergent and in large measure even mutually incompatible.

The birth of modern science in the seventeenth century brought with it a firm conviction that scientific theory must be founded upon and suppor-ted by observed factual and experimental evidence, and no respectable scientist since then has ever regarded a theory as established until some experimental confirmation, considered sufficient by the scientific com-munity, has been produced. This dependence of scientific knowledge upon observation and experiment is what is meant by empiricism in science. But the precise function of observation and its relation to theory in the methodology of science is a matter to be further investigated.

Philosophical Empiricism, on the other hand, is something much more radical and deep-seated. It is a theory of knowledge, an epistemology, which carries with it implications for scientific method, but which can itself claim empirical support only if and so far as the actual practice of scientists conforms to its requirements. Philosophical Empiricism is not just a methodology of science; it is a theory of the nature of knowledge as such, and whether or not it is empirical in the first sense I have distin-guished is a further question.

I do not propose to review the long history of philosophical Empiricism or to list its numerous varieties — for not all theories which accept the title agree in detail. It will be enough to observe that in its modern forms the philosophic theory was largely inspired by the new emphasis on empirical evidence in seventeenth century science, and especially by the enthusiasm for experimental methods expressed by Francis Bacon in his *Novum Or-ganum*. It must be noticed, however, that Bacon did not develop an epistemology, but only a methodology of science, and one that does not necessarily involve empiricism in the second sense of the term. He protested against the prejudices of the learned and of the vulgar, against fruitless debate without systematic investigation, and he insisted upon the importance of experiment, but he did not ground these views on any explicit philosophical theory of knowledge or reality.

Modern philosophical Empiricism proper was founded by Thomas Hobbes and John Locke; but I shall not expound their theories or that of any other individual philosopher. I shall only outline in brief (and I hope without undue misrepresentation of any particular thinker) the main representative tenets of philosophical Empiricism in general, note its consequences for scientific method, and then turn to the actual procedure of practising scientists in order to discover whether it supports the philosophical theory.

The first and most fundamental principle of theoretical Empiricism is that all factual knowledge about the world ultimately derives from sensation. This is perhaps a rather crude statement of the principle, but though it may need refinement and qualification, it does not seriously misrepresent the tradition. Sensations are held to be passively received and to reveal to the knowing subject those basic qualities by combination of which physical objects are built up. The rest is a matter of construction, arrangement and concatenation of these, which issues as a picture of a world of material things in specific relations.

Some might wish to deny that Empiricists derive all knowledge from sensation. Logical truths, they will say, and what David Hume called 'relations of ideas', as opposed to 'matters of fact', are, as he put it, 'discoverable by the mere operation of thought without dependence on what is anywhere existent in the universe'.[1] But logical truths, for Empiricists, are devoid of factual content and express only linguistic equivalences, so that it is doubtful whether they should rank as knowledge in any proper sense of the word. Even so, if statements of linguistic equivalence are to have any content whatever, it must, on this theory, derive from sense. As to Hume's 'relations of ideas', he was quite adamant in his insistence that all ideas are merely fainter copies of sensory impressions, and what is 'discoverable by the mere operation of thought' is, for him, discoverable by thought's operation only upon ideas or impressions, for there is no other matter for it to work upon. Abstract ideas, apart from particular impressions or their ideal replicae, Hume, following Berkeley, rejects without reserve. So I think I can leave my initial statement standing that for Empiricism the original source of all knowledge is sense.

If more testimony is desired I have only to quote Hume once again. In

---

[1] David Hume, *An Enquiry Concerning Human Understanding*,

his *Treatise of Human Nature* he writes:[1]

> Now since nothing is ever present to the mind but perceptions, and
> since all ideas are derived from something antecedently present to the
> mind; it follows, that 'tis impossible for us so much as to conceive or
> form an idea of anything specifically different from ideas and
> impressions. Let us fix our attention out of ourselves as much as
> possible: Let us chace our imagination to the heavens, or the utmost
> limits of the universe; we never really advance a step beyond ourselves,
> nor can we conceive any kind of existence, but those perceptions,
> which have appeared in that narrow compass. This is the universe of the
> imagination, nor have we any idea but what is there produced.

It is further maintained that all sensuous impressions are 'Particular
existences' and so likewise are the simple ideas derived from them. The
former, in more recent terminology, are called sense-data and the latter
their imaginative reproduction. And though our minds can combine or
separate them in any way it pleases in imagination, and can compare and
relate their qualities, it cannot create them *ab initio* and can only accept
impressions as they occur to it, in continuous succession. Moreover, their
intrinsic character reveals no feature which can determine how, or in what
order, they should occur; so that there is no evident connexion between
any two of them, and in consequence the occurrence of none of them can
be inferred from that of any other.

It follows that the only ground we can have for the prediction of future
experience is our expectation that what has in the past frequently
occurred in conjunction will be similarly conjoined in the future. For apart
from the frequent conjunction of ideas in the past, there is nothing to
indicate in what order they may occur in the future. But frequent
conjunction leads the mind to expect similar recurrences. Thus if thunder
has, in our past experience, constantly followed lightning, we expect that
this conjunction will recur, and when we see the flash we shall listen for
the rumble as its consequent, or if we hear the crash we shall presume that
the lightning occurred immediately prior to it. All inference to matters of
fact, according to the Empiricist doctrine, is and can only be of this
inductive character.

Inference of any other kind depends, according to Hume, upon
comparison of ideas or impressions (or both) which are immediately
present to the mind. More recent writers have stressed its purely analytic
character. It elaborates only the consequences of the definitions of terms
and is thus essentially tautological and can lead to no new information.
This is the character, for Empiricism, of all deductive reasoning. Any and

---

[1]   Book I, pt ii, section vi.

every synthetic inference, yielding conclusions which are not contained in the premises, can only be inductive.

It would be altogether mistaken to form the impression (should anybody be so inclined) that, because I have quoted Hume, Empiricism may be dismissed as a philosophical doctrine which went out of commission in the eighteenth century. Not only did John Stuart Mill continue the tradition in the nineteenth, but it has been predominant among philosophers of our own day in the English speaking world and very influential outside it. But while contemporary thinkers, like Bertrand Russell, G.E. Moore, Wittgenstein and Carnap have introduced complications and sophistications, the fundamental tenets remain the same and Hume's statement of the theory is still the most consistent, most uncompromising and most powerful. Accordingly, at least until the last decade, current philosophy of science has been largely concerned with developing the consequences of philosophical Empiricism for scientific methodology, and has concluded, in conformity with the outline I have given, that scientific reasoning is, and like any other reasoning only can be, either deductive, which is purely analytic and tautological, or inductive, deriving general laws from particular observed instances and making predictions on the basis of such laws. An elegant and detailed account of how these two types of reasoning are combined in scientific method is set out in Professor R.B. Braithwaite's book, *Scientific Explanation*, as well as in many other modern texts, which leave no doubt of the current prevalence of the theory.

Unfortunately, difficulties immediately suggest themselves, for the main pride and special achievement of science has been the making of discoveries, and if its methods were restricted to the two forms of reasoning alleged it could never discover anything new, unless by direct observation, for which no special method seems necessary. That nothing new can be discovered by purely analytic deduction everybody will agree — and all Empiricists assert. But it is less obvious that inductive inference is equally sterile. For all that can legitimise its conclusion is the frequent conjunction of events in past experience, and the only conclusion *that* can support is the probable repetition of the past conjunction. Consequently induction can do no more than underline what is already known. Neither of these forms of reasoning could predict the occurrence of a conjunction that has never previously been observed, nor do Empiricists claim that they could.

It may be said, however, that although new knowledge cannot be reached by deduction alone, or by induction alone, yet in combination they can reveal the unexpected. If this is so, I cannot understand how. It is usually maintained that the purely formal structure of a deductive system is an uninterpreted calculus, consisting of formulae constructed from symbols representing variables. The calculus operates according to set rules prescribing the method of transformation of the formulae, so that from certain equivalences others can be derived. We interpret the calculus by substituting empirical terms, denoting observables, for the variables; then we can deduce from certain empirical statements others which we have not yet observed but can now put to the test of experiment.

This, however, does not seem to me to be feasible, because the deductive system is analytic and no conclusion can be drawn by its means which contains anything not already contained in the premisses. So even if the premisses are empirical all that could be derived from them by pure deduction would be what had already been observed, though now stated in a new way. Any formula in a calculus, if validly derived by substitution from any other, must be equivalent to that for which it is substituted. So the meaning of any statement resulting from the replacement of the variables by empirical terms must be the same as any other from which it could validly be derived. If new information of any sort is to be acquired by 'deduction' it must be some sort of deduction other than what Empiricists will allow.

How then does the scientist make discoveries? Must he wait until he observes new phenomena by chance? Some scientific discoveries do seem to have been accidental, but serendipity is exceptional and its accidental character is largely a deceptive appearance. Is it, perhaps, that the methodology of scientific experimentation, on the necessity of which Bacon was so insistent, holds the secret of discovery. In some measure I believe that it does, but it is not sufficient by itself. And if it does, traditional Empiricism has not revealed that secret, for it cannot be with the help of deduction or induction that experiment can discover anything *new*, and, if it does not do so by sheer accident, what kind of logic must be involved?

Moreover, a very little reflection on the history of science soon reveals that some of the most significant and spectacular discoveries have been made independently of any new observations, others have been predictions of what nobody had hitherto observed, and others again have been of objects or processes that could not be observed at all. In some cases the discoveries were of facts which could not at the time be observed with the means then at the disposal of scientists; in other cases they were literally unobservable. Numerous examples are available of both these types. One example of the first is the discovery of molecular structure, and an example of the second is the discovery of the precession of the perihelion of Mercury.

Even a less controversial case, like the discovery of Uranus, was not just the direct observation of a new phenomenon. In fact it was not a new observation at all, for Uranus had been sighted twenty-two times before it was 'discovered'. Even Herschel, while mapping the heavens, when he came upon the unexpected object, took it to be a comet. And he did so, not entirely on the basis of what he saw, but largely in consequence of theoretical assumptions. Only after elaborate mathematical calculations to determine the orbit of the alleged comet was it discovered to be a planet, and needless to say no orbit as such can be directly observed. It has to be inferred from a conjunction of observation, measurements and calculation. Thus discovery *is* the fruit of inference, but not of purely analytic deduction which cannot produce new knowledge, nor of induction which can only repeat the old. At no stage in Herschel's proceeding did he, or anybody else, argue that because the new celestial body appeared as it did, or moved as calculated, it could be expected to do so again in the future. Such an inference would have been of no interest. What excited astronomers and the world at large was that an eighth planet had swum into the ken of mankind. A new and hitherto unknown fact had been revealed.

I am not suggesting that observation and experiment are unimportant factors in scientific method; quite the contrary. They are undoubtedly quite indispensable and it is precisely to them that the description of science as empirical refers. But the relation between observation and theory is not, in my view, what traditional Empiricism alleges. No observation is intelligible and no experiment would be made apart from theory, which is not only the conclusion drawn from them, but is also the means of interpreting and recognising what is observed, as well as of conceiving and designing experiments. Observation may never be merely random and haphazard if it is to be scientific; but, without a prior hypothesis, random and haphazard is all it could be. Experiment is actually the question that the scientist puts to Nature, and no question arises unless some theory is already being entertained. Further, all observation, even the most naive, is an interpretation, in the light of prior knowledge, of presented 'data' (though I use that word with reservation, because nothing intelligible is ever merely 'given'). Experiment is part of the scientist's endeavour to develop the implications of hypotheses already conceived. And it is in terms of theories already established and accepted that he interprets his results.

But neither the accepted theories nor the hypothesis to be tested are products of inductive inference of the sort envisaged by philosophical Empiricism. Arguments of the form 'AB frequently, therefore probably AB always' may be encountered in therapeutic sciences, like Medicine, but they are never more than preliminary and no scientist bent on discovery will be content with such reasoning. Practitioners may for a time rely on what are called 'purely empirical' conjunctions. For instance, acupuncture has been found, whenever skilfully applied, to have certain effects; therefore, if similarly applied again, similar effects may be expected. But the scientific physiologist will want to discover why acupuncture has these effects and will look for more systematic connections. Constant conjunction is indeed an indication that systematic relationships exist and may be discovered so that the argument 'AB frequently, therefore perhaps AB always' is only a first step.

Even so, some prior theory, some suggested hypothesis, is necessary before a constant conjunction appears significant, and without the theory no correlation may even be noticed. Moreover an important condition is that the prior theory should be in some way defective and should have given rise to difficulties and conflicts. For example, in the early days of chemistry, it was only when the phlogiston theory began to give trouble that attention was given to the fact that substances increased in weight when burnt. The fact itself had been noticed as early as 1630 by Jean Rey, but so long as the idea of phlogiston seemed useful (and in its day it was far more fruitful than is often imagined) the only interest the augmentation in weight aroused was as a slight anomaly to be explained away. However, as the pneumatic chemists of the eighteenth century came upon various 'airs' some of which did and some of which did not support combustion, some of which burned in air and others not, the phlogiston explanation gave rise to numerous contradictions, a list of which is given by Lavoisier in the first section of his *Opuscules Physique et Chymique*. He therefore proposed the hypothesis that when substances burned and metals calcined they absorbed some portion of the surrounding air. At the same time Guyton de Morveau performed a series of experiments demonstrating the constant augmentation of weight accompanying combustion, the clue which Lavoisier followed (among others) in a more famous series of experiments establishing the theory of oxidation.

We can observe from this example first that there existed a prior theory which was proving unsatisfactory; secondly, that the contradictions arising from it raised new questions, which prompted experimentation and observation revealing constant conjunctions. Thirdly, these gave rise to a new tentative hypothesis, followed, fourthly, by further experiments to test and confirm the new theory.

An important feature of this development is that, if de Morveau's experiments seemed to reveal a constant conjunction, Lavoisier's were neither designed to do so nor produced one as their result. The experiments were diverse in character, each produced a different result, none were merely repetitive; but all the results fitted together systematically and each supported all the rest, so that they formed an interrelated system of evidence of mutually dependent facts. The new theory stated the principle of relationship that made the diverse phenomena hang together coherently, as the old theory had tried but had failed to do.

To these characteristics of scientific method I shall have occasion to refer again, but we may observe immediately that so-called inductive argument plays a relatively minor part. In fact, it is demonstrably false that scientists always derive their theories by generalisation from repeated conjunction of particular phenomena. Undoubtedly they do, on appropriate occasions, use statistical methods to evaluate evidence. But not all, and frequently not the most important, scientific theories have been reached by any method remotely resembling 'induction' of the traditional Empiricist pattern. An outstanding example (but certainly not the only one) is the heliocentric hypothesis of Copernicus, which was not prompted by any special observations. In fact, it would be difficult to imagine any naked eye observations of the heavens (and none other were available at the time) from which such a hypothesis could have been generalised. No observation of the diurnal motion of the heavenly bodies reveals the fact that the earth (or any other planet) revolves round the sun, and no inductive generalisation from what is constantly observed gives this conclusion. What Copernicus did was to revive a theory suggested centuries earlier by Aristarchus of Samos to explain data which, as sensuously observed, could mean nothing intelligible without some theory in terms of which they could be interpreted. Nor was Copernicus' system for interpreting the movement of heavenly bodies less complicated or more successful as a means of prediction than Ptolemy's, which it was designed to replace. Its sole claim to superiority, and the source of its appeal to Copernicus' followers, was its greater coherent unity, the merit which he himself emphasised in recommending it to Pope Pius III.

Among contemporary philosophers, Sir Karl Popper first drew attention to the fact that induction was not the typical form of scientific reasoning. He rejected it also for philosophical reasons which, important as they are, I do not propose to review.[1] The method in his view is hypothetico-deductive and he would respond to my question about scientific discovery by denying that it is ever a matter of logic. What scientists discover are new theories and these are pure conjecture, to which logic does not apply. One conceived, consequences can be deduced from a hypothesis which are subject to experiment and observation. Thus we may test the hypothesis; but a favourable experimental result does not verify it. It leaves it unrefuted, but verification by inductive reasoning is never possible for no amount of favourable evidence is ever enough. On the other hand, one unfavourable instance is sufficient to falsify the hypothesis. So the endeavour of science is always to falsify and hypotheses survive only as long as that endeavour fails.

The answer to my question about the logic of discovery, on this view, would be that there is none, for no logical account of it can ever be given. Logic becomes applicable only in assessing the arguments by which scientists seek to falsify theories, or when occasion arises to justify their retention. They discover them by the exercise of their own genius which is

---

[1] I have done so elsewhere. See *Hypothesis and Perception*, chs II, IV.

explicable, if at all, only by psychology and follows no logical rules. This is today a widely accepted doctrine and, of course, it is true both that arguments in defence or in refutation of scientific theories must be logically validated, and that genius is largely unaccountable, in the sense that insight is a talent for the acquisition of which there are no rules. But if genius is needed to make scientific discoveries it does not follow that no logical process is involved in the activity, any more than it follows from the fact that genius is needed for the composition of a symphony that there are no principles of harmony or counterpoint.

There are good reasons for denying the division of scientific procedure into what have been called 'the context of discovery' and 'the context of justification'. The two processes are inextricably intertwined and I hope to be able to indicate, if not to demonstrate conclusively, that a logic of some sort is intrinsic to both.

Professor Popper seems to me to be certainly right in his view that consequences are deduced from hypotheses which are then tested by observation. But if so the deduction must be of a kind which can develop new facts. If it were purely analytic all we could derive by its means would be either alternative forms of the hypothesis or alternative formulations of initial conditions brought under the supposed law (the hypothesis having the form of an assumed law of nature). But this would give us nothing to investigate experimentally. The argument should run:

If hypothesis *H* is true, under conditions *a*, *b*, *c*, (which we have experienced and can reproduce) result *R* would occur (which has not yet been observed),

and that would be a synthetic proposition which could not be the product of purely formal deduction. Nobody, least of all Popper, would regard it as an inductive argument. So the question remains, What kind of logic is involved? Even in hypothetico-deductive procedure, it is not what Empiricism could consistently admit.

Professor Popper has put us upon a new path but he has not yet led us out of the wood. Hypotheses are not as a rule, or typically, mere guesses, and they are prompted by rational considerations. Some kind of logical account of them should therefore be possible. In the history of science we constantly find that new hypotheses are modifications and adaptations, of older ones, the breakdown of which is heralded by the emergence of contradiction in the course of developing their consequences. The success or failure of a hypothesis depends on the extent to which it can disclose systematic relationship among the observed phenomena consistently and over a comprehensive range, and when it fails it gives rise to new questions and efforts at reconstruction in order to resolve the conflicts.

But the method of empirical science does not centre purely on efforts at falsification. When awkward cases are found in the course of scientific research the theory affected is not immediately rejected. The matter is usually held in abeyance, pending closer investigation, for scientists do not — they cannot afford to — reject an effective explanatory system in deference to isolated unassimilable instances. The anomalies are not altogether ignored, but a persistent effort is made to adjust or modify the principles of the system so that the difficulties will be overcome. When many such anomalies have accumulated and when they involve serious contradictions within the system drastic modifications of the conceptual scheme may be demanded, and when such epoch-marking changes do occur they alter the whole aspect of the science concerned. But contrary to common belief, they are not altogether discontinuous with the theories they replace.

The historical example to which appeal is most frequently made in support of Empiricism is Galileo's discovery of the law of falling bodies. This is usually taken as the turning point at which science adopted empirical methods and broke away from metaphysics. It may be useful therefore to consider the facts with some care. The law is commonly supposed to have been a generalisation from experimental results obtained by Galileo when he dropped weights from the leaning tower of Pisa and rolled balls down inclined planes. Just what experiments Galileo performed we do not precisely know, for he does not describe them in the treatise in which he set out his theory, and he demonstrates it, for the most part, without reference to experimental results. Moreover, if he did perform the appropriate experiments he could not with the means at his disposal have measured distances and velocities with sufficient accuracy to derive his laws. Worse still, if he had been able to measure precisely, he would have obtained results which refuted his theories and supported that of his opponents. We may assert with confidence therefore, that the law was not the conclusion of an inductive argument. Nor is it pure conjecture or random guesswork. The theory is set out in deductive form by Galileo. But the deduction is not used to derive observable consequences and neither Galileo nor his successors made experimental attempts to falsify the theory. Had they done so, the results of the alleged experiments from the leaning tower, accurately measured, would have been sufficient refutation and the hypothesis should have been rejected.

That the law is a principle serving to systematise our experience of phenomena of motion is too obvious to require emphasis, for it relates systematically the behaviour of falling bodies, of objects sliding down inclined planes, of projectiles and of weights propelled by impressed forces. Newton later correlated it further with Kepler's laws of planetary motion to evolve a single system of mechanics, celestial and terrestrial.

The method of derivation, we find when we examine Galileo's argument, relates empirical facts and deductive reasoning in a manner quite foreign to the teachings of philosophical Empiricism; for, according to that, deduction is purely analytic and cannot produce new factual information. Yet this is what Galileo succeeds in doing. I shall confine myself to only one of his demonstrations which seems to me specially typical and illuminating. The law to be established is stated as follows:

> The momenta or speeds of one and the same moving body (falling along an inclined plane) vary with the inclination of the plane (from the horizontal).[1]

First we must notice that Galileo uses the word 'momentum' in almost precisely the sense given to the term 'impetus' (which he sometimes substitutes for it) by the thirteenth century Parisian scholars. They had introduced the concept to remedy difficulties arising out of Aristotle's theory.

A digression here is perhaps justified to observe this source of Galileo's thinking in more detail. Aristotle, as is well-known, taught that bodies moved only if violently dislodged from their normal place. They moved therefore only either under impulsion, or naturally if returning to their proper place in the universe. Two major difficulties, however, arose from this theory. First, falling bodies moved continuously faster as they approached the earth, and the Aristotelian explanation that they increased their speed from joy at the nearer approach to their natural home would not account for the fact that a body dropped from a greater height accelerated more than one falling from a lower point despite equal proximity to the earth. Secondly, the motion of projectiles could not be accounted for on this theory. Why did the arrow, for instance, not drop directly from the released bow-string? Peripatetics had tried to argue that the force of the air rushing into the space left by the moving arrow kept it in motion – but why then should it ever stop? One could not, without contradiction, invoke air pressure both to propel the arrow and to bring it to rest. Buridan solved this problem by propounding the theory of impetus, according to which motion automatically engendered in the body a nisus to continue in motion. This impetus gradually died out, in the same sort of way as a hot poker gradually cools. Falling bodies would thus gather impetus as they fell and it would increase in proportion to the time and distance through which they moved, and it could now be maintained without contradiction that projectiles would be kept in motion by their impetus which would be progressively overcome by air resistance.

It is precisely this quantity of motion proportional to time and distance that Galileo calls 'momentum' and the relation of the concept so used to

---

[1] *Dialogues Concerning Two New Sciences*, trans Crew, de Salvio and Favaro (Evanston, Illinois, 1950) p. 176.

the modern conception is much more obvious. Thus we may trace a continuous conceptual development from Aristotelian physics to Newtonian. The process of development is also clear. Aristotle systematised the observed phenomena in one way, but his system was not coherent. It led to contradictions. Buridan modified it so as to remove these. But when Copernicus introduced the heliocentric hypothesis new conflicts arose due to the alleged motion of the earth. For instance, if the earth was not the centre of the universe why should it be the natural place of heavy bodies? Galileo was concerned to remove these conflicts and was in the process of evolving a new mechanics, which would account for everything that the old one had accommodated, as well as conform to the new celestial hypothesis. Here then we find our clue to the origin of new theories. It is not simply guess-work or mere conjecture, nor is it generalisation from numerous similar conjunctions of events, but it is a step in the successive adjustments of an explanatory system, designed to remove contradictions.

Let me now return to Galileo's form of reasoning to prove the law I have quoted. Still following Aristotle he points out that heavy bodies fall vertically towards the centre of the earth and that no heavy body has any natural tendency to move upwards. Accordingly a body at rest on a horizontal plane will have no tendency to move and will offer no resistance to external lateral forces. If the plane is inclined, the body will tend to move downward, but the 'momentum' acquired by a falling body will be greatest when it falls vertically. If it falls along an inclined plane this momentum will be proportionately less.

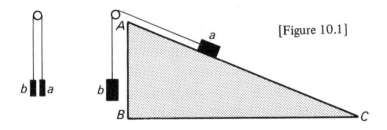

[Figure 10.1]

Now imagine two weights *a* and *b* hanging over a pulley. To balance, the weights must be equal. But if one of them, *a*, is placed on an inclined plane, it will have to be heavier than the other, *b*, which hangs vertically, because its 'momentum' will be decreased by the support of the incline. If the supporting surface were horizontal, no weight at all would be required hanging vertically to balance it; but, as the plane inclines from the horizontal, the balancing weight must increase. The momenta of the bodies are represented by the distance each would fall freely in equal times. The force, in both cases, acts along the vertical and so is proportional to the vertical distance moved. Thus, moving freely, an equal weight falling vertically would move further than one on an incline, in the proportion of the length of the incline to its height. The relation in weight of two bodies mutually attached so as to balance each other, in the manner shown, would have to be in the inverse proportion to these lengths: that is, the weight of *b* to that of *a* must be in the proportion of the height, AB, to the length, AC, of the incline. Hence the momentum of a body falling along an inclined plane will be proportional to the inclination of the plane from the horizontal.

This reasoning is obviously a form of deduction and is partly geometrical, partly arithmetic, but the conclusion concerns matters of fact and gives factual information about the movement of a body along an inclined plane, that is not contained in the premiss about vertical motion. Whether or not Galileo ever performed the experiment he does not base the reasoning on any record of experimental results, nor does he claim that he ever checked his conclusion experimentally. Clearly the reasoning is cogent without any such support. Yet it does depend on empirical knowledge about falling bodies and is not purely *a priori*. For the knowledge is assumed that bodies fall more rapidly on a vertical course than along an incline and that in both cases they accelerate. The reasoning is neither inductive nor purely analytic and it does not seem, either, to be a merely additive combination of the two. Galileo does not argue or assume the argument that bodies have been frequently observed to fall thus and so, and will therefore do so as a general rule. Nor does he substitute empirical quantities for the variables in an algorism and calculate an answer.

What he is doing is presuming a systematic relationship between certain concepts: weight, momentum, time, distance and motion; as well as geometrical and arithmetic relationships mathematically determined, and by applying to this system certain defined structures, reading off a determinate conclusion. The reasoning is *constructive* of system rather than inductive or deductive, and seems to demand a logic akin to both at once yet identical with neither. What this logic is precisely, nobody has yet fully worked out, but there is a clear need for research into the matter.

The limited conclusions that I wish to draw from what I have said are: (1) that empiricism in science — the appeal to common experience, to observation and contrived experiment — neither entails nor supports the epistemology of philosophical Empiricism; (2) that the methods of science and the forms of scientific argument are not what philosophical Empiricism requires: they are not inductive, proceeding from observed particular cases of conjunction to a general statement of universal conjunction; neither are they purely formal deduction from conjectured hypotheses, nor do they restrict themselves to seeking purely empirical falsification of such hypotheses; (3) that scientific theories are conceptual schemes serving to organise our perceptual experience in systematic ways, and they succeed — that is, their explanatory efficacy is greater — when they do so over the widest range and with the greatest consistency, or absence of internal conflict; (4) that hypotheses are not created *ex nihilo* or arbitrarily proposed. They are developed by continuous modification and adaptation from earlier theories — a process prompted by the generation of conflict within the earlier structures as they are applied to wider ranges of fact; (5) that the form of scientific argument is accordingly constructive of systems of evidence, the elements of which are diverse yet mutually supporting. It has therefore a deductive aspect as well as empirical content — a dual inductive-deductive character.

What the precise logic of this form of reasoning may be I do not claim to know. It presents a problem which I am as yet unable to solve. Nor do I claim to have established conclusively all the theses I have listed, only to have adduced some evidence for them. If they are accepted and developed they should give the philosophy of science a new direction and a new structure, and should make the spectacular successes of science more intelligible.

11

WHY SHOULD THE SCIENCE OF NATURE BE EMPIRICAL?

L. Jonathan Cohen

In the past empiricist[1]philosophy has urged one or other or both of two interconnected, and sometimes interconfused, theses. The first has been a thesis about the causal origins of certain beliefs, the second a thesis about the proper criteria for appraising these beliefs. The causal thesis is that all beliefs about the structure and contents of the natural world are the end-product of a process that originates wholly in individual experiences of seeing, hearing, smelling, tasting, or touching. The criterial thesis is that all these beliefs are ultimately to be appraised for their truth, soundness or acceptability in terms of the data afforded by such perceptual acts. Of recent years the causal version of empiricism has been much attacked, primarily in regard to its implications about language-learning. The language in terms of which our beliefs are constructed is heavily conditioned, we are told, by certain congenital features of the human brain. But, whenever Chomsky and his followers have assailed the causal version of empiricism, they have always been careful to claim for their doctrines the warrant of empirical evidence. They have never questioned the correctness of the criterial version of empiricism.

Yet that question certainly looks as though it can be raised. No small part of the point of *causal* empiricism, from Hume's time onwards, has been to justify *criterial empiricism*. If all our knowledge originates in sensory perceptions, then — it may be argued — claims to knowledge must always be checked against appropriate perceptual data. So if causal empiricism is undermined, perhaps criterial empiricism can no longer be defended?

In this lecture I want to discuss the status — the validity — of criterial empiricism. But I shall seek to discuss it in a way that does not depend on

---

[1] I use this term in the sense in which it is normally used by modern historians of philosophy, not in that in which both Bacon and Mill condemned empiricism: cf. J. Jonathan Cohen, *The Diversity of Meaning*, 2nd ed. (London 1966) p. 326.

the outcome of the issue between Chomsky and his opponents; and I have three reasons for so doing.

First, causal empiricism, in the form in which it is currently supported or attacked, purports to be a scientific hypothesis, to which some findings of linguistic, psychological and neuro-physiological research are relevant. Criterial empiricism, on the other hand, is a philosophical or methodological theory and applies equally to all scientific hypotheses. It is therefore the more fundamental issue.

Secondly, to discuss the psychology of learning in terms of a dichotomous opposition between empiricism and rationalism, as Chomsky often does, is rather to misrepresent the problem by understating its complexity. Obviously there can be no learning at all, unless some learning-mechanisms or learning-strategies, or the conditions for their development, are innate in the child. Even Hume supposed an innate mechanism of association. So the psychological problem that has to be solved concerns the number, variety and specificity of these mechanisms or strategies and the constraints that control their functioning. And that problem has many more than two possible solutions.

Thirdly, much of what has been said recently about language-learning is either speculative or programmatic, or rests on a controversial interpretation of the data. Until the definitive neuro-physiological findings are in, philosophers do best to avoid resting any arguments on assumptions about what these findings will be.

So my review of the case for criterial empiricism is designed to proceed independently of current disputes about the psychology of learning. Perhaps someone may object therefore that, if I am putting the problem of causal empiricism on one side, I am shelving what is now the only live issue in debates about empiricism. "Plato's epistemology", he may say, "has long since lost all its adherents, and so too have the epistemologies of Descartes, Spinoza and Leibniz. No one now supposes that theories about the structure of reality are to be appraised in the light of their resistance to *a priori* criticism or their deducibility from self-evident first principles. All philosophers of science now, even Quineians, are criterial empiricists. Their disagreements are solely about the nature, scope, presuppositions, and relative power of the relevant empirical criteria. So why waste time on trying to justify a general position that no one calls into question?"

Well, the short answer to such an objection is that I am now calling the position into question in order to see how defensible it is. The more widely a principle is taken for granted, the more important that philosophers should sometimes examine its credentials. But there might also be a longer answer, relating to current changes in cultural values. Discontent with the quality of life effected by modern technology sometimes engenders a certain disillusionment with the achievements of natural science as a study of the nature of reality. The fundamental truths about reality, it is sometimes felt, must be more beneficial to their discoverers than modern science has been. Anyone who thinks like this may well be tempted to appraise hypotheses by other criteria than those which natural scientists currently honour. Appeals to the revelations of an inner light, for example, – to private states of consciousness, whether naturally or artificially induced, rather than to publicly checkable evidence – seem rather commoner in the present generation than they have been for quite a while.

Of course, this line of attack on criterial empiricism is not a very cogent one. It rests on the anthropocentric assumption that the growth of human knowledge – in whatever way that knowledge be acquired – must, on balance, be beneficial to humanity. But though this assumption has been widely held and has done much, since Francis Bacon's day, to promote the progress of science, it too is open to question. Though Bacon encouraged seekers after knowledge to abandon enquiry into the ends or purposes of natural phenomena, he may have been rather too ready to assume an end or purpose for the acquisition of knowledge. If there is no reason to suppose that reality is particularly friendly to the human race, there is always a risk that the use of knowledge for human purposes – even when associated with the best of intentions – may have bad unforeseen by-products. And this is true whatever the method by which knowledge is sought. The evidence of an inner light is in no better a position here than the evidence of the senses. Hence current worries about the exploitation of the biosphere are not a valid ground for casting doubt on the validity of criterial empiricism. Nevertheless, when once the validity of a widely accepted principle has come to be doubted, even if for bad reasons, a case arises for re-examining what stands in its favour. So let us consider in turn the main arguments that have been put forward in support of criterial empiricism.

II

One classical argument for criterial empiricism ran from a thesis about about the nature of human thinking. According to this thesis thinking, in its full dress form, involves a kind of imaginative recreation of perceptual experience. The elements composing our thoughts are copies of previous perceptions, and the patterns in which those elements are combined mirror actual or possible patterns in the world of our sensory experience. It follows, if this is correct, that the truth of a thought must always be appraised by reference to the perceptual realities which it purports to represent.

But, notoriously, this thesis about the nature of human thinking turned out to be untenable. Not only could it afford no satisfactory account of thoughts about logical or temporal relations, or of the difference between entertaining, affirming, questioning or desiderating the truth of a particular thought. It also failed altogether to allow for the unambiguous representation of sorts or qualities. Unless accompanied by some conventionally interpretable tag or title, we just do not know how to take the picture of a man, for example, that we see on the wall of an art gallery. But just the same ambiguity arises about such a picture in the mind. Is it the thought of a living creature, a human being, a man, a young man, a dark-haired young man, a dark-haired young man holding a book, a student, or the thinker's (painter's) son? Clearly thinking cannot be regarded as a process by which imagination mimics perception, without having to add so many qualifications and appendices to the thesis that it ceases to afford any obvious support for criterial empiricism.

Another classical argument ran from a thesis about the nature of existence, rather than about that of thinking. At its strongest this thesis was that existence consists in being perceived, and weaker versions held, in various ways, that assertions of existence were assertions of the availability of certain perceptions under appropriate circumstances. If such a phenomenalist doctrine were true, every statement about existent entities would be a statement about perceivables and thus exposed to empirical checks. Criterial empiricism would be well-founded. But even the weaker form of phenomenalist doctrine is too difficult to reconcile with the actual course of scientific development for the doctrine to be able to underwrite the criteria of appraisal by which that development is normally assessed.

First, one has to recognise that even in its weaker form the doctrine inherits an anthropocentric point of view from its theistic origins in the philosophy of Bishop Berkeley and his forebears. In the older, teleological framework nature existed primarily for the use and enjoyment of man. In the new phenomenalism nature exists for human perception. Or at any rate, just as direct or indirect utilisability by man was a necessary condition for the existence of any particular thing according to the older outlook, so too perceivability by man was a necessary condition for the existence of any particular thing according to the newer outlook. But a science that can locate the human species in just one of very many millions of niches within the vast ladder of terrestrial evolution, and can then locate this particular ladder of evolution within just one of very many millions of solar systems within the universe — such a science hardly coheres with the thesis that human perceptual powers are the measure of natural reality. Once the cosmological status of man has been cut down by modern science to its proper size, it is absurd to suppose that human sensory organs have any special privilege in determining what exists in the universe. Why should not the objects of other animals' senses also be credited with existence? Even on this planet termites, snails and flatworms, for example, are apparently sensitive to magnetic fields. And elephant fishes are so constituted that both conducting and non-conducting objects alter the pattern of the electric field around the head of the fish and thus presumably affect the pattern of the nerve impulses from its sensory receptors. Since a human being is electro-magnetically blind by comparison with these creatures, we have to grant that they may have direct perceptual access to features of the world that we can know only by inference – much as, among human beings, the sighted have direct access to features that the visually blind can know only by inference.

Of course, earth-bound as they are, human philosophers have naturally tended to give a special ontological status to the medium-size concentrations of matter that we call physical objects; and it is even claimed sometimes that these entities must be *the* paradigms of existence, since existence presupposes reidentifiability and an entity is reidentifiable only if it has a distinct continuous history in space and time. But suppose a remote intelligence whose perceptual modalities are sensitive only to radio-signals, to the wavelengths and intensities of these signals, and to the directions from which they come. Then this intelligence might well reidentify the source of a particular pattern of intermittent transmission, even though that source was not known to have either the relative size, or the concentration in space, or the continuity in time, that we attribute characteristically to physical objects.

Nor will it do to generalise the doctrine of phenomenalism, in an attempt to avoid excessive anthropocentrism and allow for the exotic sensory potentials that alien intelligences may possess elsewhere in the universe and some terrestrial animals, like elephant fish, are already known to have. A sufficiently generalised definition of perception is in any case difficult to contrive, since in its ordinary meaning the term "perception" is closely tied to the seeing, hearing, smelling, etc. with which we are all familiar. One might begin by attempting a generalised definition of a sensory mechanism as a channel through which events external to an organism cause information (in the transmission-theoretic sense) to pass into a control-centre within the organism. One might then hope to indicate a generalised sense for the term "perception" by saying that perception, in this generalised sense, stands to sensory mechanisms, in the generalised sense that I have just defined, as perception, in the ordinary, narrow sense stands to the familiar organs of sight, hearing, smell, etc.[1] A correspondingly generalised phenomenalism would then claim that nothing exists unless it is perceivable, in this generalised sense, by some organism. But this kind of phenomenalism would be correspondingly useless for

---

[1] There are difficulties in working out the implications of this analogy, as C.A.J. Coady, 'The Senses of Martians', *Philosophical Review*, 83 (1974) pp.107ff., has shown, criticising H. P. Grice, 'Some Remarks about the Senses', in R. J. Butler, (ed), *Analytical Philosophy* (Oxford 1962) p. 133ff.   But these difficulties need not concern us here, since they tend to reinforce, rather than weaken, the tenor of my own argument.

buttressing a defence of the normal form of criterial empiricism. It could only support a much weaker, extended form of criterial empiricism, according to which every claim to knowledge about the world is exposed to empirical checks of some kind, but not necessarily to checks that human beings are equipped to operate. And in any case the old objection to phenomenalism can now be generalised also. The new phenomalism, we can say, is biocentric, just as the old one was anthropocentric. When one considers how small a part living organisms actually play — so far as we know — in the vast drama of the cosmos, there seems no good reason to suppose that every existent must be perceivable by some living organism.

But phenomenalism is also unfitted on other grounds to provide a foundation for the epistemology of modern science. It enforces an implausibly discontinuous interpretation of scientific theories. Terms denoting structures above a certain threshold of size are to be interpreted as denoting structures of their professed size, while terms purporting to denote certain structures *below* that threshold are to be interpreted as in fact denoting other kinds of structure *above* it. Bacteria, viruses, electrons etc. become congeries of macroscopic phenomena or the dispositions to exhibit them. Yet if mice are smaller than elephants, and mites than mice, why should not bacteria be conceived of as being smaller than mites and viruses than bacteria? If you can recognise under a microscope the same macrostructures that you can see with the naked eye, why should you not attribute the same degree of reality to the microstructures that you now discern alongside them? The same dimensions of shape, mass, etc. are at issue — only smaller determinations of them. Certainly the scientific imagination would be immensely handicapped if all hypotheses making extrapolations and projections below a certain threshold of magnitude were considered *a priori* false in their normal, literal sense. A defence of criterial empiricism is not worth much if it forces reinterpretations on us that drain away so much content from the scientific theories with the appraisal of which criterial empiricism is concerned. Indeed a defence of criterial empiricism that contracts the subject-matter of science within the frontiers of the perceivable involves a kind of *ignoratio elenchi*, or at least an implied claim that no real problem exists. After all, statements about the perceivable have always invited perceptual checks. Serious problems about the application of empirical criteria begin to arise only when we come to consider statements about underlying principles, hidden causes, fundamental structures, and so on.

III

Since therefore neither of the two classical arguments for criterial empiricism is acceptable, we must now turn to consider some other defences that have been, or might be, proposed. Of these the first to deserve examination is undoubtedly the verification principle. If — as this principle once claimed — no statement is cognitively meaningful unless it is either analytic or empirically verifiable, in some appropriate sense, then every meaningful statement about the real world is open to appropriate checks against perceptual data. Where empirical verifiability is a necessary condition for meaningfulness, empirical evidence provides the touch-stone of truth.

Not that the primary purpose of the verification principle was to constitute a prop for criterial empiricism. Rather the purpose of the verificationist programme was to demarcate the limits of intellectual respectability. It *assumed* the validity of criterial empiricism — it *assumed* that beliefs about nature should be empirically attestable — and on the basis of this assumption it proceeded to discredit those categories of statement that did not meet the required standard. Still, if we could formulate such a principle successfully, it could be turned round to provide some kind of justification for criterial empiricism. If we had a principle that would neatly divide all propositions into two piles, into the first of which fell all, and only, obviously respectable propositions and into the second of which fell all obviously disreputable and dubious ones, the principle would acquire a good deal of cogency from its ability to make such a division. And if the cardinal issue in achieving this division was empirical verifiability criterial empiricism would acquire a good deal of support therefrom. But this way of supporting criterial empiricism depends entirely on our success in formulating a principle that will in fact divide the respectable sheep from the disreputable goats.

For over twenty years it has been widely held that any attempt to formulate such a principle is doomed to failure, at least if the attempt proceeds along anything like the same lines as those proposed over a quarter of a century ago by Ayer. This conclusion is, I think, correct, but not for the reasons normally given, and a re-examination of the issue is well worth while.

The terms in which the problem was discussed in the 1930's and 1940's were quite restrictive. The required principle was conceived as being free to invoke an unexceptionable class of observation-statements, whose empirical verifiability and falsifiability were not in question. It could employ standard modes of logical quantification and truth-functional composition, and standard concepts of analyticity and deducibility. With this jejune apparatus a hallmark had somehow to be described that would attest the purity of genuine scientific theories, however abstruse their terminology, and would exclude any synthetic theorising of an intellectually disreputable nature.

Ayer's 1946 proposal was that a sentence S should be regarded as literally meaningful if it is either analytic or directly or indirectly verifiable, (or, presumably, the negation of such a sentence). S is directly verifiable if either S is itself an observation-statement, or, like 'All crows are black', say, S is such that in conjunction with one or more observation-statements it entails at least one observation-statement which is not deducible from these other premises alone. S was indirectly verifiable on Ayer's view – and this was presumably the category that took care of scientific theories about underlying structures, hidden causes, etc. – if two conditions are satisfied: first, in conjunction with certain other premises S must entail one or more directly verifiable statements that are not deducible from these other premises alone, and secondly, these other premises must not include any statement that is not either analytic, or directly verifiable or capable of being independently established as indirectly verifiable.

Against this proposal Church pointed out, ingeniously enough, that, if there are any three observation sentences none of which entails any of the others, then it is possible to construct appropriate additional premises to be conjoined with any sentence whatsoever, or its denial, so as to guarantee indirect verifiability for that sentence, or its denial, as the case may be. Also, as Hempel pointed out, whatever consequences can be deduced from S with the help of permissible subsidiary hypotheses can also be deduced from S & N by means of the same subsidiary hypotheses, where N is any sentence you please. So the whole of any conjunction became literally meaningful on Ayer's view, just so long as one conjunct in it was indirectly verifiable. Moreover, if you accept that any conjunct in a meaningful conjunction is also meaningful, Hempel's argument shows that Ayer's proposal allows any sentence N whatever to be meaningful, just so long as at least one sentence is indirectly verifiable.

Thereafter some half-hearted and unsuccessful attempts were made to patch up Ayer's proposal. But the whole enterprise was soon abandoned, in favour of an equally unsuccessful attempt to characterise unobjectionable predicates rather than unobjectionable sentences. Yet the original enterprise was never *proved* to be incapable of success. And in fact a fairly simple stratagem would have protected Ayer's principle against the kind of counter-examples with which Church and Hempel attacked it. These counter-examples all purported to show that the principle was too liberal: it could let in a sentence S whose actual content contributed nothing at all to the content of the observation-sentences that testified to S's respectability by being eventually deducible from the conjunction of S with certain other premises. Hence the counter-examples can be ruled out by the not unreasonable requirement that every component of S *must* contribute somehow, via its actual content, to the requisite deducibility of observation-sentences. There must be no superfluity in the content of S – nothing superfluous to S's empirical orientation.

More specifically, we must add the following as conditions on Ayer's criteria of direct and indirect verifiability, respectively. So far as the criterion of direct verifiability for S is concerned, there must be no set Σ of sentences such that:

(i) the conjunction of the members of Σ, but of no proper sub-set of Σ, is logically equivalent to the conjunction of S and any observation-statement (or conjunction of observation-statements) that is its auxiliary premiss, and

(ii) all observation-statements deducible from the conjunction of S and its auxiliary premiss are also deducible from a proper sub-set of Σ, where the member or members of the complementary sub-set of Σ are not directly or indirectly verifiable independently by Ayer's criteria.

In other words there must be no equivalent conjunction that is as small as it could be without losing logical equivalence but could afford to be even smaller without losing any of its power to imply observation-statements. Correspondingly, so far as indirect verifiability is concerned, there must be no set Σ of sentences such that:

(i) the conjunction of the members of Σ, but of no proper sub-set of Σ, is logically equivalent to the conjunction of S and the appropriate auxiliary premisses and any observation statements that need to be premissed to attest the direct or indirect verifiability of these auxiliary premisses, and

(ii) all observation-statements deducible from the conjunction of S and those other statements are also deducible from a proper sub-set of Σ and the member or members of the complementary sub-set are not directly or indirectly verifiable independently by Ayer's criteria.

It will be found that (at the cost of insisting on a certain economy of formulation in scientific theories) the addition of these conditions to Ayer's criteria produces a principle immune to all objections of the kind that Church and Hempel raised against Ayer.[1] But it does not follow that

---

[1] The immunity to Hempel's objection is obvious. Church supposed three observation-statements, O_1, O_2 and O_3, such that none of them alone entailed any of the others. He then argued, for any S, that by Ayer's definition $(-O_1\&O_2)v(O_3\&-S)$ is directly verifiable, because with O_1 it entails O_3. Then this directly verifiable sentence when conjoined with S entails O_2. So S is indirectly verifiable (unless it happens that $(-O_1\&O_2)v(O_3\&-S)$ alone entails O_2, in which case $-S\&O_3$ entails O_2, so that $-S$ is directly verifiable. My proviso blocks such a move, $(-O_1\&O_2)v(O_3\&-S)$ becomes not directly verifiable unless S is observational, because $O_1\&((-O_1\&O_2)v(O_3\&-S))$ has an equivalent, $O_1\&O_3\&-S$, from which one conjunct, $-S$, can be dropped without omitting any observational content. There are, of course, problems about whether verifiability is effectively computable, but these apply to Ayer's conditions as well as to my own. Cf. A. Church in *Jour. Symb. Log.*, 14 (1949) pp. 52–3.

the revised form of the principle will not provide a satisfactory hallmark of respectability. Far from it. We encounter now a deeper difficulty — philosophical rather than logical — which forces us to regard the terms in which the problem was originally discussed as being too restrictive.

The point, in a nutshell, is this. How do we bridge the logical gap between the predicates occurring in a scientific theory about underlying structures or hidden causes and the predicates occurring in observational sentences? Directly verifiable sentences certainly cannot do this, because at best they lead us only from one set of observational predicates to another. Nor can the gap be bridged by any set, however large, of indirectly verifiable sentences. What we need is a sentence that will connect each theoretical term with some set of directly verifiable sentences. A theory about sub-atomic particles, say, needs to be connected to appropriate experimentally testable generalisations about the movements of pointers on dials, the appearance of scratch-marks on photographic plates, and so on. So one end of the bridge must always be a theoretical term (or terms) and the bridge cannot therefore be a directly verifiable sentence. But though any non-analytic, non-observational, non-directly-verifiable sentence that is invoked, as an additional premiss, in showing a scientific theory to be literally significant must, according to Ayer's principle, be capable of being independently established as indirectly verifiable, any attempt to establish the indirect verifiability of such a bridging proposition (which always has a theoretical term at one end) collapses into an infinite regress.

Of course, a thorough-going phenomenalist analysis of theoretical terms avoids this difficulty, because it can invoke analytic bridging propositions. But if we are agreed, for the reasons already given, that no such phenomenalist analysis is acceptable, we must expect any appropriate bridging propositions to be non-analytic. The connection between the movements of the sub-atomic particles accelerated by the cyclotron and the scratch-marks on the photographic plates, for example, is a causal one. We are thus left inevitably with the conclusion that no satisfactory verification principle can be formulated within the framework to which the verificationist enterprise was originally restricted. This framework allowed the use of standard logical concepts and operations, plus the concept of an observation-statement. But what turns out to be needed also for each theoretical term, if a phenomenalist analysis is to be rejected, is at least one non-analytic bridging postulate. We have to be able to assume the truth of at least one non-analytic proposition connecting the theoretical term with observational predicates. The price of a realist interpretation is thus that the verifiability of a scientific theory turns out to be a question of fact, not of linguistic analysis — a question for scientists, not philosophers.

It follows that the limits of verifiability at a particular date are set in practice by the range of accepted bridging propositions, though these propositions are themselves subject to modification or recall in the light of experience with the theories that they help in testing. Time, for example, is perhaps one of the earliest and most important theoretical concepts in the history of science. We have to compare intervals of time, or measure its passage, by observing some associated process of change. The more uniform this process is, the more accurate our comparisons or measurements can be. Initially, say, the intervals between one noon and the next are taken[1] to be uniform. But as waterclocks replaced sundials, and then various forms of mechanical escapement were introduced, and then electric or atomic clocks took the place of spring-driven ones, more and more accurate measurements have become possible. Correspondingly theories making predictions about velocities in more and more exact forms have become empirically verifiable. In short science is constantly expanding the realm of empirical verifiability. The terms in which the verificationist enterprise was originally discussed allowed no room for this process of expansion. They implied a static domain of verifiability, the frontiers of which could be determined by any philosopher with sufficient linguistic knowledge and logical acumen. But, as we have seen, this is a misleading conception of the situation. *It is not empiricism that sets permanent limits to science, as the phenomenalist claims, but science that progressively extends the horizons of empiricism.*

So the verificationist enterprise can afford no support or defence for criterial empiricism. It might have done this if a verification principle could have relied solely on the concept of an observation statement, alongside logical machinery, in order to divide intellectually respectable propositions from intellectually disreputable ones. If observational verifiability were thus shown to be critical for significance, the validity of criterial empiricism could hardly be made to stand out more clearly. But when we find that the concept of an observation statement is not enough for this purpose — when we find it necessary to pray in aid at any one time those bridging propositions that happen to be acceptable at that time — the picture becomes somewhat clouded. It would be open to an opponent of criterial empiricism, for example, to construe the need for such bridging propositions as suggesting a certain indirectness or second-handness about empirical knowledge. "Might it not be simpler", he could ask, "if we had a conception of what is fundamental in reality, and a way of checking fundamental theories, that operated less indirectly? A fundamental theory could then be said to be significant if it were directly verifiable in this way, without any need to invoke bridging propositions that are of by no means

---

[1] No doubt this often conformed to many people's subjective sense of time. But no one supposes that sense to be a reliable source of empirical data: hence the need for clocks.

certain truth." However difficult it may be for a philosopher to make the details of such an anti-empiricist epistemology plausible, one must accept that its *prima facie* possibility blocks the road that might have led from the verification principle to a defence of criterial empiricism.

IV

So let us consider some other possible lines of defence. Obviously one of these is to argue from the very great apparent success that has so far attended the orientation of science towards criterial empiricism. If — it might be said — appraisal by reference to empirical criteria has endorsed so many fruitful hypotheses, especially in the past three or four centuries, and has thus underwritten the triumphs of modern technology, there can hardly be much amiss with it as a method of checking theories about the structure and contents of the natural world.

Such an argument has an impressive force when one first considers it. It is undoubtedly the commonsense argument *par excellence* for the aims and methods of modern science. But as a defence of criterial empiricism its logic is unfortunately rather weak. First, it is inherently question-begging so far as it is concerned with scientific predictions, since the alleged successes to which it appeals are themselves apparently to be attested by empirical evidence. Secondly, so far as it is concerned with the use made of these predictions, it is undercut by that form of opposition to criterial empiricism which springs from discontent with the quality of life effected by modern technology and a consequential disillusionment with the achievements of natural science as a study of the nature of reality. If empirical science has not been so successful after all, criterial empiricism is weakened rather than strengthened by a consideration of scientific achievements. Thirdly, the argument credits a certain philosophy with what are in fact the achievements of science. The argument would therefore be open to criticism by anyone who wanted to account for scientific achievement in a way that did not attach so much importance to procedures of empirical verification. If fundamental theories are best checked by examining their deducibility from self-evident first principles, for example, the empirical criteria that have been popular in the scientific practice of the last few centuries must afford rather a second-best type of support. So in any case, on this view, it is Cartesian rationalism that would take the credit for scientific achievement in a world in which scientists checked their theories properly, and perhaps if they did do this the triumphs of modern science would be even greater.

One sometimes also hears criterial empiricism defended by reference to the need for scientists to employ inter-personally acceptable standards of evidence. Introspection, intuition, self-evidence, etc. all suffer, it may be claimed, from the disadvantage that on controversial issues they often tend to produce different judgements in different people. What is self-evident to me may perhaps seem rather dubious to you. Perceptual sensations, on the other hand, and, above all, visual sensations, tend towards unanimity. Once certain well-known illusions, like mirages, and perceptual handicaps, like colour blindness, are discounted, there is no serious room for disagreement between normal adults about what they do or do not see. Hence the validity of criterial empiricism depends, it may be said, on the indisputable objectivity of perceptual evidence. With such evidence available as a touchstone, it is reasonable to hope, in any particular field of enquiry, that one theory may turn out to be objectively preferable to any of its rivals.

But if the aim of scientific enquiry is to get as near as possible to the truth, i.e. to the description of things and their connections as they actually are, it is not at all clear why human unanimity should be intrinsic to the process. Certainly people have often in the past agreed about propositions that we should now take to be false, and also they have often disagreed among one another about propositions that we should now all take to be true. So unanimity of opinion at one time is no guarantee of unanimity at a later date, nor is lack of unanimity at one time a sure sign that people will always disagree.

Moreover, unanimity at the perceptual level by no means guarantees unanimity of preference in relation to theories about fundamental structures and hidden causes. An indefinitely wide variety of theories can be made to fit any given set of perceptual data, as has been remarked by Popper, Goodman and many other philosophers of science. So an opponent of criterial empiricism can always object that the price it pays for unanimity at the perceptual level is the opening up of a very wide area of indeterminacy at the theoretical level. Might it not be better, he would urge, to prefer a criterion of knowledge (like deducibility from self-evident axioms) that operates more univocally in relation to choice of theory, even if the price paid for this is a greater risk of disagreement about which theory the criterion actually endorses in relation to a particular problem? That way we might have at least somebody espousing the true theory, in a determinate form, and everyone would at least feel entitled to claim the truth of his favoured theory. But if we accept an empiricist epistemology the concept of *the* truth seems to lack any determinate criteria of application at the theoretical level. A lot of different theories might be held, each fitting the perceptual data, but none of their adherents would feel entitled to claim the truth of his favoured theory.

I conclude that though the argument from the value of perceptual unanimity has at first sight a strong methodological appeal it cannot be made to clinch the matter. A determined opponent of criterial empiricism can put forward the fact that empirical evidence is characteristically ambiguous in its indication of which theory to prefer, in order to counterbalance the fact that perceptual data themselves, when we recognise them as such, are not characteristically disputable.

Nor indeed is the line between perceptual datum and theoretical interpretation always sufficiently sharp for it to be clear where exactly this benefit of indisputability belongs. When we measure length by the superposition of a metal rod, for example, how much theory is involved in the choice of a unit of measurement, in the calibration of the rod and in assumptions about the stability of the metal? It may be tempting to say that some piece of experimental material was just "perceived" to have a length of two centimetres. But that kind of perception is undoubtedly theory-laden, as many philosophers have remarked.[1]

V

I have now examined in turn five possible defences, or justifications, of criterial empiricism. None of them, as it turns out, is tenable. So what are we to say? Is criterial empiricism some ultimate principle of human thought which can be stated and adopted but is incapable of rational justification? Or is there some other and more appropriate form of defence for it than the arguments I have already examined? I am reluctant to accept that a principle which in the seventeenth and eighteenth centuries was so much a subject of philosophical controversy, and at the present time is so integral to the actual conduct of scientific enquiry, should be treated as a matter solely for arbitrary, non-rational adoption or rejection. So I am inclined to suggest a new and different line of justification for the principle. But I am well aware of the danger that where so many defences have proved, under closer scrutiny, to be weaker than they at first sight appeared, my own suggestion may turn out in the end to have weaknesses that I cannot at present discern.

I begin by assuming that, at any one time or relative to any one context of enquiry, there is a category of observational belief which is not intrinsically illusory. That is to say, I assume that some statements by human beings, in which they sincerely purport to describe features of their immediate environment, are true. More specifically, for example, when people report that the movement of one billiard ball has been followed by the movement of another or that a pointer on a certain dial overlaps a particular line, they are at least sometimes – when their reports are sufficiently accurate – reporting features of the real world. Unless some such assumption is made the usual distinction between perceptual reality and perceptual illusion seems quite unintelligible. For the distinction has to be learned through perceptual practice. And if the sight of a puddle in the road, say, as distinct from a mirage, is to be cited as a typical example

---

[1] For present purposes it suffices to distinguish between *relatively* observational and *relatively* theoretical entities, as M. Hesse does in her *The Structure of Scientific Inference* (London 1974) ch.1.

of a non-illusory perception, then puddles are part of the real world.

This form of argument is often called a "paradigm-case" argument. But whatever the difficulties about such an argument in other fields, here it does suffice to show that at any one time, or in any one context of enquiry, some types of statement about the real world are subject to observational verification and falsification. What then needs also to be shown is that any statement or theory about *underlying* features of the real world — features which are not, and are not claimed to be, open to direct observation — should be made subject to some kind of observational check, albeit an indirect one. My argument for saying that it should will rest essentially on a double appeal to the generally accepted need for maximum comprehensiveness of scope, and economy in number, in regard to our theories about any subject-matter whatever. This is a principle that almost all modern philosophers of science, from Bacon and Whewell to Popper and Nagel, have propounded and almost all theoretical scientists have implicitly accepted. It is a principle that can be shown to be integral to all inductive reasoning, whether this be about nature, numbers, morality, or any other subject-matter.[1]

The first use of this principle I propose to make is to argue that considerations of comprehensiveness and economy should lead us to suppose that systematic connections can be discovered (if we search long enough and hard enough) between the realities we perceive and the underlying realities about which we hypothesise. To explain the former (perceivable realities) in terms of the latter (underlying realities) has, of course, long been a principal objective of scientific enquiry. But in the present problem we cannot argue from scientific practice, since if criterial empiricism is wrong modern scientific practice would be wrong also. I therefore argue instead from the need to suppose a single system of reality, whether perceivable or imperceivable to human beings, in order to achieve maximum comprehensiveness and economy in our theories about reality. No refined analysis of the concept of theoretical economy is needed for this point to be evident.

But, even if you accept that hypotheses about underlying reality should be systematically connected with statements about observable reality, you do not thereby accept that the fundamental hypotheses should be subject to empirical checks. It would be possible to hold instead that the validity of the fundamental hypotheses depends on, say, their deducibility from self-evident first principles, and that the art of scientific explanation

---

[1]   Cf. Jonathan Cohen, 'The Inductive Logic of Progressive Problem-Shifts', *Revue Internationale de Philosophie*, 95–6 (1971) pp.62ff., and, for inductive reasoning outside natural science, see L. Jonathan Cohen, *The Implications of Induction* (1970) sections 17–18.

consists in finding hypotheses so deducible which can be connected in some appropriate fashion with observable facts requiring explanation. So the defence of criterial empiricism necessitates a second appeal here to the need for comprehensiveness and economy. If comprehensiveness and economy were of no importance and the fundamental hypotheses were attestable in some non-empirical way, then each species of observable fact requiring explanation could be explained by a separate hypothesis about underlying reality. For each species of observable fact we might posit an underlying form, perhaps, or even a deity, so long as the existence of each such form or deity could be supported in some appropriate non-empirical way. But if considerations of comprehensiveness and economy are overriding, then whatever support of this kind may be available for a hypothesis, the overriding consideration will always be: how many different species of observable facts does it explain? The overriding criteria of merit will be empirical ones — which is what had to be shown. That is, the hypothesis that was introduced to explain one range of phenomena in a certain field of enquiry must prove its worth by explaining another, and the hypothesis that was favoured because it covered the whole range of known phenomena in that field must prove its worth by predicting (and explaining) some hitherto unknown type of phenomenon.

This is too familiar a characteristic of modern science to need illustration or detailed analysis here. But I emphasise again that I am not trying to labour the obvious point that this is in practice how fundamental theories are taken to be confirmed. My point is rather that the overriding need for such empirical confirmation, whether in human sciences or in the scientific enquiries of extraterrestrial creatures, follows directly from the methodological requirement of comprehensiveness and economy in the construction of fundamental hypotheses. *The need to invoke empirical criteria for the validity of our fundamental explanations is forced on us by the desire to make our explanations as unified and comprehensive as possible.* There is no more to it than that. No appeals to the nature of thought or cognitive meaning, or to the value of public testability, are necessary. The defence of criterial empiricism may, it seems, be based securely on the requirement of maximum comprehensiveness and economy, since whatever the difficulties that may be involved in giving an exact analysis of this requirement the requirement itself is essentially a quite general and *a priori* one, applying to any subject-matter whatever, whether empirical or non-empirical. It is thus inductive logic that, at bottom, justifies empiricism, not empiricism that needs to justify the use of inductive logic or to demonstrate the rationality of inductive reasoning.

12

THE EMPIRICIST ACCOUNT OF DISPOSITIONS

R. S. Woolhouse

Nelson Goodman has written that

> Besides the observable properties it exhibits and the actual processes it undergoes, a thing is full of threats and promises. The dispositions or capacities of a thing — its flexibility, its inflammability, its solubility — are no less important to us than its overt behaviour, but they strike us by comparison as rather ethereal. And so we are moved to inquire whether we can bring them down to earth; whether, that is, we can explain disposition terms without any reference to occult powers.[1]

The desire to bring things 'down to earth', to reduce the occult and ethereal to the overt, is a characteristic of empiricism. It shows itself in such claims as that statements about material objects can be translated without residue into statements about sense-data, that simple statements about minds are really more complicated statements about bodies, and, in the present case, in the idea that statements attributing dispositions to an object are equivalent to other statements about the object's observable properties or manifest behaviour.

Of course it belongs to the notion of a disposition that an iron bar may yet be flexible without at any time manifesting it; a bar which is flexible need not, at any time, actually be bending. So in thinking about dispositions we must think, not in terms of categorical or actual manifest happenings or events, not in terms of what has been, is, or will be happening, but in those of what would have happened or would happen in certain conditions. The idea thus emerges that a statement such as 'this iron bar is flexible' whilst apparently categorical in form is really hypothetical. But whilst hypotheticals doubtless are involved in the

---

[1] N. Goodman, *Fact, Fiction, and Forecast*, 2nd ed. (Indianapolis, Indiana, 1965) p. 40.

analysis of at least many categorical disposition statements it seems to me that they are not of the sort or involved in the way the empiricist supposes – though whether this amounts to saying that such statements are *not* disguised hypotheticals depends, we shall see, on the particular case. But that they are of the sort the empiricist supposes is so much a received doctrine that any analysis in their terms has come to be known as 'a dispositional analysis'. Our notion of a disposition is ceasing to be a touch-stone for the correctness of the empiricist account, and the account itself is coming to be constitutive of our notion. Unless the rather impoverished things suggested by empiricism have already become what dispositions are to us in our natural moments my claim that the 'dispositional analysis' of dispositions is incorrect will be intelligible in its content and paradoxical only in its superficial form.

The desire that dispositions be brought down to earth shows itself also in the typical empiricist claim that though the success science has met with, in giving theoretical explanations of why things have the dispositions they do, might lead us to think that (at least many) dispositions have categorical bases this is at best a *contingent* truth. This aspect too of empiricism about dispositions seems to me to be false. In the light of what I shall suggest as the correct account of the relation between dispositions and their manifestations it will appear that dispositions *necessarily* have categorical bases; it is an intimate feature of our unbiased and unre-constituted notion that they have them.

I have already introduced the idea that to say of an iron bar that it is flexible is in effect to say that it bends when under pressure, that it would bend if pressure were applied to it. But in attributing flexibility to something we mean not merely that were it under pressure *now* it would bend but, more strongly, that if *ever* it were to come under pressure it would bend. Thus a form such as

(1) Dx

where 'D' stands for some disposition such as flexibility is to be equated with the universally temporally quantified form

(2) $(t) (Oxt \rightarrow Rxt)$

where 'O' stands for some operation such as the application of pressure, 'R' for some reaction such as that of bending and where, for reasons initially made clear in this context by Carnap, '$\rightarrow$' will need to be taken as something stronger than truth-functional material implication, as some sort of causal or nomological implication.

What is in effect this equation is made in at least some moments of the writings of Carnap, Hempel, and Pap.[1] And it is made by Ryle who says

---

[1] R. Carnap, 'Testability and Meaning', *Classics of Analytic Philosophy*, ed. R.R. Ammerman (New York, 1965) p. 145, and 'Methodological Character of Theoretical Concepts', *Minnesota Studies in the Philosophy of Science*, I, ed. H. Feigl, M. Scriven
continued on next page

that to say of a piece of glass that it is brittle 'is to say that if it *ever* is, or *ever* had been, struck or strained, it would fly or have flown into fragments'. And again, that 'to say of this lump of sugar that it is soluble is to say that it would dissolve, if submerged anywhere, *at any time* and in any parcel of water'.[1]

It is clear, however, that more needs to be said. For there remains to be taken into account the fact that dispositions may be permanent, or may come or go: our bar may, after suitable treatment, come to lose its flexibility. Now Ryle explicitly draws attention to this fact in a later passage. But his dealings with it imply that (2) does not after all give the form of dispositions in general but only of *permanent* ones in particular, that (2) gives the form not of (1) but of

(1 perm)   At all times Dx

And there must be something wrong here, for Ryle had initially arrived at (2) without mention of the fact that dispositions may come or go, or may be permanent. Though as Carnap, Hempel, Pap, and others in their tradition, arrive at what is in effect the same place as Ryle when they[2] recognise in their formulae if not in their verbal discussion that dispositions can come and go, the empiricist's reaction would presumably be that all that is wrong is a simple inexplicable error on Ryle's part. The empiricist's considered view would be that (2), as its universal quanti-fication over time makes clear, does not give the form of dispositions in general but only of permanent ones in particular; that it is true only of a bar which is permanently, always, flexible that if *ever at any time* it were subject to pressure it would bend; that (2) gives the form not of (1) but of (1 perm). But it is precisely here, it seems to me, that the empiricist begins to go wrong; it is precisely here that he begins to do violence to our actual notion of a disposition.

(continued from page 185)
(Minneapolis, 1956) p. 63; C. G. Hempel, *Aspects of Scientific Explantation* (New York, 1965) p. 109; A. Pap, 'Are physical magnitudes operationally definable?', *Measurement: Definitions and Theories*, ed. C.W. Churchman, P. Tatoosh (New York, 1959) p. 178.
[1]   G. Ryle, *The Concept of Mind* (London, 1949) pp. 43, 123 (my italics).
[2]   Usually one finds something like 'x is D at t_1' being equated with something like 'Oxt$_1$Rxt$_1$' so that, presumably, (1 perm) would be equated with (2). See Carnap's 'Logical Foundations of the Unity of Science', *Readings in Philosophical Analysis*, ed. H. Feigl, W. Sellars (New York, 1949) p. 416; Hempel's 'Methods of concept formation in science', *Foundations of the Unity of Science*, II, ed. O Neurath, R. Carnap, C. Morris (Chicago and London, 1970) pp. 676–7; Pap's 'Are physical magnitudes operationally definable?', pp. 178–80, *An Introduction to the Philosophy of Science* (London, 1963) p. 280, and 'Dispositional concepts and extensional logic', *Minnesota Studies in the Philosophy of Science*, II, ed. H. Feigl, M. Scriven, G. Maxwell (Minneapolis, 1958) p. 198. See also R. B. Braithwaite, 'The nature of believing', *Knowledge and Belief*, ed. A. Phillips Griffiths (London, 1967) p. 35; J.L. Mackie, *Truth Probability and Paradox* (London, 1973) pp. 123–7; and H. H. Price, *Belief* (London, 1969) pp. 246–7.

By 'our actual notion of a disposition' I mean that notion which if we are honest would not lead to an unsympathetic 'No' to Sellars[1] when he asks, 'Is there no temptation to think of . . . [some inflammable] paper as having the settled intention to burn when and if fire approaches (though without having decided to do so)? or, perhaps, as "resigned" to burn in these circumstan[c]es?'. I mean that notion which Goodman's metaphor, with which I began, of dispositions as threats or promises, so aptly captures. And it is by attending to the aptness of these metaphors that I hope to show that the fact that dispositions may be permanent, may come or go, does not reflect on (2) as the analysis of (1) in the way that an empiricist would suggest.

What is perhaps the most obvious thing here is that at least in many cases both dispositions and threats/promises/intentions speak generally for the future and not merely particularly for the present: a man may threaten not merely to resist any pressure that may be brought to bear on him *now*, but to resist it if at *any time* it is brought to bear. Thus, paralleling this, Ryle quite rightly says that to say that this piece of glass is brittle is to say that were it *ever* struck or strained it would fly into fragments; he does not say merely 'were the glass struck *now* it would fly into fragments'.

I say that 'at least in many cases' both dispositions and threats/ promises/intentions speak generally for the future and not merely particularly for the present, for they do not do so in all. With threats, promises, and intentions this is clear. One man's threat may be to resist pressure if *at any time* it is brought to bear. But another's may be only to resist pressure if it is brought to bear *now*, or only to resist *next week's* pressure, or only to resist *tomorrow's*. It is not so immediately clear, however, that dispositions can differ amongst themselves in this way and so not so clear what is involved in saying that flexibility is a disposition to bend if *at any time* subjected to pressure. But if we consider the dispositions of man-made devices the possibility of different cases is clear. A standard doorbell in working order is disposed to ring if *at any time* it is pressed. But a non-standard bell may easily be devised so as to be only disposed to ring if pressed on weekdays, or if pressed next week.[2] So dispositions, like threats, intentions, and promises, may differ in the extent to which they speak for or pertain to the future. For convenience, however, I shall continue to speak as though all were of the usual type like flexibility which is the disposition to bend *at any time* under pressure.

Further to this fact that both dispositions, and threats/promises/ intentions may be compared in the extent to which they speak for or pertain to the future there is a less obvious but quite different and equally important aspect of their metaphorical identity. This is that claims about dispositions and threats/promises have in common a difference from certain superficially similar predictive claims.

---

[1] W. S. Sellars, *Philosophical Perspectives* (Springfield, Illinois, 1969) p. 119.
[2] For further discussion and the logic of such bells see my 'Tensed Modalities', *Journal of Philosophical Logic*, II (1973).

What is the difference between saying that someone has threatened or promised and therefore *intends*, to resist pressure whenever it might be brought to bear, and *predicting* that he will? One thing, of course, is that I might say that someone has threatened and therefore so intends even though I believe that, through weakness of character and will, he will not, in the event, be true to his intent, carry out his threat. And in this case though I claim that he does intend I have good reason for not making the predictive claim. But even if we neglect this there is another important difference. This is that my claim about the man's intentions does not relate to his future actions in the simple way my predictive claim does. For, if at some future time, pressure is brought to bear without his even attempting to resist it, then, *it follows*, I was simply wrong when I said, *predictively*, that he would resist pressure *whenever* it might be brought to bear. But in these circumstances it does *not* follow that I was wrong in saying that he intended to resist pressure *whenever* it might be brought to bear. For, quite simply, the threat may indeed have been made, but later withdrawn; the intention may have been abandoned. In the case of threats, promises, intentions, there are two possibilities; in the simple predictive case there are not. If at some time the man turns out not to be resisting pressure then my prediction about his future actions was simply false; but, as to my claim about his threatened intent, *either* the threat was at no time in force because it was never made (in which case my claim was false) *or* it was made, in force for a time, and then, later, withdrawn (in which case my claim was not false).

In connexion with threats about future actions it can be *true* of a man *today*, yet *false* of him *tomorrow*, that he is going to resist pressure *at all times*. But in connexion with those future actions taken in themselves, though it can be true today of a man that he will resist pressure *at all times*, it is not a truth which particularly concerns today, because if it is true today then, necessarily, it is true tomorrow. If tomorrow's events show it not to be true then it was not, after all, true today. Despite what we may think today, tomorrow's events can show, as a matter of straightforward deductive falsification, that it just is not true that the man will resist pressure *whenever* it is brought to bear. But they cannot show that there was not *today* a threatened intent to resist pressure *whenever* it might be brought to bear.

It is in facts such as these that there lies a further basis for the metaphor of dispositions as threats or promises. They are similar not only in the relatively superficial way that both may speak for or pertain to the future in that both may involve something of the universally quantified form of

(2) (t) (Oxt→Rxt)

but also in the deeper way that this voice may simply become silent. Just as a promise or threat may be withdrawn, an intention given up, so an object may come to lose a disposition.

Thus we have returned to the fact that (2), at least without further explanation, will not do as the analysis of (1). For according to the most obvious interpretation of (2) — and this is the interpretation the empiricist gives to it — to say of something that it is flexible is to say, *as a matter of prediction*, that it will bend if *at any time* pressure is applied to it. And this *predictive* claim would be shown up as false if there ever were a time at which, even though under pressure, the thing did not bend. But to make a temporally unrestricted predictive claim about something is not at all the same as to claim that it has a disposition. To claim that something is flexible is to make a *present tense* claim, the claim that it *is now* the case that it would bend if ever pressure were applied to it. So unless something further is said about (2) and its interpretation as a predictive claim avoided the attribution of a disposition will collapse into a temporally general claim about future behaviour. It is, of course, because he does interpret it as a predictive claim that the empiricist, when he recognises that dispositions need not be permanent, turns round and says that (2) gives the form only of permanent dispositions. But the time to consider this mistaken reaction fully is not quite yet.

Since there is, as we have seen, a difference between the temporal generality of a typical predictive claim and the temporal generality involved in a typical claim about disposition or an intention we need to bear in mind two different readings or interpretations of (2). I shall call these the *predictive* and the *dispositional* readings. When (2) is taken predictively, in which case I shall refer to it as '(2P)', it is understood as a form which *cannot* be satisfied by something which at some time is both under pressure and not bending. When (2) is taken dispositionally, in which case I shall refer to it as '(2D)', it is understood as a form which *can* be satisfied by something which at some time is both under pressure and not bending. As yet, of course, our grasp of (2D), the dispositional reading of (2), is less than perfect. But that and how it differs from the more easily grasped (2P) is clear.

Now the fact that something can have a certain disposition at one time which it does not have at another is simply the fact that (1) is such that something may satisfy it at one time and not at another. So the first step to taking it into account is to recognise that (2), as the analysis of (1), must itself be such that something may satisfy it at one time and not at another. In fact, of course, this is simply to acknowledge the dispositional reading of (2). For it is precisely in this that (2D), the dispositional reading of (2), differs from (2P), the predictive reading. *Ex hypothesi* (2P) is such that something fails to satisfy it if there ever is a time at which it is under pressure and not bending, and hence such that something which ever fails to satisfy it always fails to satisfy it. (2P), that is, is not such that something may satisfy it at one time and not at another, satisfaction of it is not relative to a time.[1] (2D), however, is *ex hypothesi* such that it can be satisfied by something which at some time is both under pressure and not bending. And this is just to say that satisfaction of it is *relative to a time*. If something is at some time both under pressure and not bending then it does not satisfy (2D) *at that time*, but it may still do so *at some other time*. The initial explanation of (2D) as a form which can be satisfied by something which at some time is both under pressure and not bending can therefore now be clarified: (2D) is a form which can be satisfied at one time, t, by something which at some *other* time, t', is under pressure and not bending.

It would appear then that in order to take account of the fact that dispositions may be permanent, or may come or go, we shall need to use some propositional operator such as the Rt-operator used by Rescher.[2] Briefly, this operator, read as 'it is the case at time t that . . .', produces out of a tensed proposition whose truth-value may vary with time, an untensed proposition, whose truth-value does not vary with time and which specifies a time at which the first proposition holds or is the case. Thus, given (2D) as the analysis of (1) and given that both are tensed such that something may satisfy them at one time and not at another, the analysis of

$$(1t_1) \quad x \text{ is D at } t_1 \quad \text{i.e. } Rt_1Dx \quad \text{i.e. } Rt_1[(1)]$$

will be

$$(2D \ t_1) \quad Rt_1[(t)(Oxt \rightarrow Rxt)] \quad \text{i.e. } Rt_1[(2D)]$$

Whilst the analysis of

$$(1 \text{ perm}) \quad x \text{ is permanently/always/at all times D} \quad \text{i.e. } (t)RtDx$$
$$\text{i.e. } (t)Rt[(1)]$$

will be

$$(2D \text{ perm}) \quad (t)Rt[(2D)] \quad \text{i.e. } (t)Rt[(t)(Oxt \rightarrow Rxt)] \ [3]$$

---

[1] It is perhaps worth making clear that in saying that (2P) is such that something fails to satisfy it if there ever is a time at which it is under pressure and not bending, and hence such that something which ever fails to satisfy it always fails to satisfy it I am not (of course) saying that if there ever is a time at which something is under pressure and not bending then at no time at which it is under pressure is it bending. That is, something which at some times is bending under pressure is not thereby something which, in the normal sense intended here, 'satisfies' (2P).

[2] N. Rescher, 'On the logic of chronological propositions', *Mind*, LXXV (1966).

[3] Having introduced the R-operator one should perhaps treat 'is under pressure' as a *one*-placed *tensed* predicate and so write 'x is under pressure at t' as 'RtOx' – and (2D t_1), for example, as 'Rt$_1$(t)(RtOx$\rightarrow$RtRx)'. But I shall continue to treat it as a *two*-placed predicate which takes as arguments an individual and a time.

Having reached this conclusion that what is needed for the analysis of 'x is permanently flexible' is something of the form of (2D perm) with its *double* universal quantification over time, I must now return to consider the typical empiricist reaction to the fact that dispositions may be permanent, may come or go. In essence it is, as I have already indicated, to say that (2) by itself does not, as might at first be thought, analyse (1), which makes no explicit mention of the transience or otherwise of the disposition, but rather, because of its universal quantification over times, already represents (2D perm) which says that x is D at all times. In order clearly to expose the mistakeness of this reaction I shall consider it as it appears in what Ryle says.

Ryle does, I have mentioned, recognise that dispositions may be permanent, or may come or go. He explicitly says that 'dispositional statements can have tenses. "He was a cigarette-smoker for a year" and "the rubber began to lose its elasticity last summer" are perfectly legitimate dispositional statements' (p. 125). The question therefore arises, How does he take this fact to reflect on (2) which, as we saw, he has in effect already given as the analysis of (1)? No direct answer is forthcoming but one may be discerned in a detail of his well-known view that disposition statements are 'inference tickets'. For Ryle adds to his observation that 'dispositional statements can have tenses', by saying that there can be 'short-term, long-term, or termless inference tickets' (p. 125). So it would seem that for Ryle the period during which something has a disposition is to be expressed by a restriction on the times over which the quantifier in (2) ranges. That is to say, according to what seems to be the thought of these later Rylean passages, (2), with its unrestricted quantification over times does not represent a form which is common to dispositions as such, be they permanent or impermanent. Rather it represents only the form of a permanent disposition; so that, in general, 'x has D between times m and n' has the analysis 'For all times *between m and n*, if x were O'd x would R'. (2), Ryle is now implying, gives the analysis of (1 perm) not of (1).

But though this view that (2), with its unrestricted temporal quantification, gives the form of (1 perm), *seems* to cope admirably well with the idea that dispositions can come and go, surely something has gone wrong in the reaching of it. For (2) was first introduced as the analysis of (1). As Ryle initially said, 'To say that this lump of sugar is soluble is to say that it would dissolve if submerged . . . *at any time*' (my italics).

We might suppose that Ryle has simply made an inexplicable mistake in first offering (2) as the analysis of (1) before going on to realise that it is the analysis of (1 perm). Or we might suppose that he is overall quite consistent and that the idea that the sugar lump is *permanently* soluble lies behind the passage just requoted. But neither of these courses is attractive. The first is not for, as we have seen, the identification of (2) with (1) is overtly made, whereas its later identification with (1 perm) is something which lies below the surface of what Ryle says. The second is not for if the thought of the sugar's being permanently soluble is of *crucial* importance to what Ryle says then why is it completely supressed and the question of permanence/impermanence raised later and as though it were a fresh matter and one worth only passing mention?

What we should suppose, I suggest, is that Ryle has confused and run together those times at which a soluble object would dissolve if it were in water, and those times at which it is soluble. Our saying that a man with an intention would resist pressure whenever it might be brought to bear, is not equivalent to and does not involve our saying that he always will so intend. We are saying that he intends that he always will do something; but not saying that he always will so intend. Similarly, our saying that a soluble object would dissolve whenever placed in water, is not equivalent to and does not involve our saying that it always will be soluble. We are saying that it has a disposition always to do something; but not saying that it always will have that disposition. From the fact that today's intention pertains to the future it does not follow that it persists into the future. And from the fact that today's disposition pertains to the future it does not follow that it persists into it. Just as we must distinguish between those times at which it is true that a man has an intention, and those times to which the content of his intention refers, so we must distinguish between there being no restriction on the times at which a permanently soluble object is soluble, and there being no restriction on the times at which a (temporarily or permanently) soluble object would dissolve if it were in water.

(2) just does not provide for both of these things. Though if it is interpreted as (2D) it *does* provide for there being no restriction on the times at which a (temporarily or permanently) soluble object would dissolve if it were in water. And if it is interpreted as (2P) it might easily be thought to provide for there being no restriction on the times at which a permanently soluble object is soluble. For (2P) and (1 perm) are alike in failing to be satisfied by something which at some time is in water and not dissolving. But over the course of what he says Ryle does try to make it cope with both. I see no reason why we should not take at its face value his initial offering of (2) as the analysis of (1) – and hence suppose that he is making its universal quantifier deal with there being no restriction on the times at which a soluble object would dissolve if it were in water. Yet, when the idea of there being no restriction on the times at which a permanently soluble object is soluble begins to obtrude he supposes that in offering the universally quantified (2) he has already (even before having thought of it!) coped with it. So he begins to write as though (2) were the analysis of (1 perm).

To realise that dispositions may be permanent, or may come or go, is to realise that (1) is tensed — and hence may be satisfied at one time and not at another. And to realise this should be to realise that anything that has been offered as the analysis of (1) — e.g. (2) — is also tensed, i.e. (2) is to be understood as (2D); so that what is needed for a permanent disposition is a further quantification over time and hence a form like (2D perm). It is simply a confusion to turn round and reinterpret (2) as (2P).

Ryle seems to think that when at time t' an object loses a disposition which it acquired at time t, it is as though a temporally restricted ticket of the form 'For all times between t and t': Oxt→Rxt' has *expired*. I am suggesting that it is rather as though a temporally unrestricted ticket of the form 'For all times: Oxt→Rxt' has *become useless* because the issuing authority has stopped that particular line of business. When an object loses a disposition it is not as though a ticket valid for a limited period has expired. Rather it is as though a termless ticket, valid for ever, is no longer being honoured and has become useless. We should deal with an impermanent disposition not by placing restrictions on the quantifier in (2P), but by adding a further suitably restricted quantifier to (2D).

In effect, then, Ryle, in moving from reading (2) as (2D) to reading it as (2P), tries to make its universal quantifier cope with *both* the fact of there being no restriction on the times at which a soluble object would dissolve if it were in water, *and* the fact of there being no restriction on the times at which a permanently soluble object is soluble. But this surely *is* a confusion. There surely are two aspects of dispositions that need separate and explicit treatment.

To begin with there is a question about a disposition's 'content'. We can ask of a man's intention, What is it an intention to do? and be given the answer, It is an intention to resist pressure *whenever* it might be brought to bear. Similarly, we can ask of an object's disposition, What is it a disposition to do? and be given the answer, It is a disposition to bend whenever subject to pressure. It is of course true that the man's intention may not have been the intention to resist pressure *whenever* it might be brought to bear, but rather the intention to resist any pressure that might be brought to bear *next week*. Whereas a bar's disposition to bend under pressure could hardly be the disposition to bend only under *next week's* pressure. There is, however, still an intelligible point in specifying the disposition as one to bend if *at any time* pressure is brought to bear — as we may remind ourselves if we consider again the dispositions of man-made devices. Most doorbells are designed to be such that they ring *whenever* pressed. But one could be built so as to ring whenever pressed *during the next two days*. No doubt it would turn out to be conceptual truth that, in their 'content', the dispositions of iron bars or elastic bands as opposed to those of devices such as bells are temporally unrestricted. But that the content of those dispositions which are usually discussed are necessarily of a temporally unrestricted nature is no reason for ignoring the question of 'content'. Still less is it a reason for confusing this question of 'content' with the second question which may be asked about a disposition.

This is the question as to how long something has had, or will have, a disposition which, whatever it is a disposition to do, it at present has. Quite apart from the content of a man's intention we can ask, When did he form it? Will he always have it? Similarly, quite apart from its content, we can ask of an object's disposition, When was it acquired, or was it, perhaps, never acquired and is never to be lost?

As far as I can see, the full recognition of both these features forces us carefully to distinguish a 'dispositional' reading of a form such as (2) from a 'predictive' reading. If, as I have argued, there are these two features, how else can we account for them except, in the specific case of (2D perm) for example, by first taking the tensed form (2D), taking care in our understanding of it to distinguish it from the quite different untensed predictive form (2P), and then by embedding it in the predictive detensing content '(t)Rt . . .', thus producing (2D perm)?

The empiricist approach to dispositions interprets hypotheticals like (2) as (2P), as untensed 'predictive' forms, rather than as (2D), as tensed 'dispositional' forms. This leads, when it is recognised that some but not all dispositions are permanent, to the supposition that (2) already pertains solely to permanent dispositions. But to suppose this is simply to confuse and collapse into one two quite separate considerations – the result being an impoverished and etiolated analysis. The empiricist is thus wrong about the nature of the hypotheticals such as (2) which are involved in the analysis of dispositions;[1] they are to be understood as tensed, as pertaining to the 'content' of the disposition, not as untensed, not as pertaining to the 'length of life' of the disposition – to take account of *that* something further is needed, as I have argued. Whether the empiricist is right or wrong to suppose that apparently categorical statements attributing a disposition are really disguised hypotheticals depends precisely on what the initial categorical statement is. Though I do not see why an object should not be disposed simply to do something (e.g. an alarm to go off at a certain time)[2] rather than to do something when something is done to it (e.g. a bell to ring when pressed at a certain time) I will allow here that a categorical tensed form such as

(1)   x is D

is equivalent to a hypothetical – given the proviso that that hypothetical is *tensed*, to be interpreted 'dispositionally' not 'predictively'. But it should certainly be denied that untensed forms such as

($1 t_1$)   x is D at t_1

[1]   I suspect that the same mistake is made about the sense-datum hypotheticals which empiricists have wanted to substitute for material object statements.
[2]   Cf. my 'Leibniz's Principle of Pre-Determinate History', *Studia Leibnitiana*, VII (1975).

or
　　(1 perm)　x is D at all times
are equivalent to hypotheticals. For though their correct analyses, (2D t₁)
and (2D perm), contain embedded hypotheticals they themselves are not
of that form.

I must now turn to the question of dispositions and categorical bases.
This is the question of whether, in D.M. Armstrong's words,

> to speak of an object's having a dispositional property entails that the
> object is in some non-dispositional state or that it has some property
> (there exists a 'categorical basis') which is responsible for the object
> manifesting certain behaviour in certain circumstances.[1]

Typically an empiricist will hold that there is not this entailment; that it is
a purely contingent matter whether a disposition has, in this way, a
categorical basis. He might admit that a scientist would do well to suppose
that dispositions are categorically based, but the belief that they are is in
no way logically forced on us: it is merely, as Bennett puts it, 'a highly
respectable regulative principle or scientific working assumption'.[2] According to the empiricist, then, the assertion that something satisfies (1)
does not *logically* involve the supposition that there is an explanation to
be given of why it would react to certain operations in certain ways. But
that this aspect of an empiricism about dispositions is false may eventually
be seen if we start again from the suggestion of (2) as the analysis of (1).

My argument has been that this suggestion should be seen as giving
expression to the thought that dispositions have a 'content' and that the
further recognition that dispositions can come and go forces us to read (2)
as (2D). One likely but ultimately unsatisfactory consequence of reading it
as (2P) is, we have seen, that it will seem then to analyse (1 perm) rather
than (1). But a further consequence of this mistake is that there will seem
to be no necessity that dispositions are categorically based.

It is, I think it should be allowed, logically possible that something
should, as a brute matter of fact and quite inexplicably, just happen to
satisfy (2P): an object which satisfies it need have no further property
which gives rise to that property which is constituted by its satisfaction of
(2P). It follows, leaving aside now any other consequence of such a
reading, that if the empiricist and an opponent, faced with (2) as the
suggested analysis of (1), were to concur in reading it as (2P) any victory
on the point that dispositions logically must have categorical bases would
be somewhat hollow. For the claim that we ought not to say of something
that it has a disposition, i.e. satisfies something of the form of (1), on the

---

[1] D. M. Armstrong, *A Materialist Theory of the Mind* (London, 1968) p.86.
[2] J. F. Bennett, *Locke, Berkeley, Hume* (Oxford, 1971) p. 105.

sole ground that it satisfies something of the form of (2P), but only on the additional ground that it has some property or is in some state which explains why it satisfies (2P), is relatively trivial and weak. According to it the *only* difference between an occasion on which we should refrain from saying that something has a disposition, satisfies something of the form of (1), and one on which we should say this, would be the fact that it *contingently happens* that the object in question is in some state which explains its satisfaction of (2P). And surely the non-verbal *substance* of the empiricist's position is safe so long as it is admitted that there could be properties which were *in all respects just like* what his opponent labels 'dispositions' except that, *it contingently happens*, they have no categorical bases.

But it has been my argument that, as the suggested analysis of (1), (2) has to be understood as (2D), not as (2P). So the concession that it is indeed logically possible that something should, as a brute matter of fact, happen to satisfy (2P) offers no real comfort to the empiricist. Moreover, if we now turn to consider (2D) and its difference from (2P), I think it will be seen that his opponent has hold of a far from superficial truth.

The difference between (2P) and (2D) is this: If at a certain time, say t, we claim that something satisfies (2P) we make a claim which is shown up as false if at some time, t or any other, the object is under pressure and not bending. Just as when we *predictively* claim at t that a man will resist pressure if at any time it is brought to bear we make a claim which is shown up as false if at some time, t or any other, he is under pressure and not resisting it. Whereas, if at t we claim that something satisfies (2D) we make a *present tense* claim which is not necessarily shown up as false if at some time (*other* than t) the object is under pressure and not bending. Just as when if at t we claim that someone *intends* to resist pressure if at any time it is brought to bear we make a present tense claim which is not necessarily shown up as false if at some time (*other* than t) he is not resisting pressure.

So, for something to *fail* to satisfy (2P) it is logically sufficient that it be, at some (it makes no matter which) time, under pressure and not bending. And its being at some time under pressure and not bending is logically sufficient not only for its failure to satisfy (2P) at *that* time (whatever it is) but also for its failure to satisfy it at *any* time. For satisfaction of (2P) is not time-relative. Thus it comes about that there being a time at which something *is* bending under pressure, whilst being neither necessary nor sufficient for the satisfaction of (2P), would be thought to provide inductive evidence for that satisfaction. And that there is more than one such time would be thought to provide more evidence still.

(2P), then, can be fully and completely understood in terms of operations and reactions. If we never subject it to pressure we can have no direct idea whether or not something satisfies (2P). But it is quite clear what we must do to find out. We must, at various times, subject it to pressure and see whether it bends. If, at one of these times, it fails to bend, then we know, as a deductive matter, that it does *not* satisfy (2P). Whereas if, at all of these times, it does bend, then we have evidence, though not 'the certainty of a demonstration' that it *does* satisfy (2P).

The situation with respect to (2D) is rather different, and crucially so. For satisfaction of (2D) is *time-relative*; something may satisfy it at one time and not at another. So there being a time at which something is under pressure and not bending is *not* a logically sufficient condition of its failure *simpliciter* to satisfy (2D). It is, though, a logically sufficient condition of its failure to satisfy (2D) *at that time*. Thus it comes about that there being a time at which something *is* bending under pressure provides evidence for the satisfaction of (2D) *at that time*; it provides no evidence for supposing that it satisfies (2D) *at any other time*. So just as bending at one time, say t_1, provides only some evidence that (2P) is satisfied, it provides only some evidence that (2D) is satisfied *at t_1*. But what, in the case of (2D) could provide more? In the case of (2P), bending under pressure at times other that t_1 provides more, for failure to bend at any one of those other times would conclusively show that (2P) is not satisfied. But bending at times other than t_1 is simply irrelevant to the question of whether (2D) is satisfied *at t_1*. So (2D) is not finally and completely intelligible in terms of operations and reactions. If something satisfies (2D) at t_1 there is something about it relevant to times other than t_1. Yet what *actually* happens at those other times is irrelevant.

There logically must, then, be something more which is relevant to the satisfaction of (2D) at a certain time, something more than behaviour under pressure at that time and something which is relevant to the fact that (2D), though it may be satisfied at one time and not at another, is a universally quantified form and refers to *all* times. And that this can be no other than a categorical basis should be plain if one thinks of the dispositions of man-made devices. When I last stressed this question of a disposition's 'content' I said that it needs explicitly to be stated that *this* bell has been designed to have the disposition of ringing whenever pressed, for *that* bell may have been designed in a way such that temporal restrictions are required to describe its dispositions. And the difference between two such bells is grounded, and can only be grounded, in the difference between their internal structures. (2D) then, unlike (2P), is not a form which something can satisfy as a brute matter of fact. To think in terms of a form like (2D) is necessarily to think in terms of categorical bases, conceived of as 'internal structures' or 'mechanisms' — even though (2D) speaks in terms only of applied pressure and bending and makes no *explicit* reference to a categorical basis. To suppose of something that it now satisfies (2D) is necessarily though implicitly to suppose that it now is structured in a way such that it would bend whenever subject to pressure. It is not to suppose predictively that it will actually bend when subject to pressure tomorrow, for dispositions may be lost and by tomorrow its structure may have been changed.

A common defence of the empiricist claim that there is no necessity for dispositions to have categorical bases is, in W. P. Alston's words, that

> If there are atomic substances with no internal structure (and this would seem to be at least logically possible) they will undoubtedly have dispositions, for they will undoubtedly react in characteristic ways to certain conditions. But since they lack any internal structure, there can be no question of various features of their structures serving as the basis for various dispositions. *Their* dispositions will be ultimate properties.[1]

But to this I would say simply that we cannot consistently and with a full understanding of what we are about attribute dispositions to supposedly 'atomic' substances. This is not to deny that such structureless substances will, as Alston says, 'undoubtedly react in characteristic ways to certain conditions'; for such behaviour need involve no more than the satisfaction of forms like (2P). It need not, and cannot if the substances really are simple, involve dispositions and the satisfaction of forms like (2D).

In conclusion I must say something about the formal logic of the two interpretations of (2), the 'predictive' and the 'dispositional'. I have argued that if, unlike the empiricist, we are to do full justice to the notion of a disposition we need to make use of tensed forms such as (2D), forms which can be untensed in various ways: (2D t_1) and (2D perm) for example. Now a necessary condition of (2D)'s being tensed is that its main connective be, as indeed it is, other than that of material implication. For on any standard account

(3) $(t)(Oxt \supset RxT)$

just is an untensed form. But if (2D) is to be tensed it is not sufficient that its main connective represent some sort of necessity. It is necessary also that it represent some sort of *tensed* necessity, that a proposition which is necessary in this sense *at one time* need not be so *at another*. This is easily seen if (2D) is rewritten, by means of an operator for 'it is causally necessary that . . .' as the strengthened material implication

(4) $L(t)(Oxt \supset Rxt)$

For (4) is simply of the form of $L[(3)]$. Thus, if (2D) is to be tensed it is necessary that the application of the operator 'L' to an *un*tensed form (e.g.

[1] W. P. Alston, 'Dispositons and Occurences', *Canadian Journal of Philosphy*, I (1971) p. 143. See also C. D. Broad, *An Examination of McTaggart's Philosophy*, I (Cambridge, 1933) p. 271; H. H. Price, *Thinking and Experience*, 2nd. ed. (London, 1969) p. 322.

(3)) should result in a tensed form.

But can we countenance the notion of tensed necessities? The fact is, I think, that we do. For, as it now appears, I have in effect been arguing that they are involved in our notion of a disposition. Perhaps someone will object that they are indeed thus involved if what I have been saying is correct; but that this, so far from showing that we do countenance tensed necessities, shows only that I *must* be wrong. But this objection will hardly do for it supposes that tensed necessities are, *a priori* and quite apart from particular examples, unacceptable. And this is simply false. A sound system can be produced[1] in which formulae of the form La are tensed whether a is tensed or not, and in which formulae of the form

(5) $Rt_1 L(t)(Oxt \supset Rxt)$

are falsified only by

(6) $Oxt_1.-Rxt_1$

and not also by, say

(7) $Oxt_2.-Rxt_2$

Such a logic is all that is needed to underpin what I have said about forms like (2D). So there is at any rate nothing formally incoherent about what I have said about the failure of empiricism, in its attempt to bring things 'down to earth', to do justice to the full richness of what I have taken to be our ordinary notion of a disposition.

---

[1] See my 'Tensed Modalities', *Journal of Philosophical Logic*, II (1973).

13

NATURE AND NECESSITY

Guy Robinson

Determinism is a spectre that has haunted our scientifically-oriented culture from the beginning. I happen to think that it is literally a 'spectre', a trick of the vision, an appearance with an internal cause only, and that it is no more than the ghost of our own conceptual determinations projected outward into a world in which it has no place and no proper being. From one point of view it is no more than an alienated fantasy involving a number of incoherent assumptions. Of these, one of the most important, and one of the most deeply eroded by much contemporary work, is the assumption that science and scientific understanding is a potentially completable system. From another point of view, however, the deterministic picture seems an inevitable product of scientific activity.

But another element in the deterministic picture is the problem I want to look at, namely: the way in which 'laws', natural or scientific, are supposed to bear on individuals, and generally the relation between laws and individuals, either individual things or individual happenings. For there is an interesting contradiction in our views here. At one moment, when we are observing or experimenting, we are perfectly clear that laws trail behind the doings of individuals; but at another moment, when we want to use those laws predictively or manipulatively, we can hardly help seeing them as having a prior, determining, existence, and the individual happening or the individual thing as subject to them. These apparently contradictory points of view are complementary and perhaps both necessary to the enterprise of science. One gives it its procedure, the other its point. Resolving the dilemma and accommodating both viewpoints is no doubt the centre of the problem of determinism.

But it is no use looking for an adequate treatment of that problem here. I only want to make the beginnings of a look at the notions of *necessity* and of the *individual*, particularly the notion of a *concrete individual,* to see whether the two can be brought into relation to each other. This will involve criticism of some of the recent attempts, (by Lewis, for example, and Plantinga), to revive the notion of *de re* necessity. All of these in purporting to attach necessities to bare individuals in the end only destroy the notion of the individual and the concrete. I want to try to go some way toward bringing this out.

Far and away the most interesting recent work in relation to the notion of the individual and its relation to modal notions is that done by Kripke since coming to the philosophic realisation that the notion of a 'possible world', that favourite of the modal logicians (his former self included), is more problematic and obscure than those notions it was meant to help clarify. (I have in mind here chiefly his long piece, 'Naming and Necessity' in the Harman and Davidson collection, *The Semantics of Natural Language.*) However, Kripke's interest there, and his methodology, turn round the problem of reference to individuals and whether this act requires us to be in possession of a unique conceptual counterpart. This question has a close relation to my problem of whether the notions of necessity and of the individual can be brought together without mutual annihilation, though my methodology and approach will be different and more unapologetically metaphysical. But we need to pause here for a moment over the problem of methodology.

In one sense there are no new philosophic problems. And around any important problem the ground will, over time, have been ploughed and re-ploughed, trodden and churned by the academic professionals until landmarks are nearly obliterated and firm footing hard to find. Even the ear for the English language (or whatever vernacular) gets debased by the coinages and the neologisms that are introduced, supposedly to clarify. Generally, whatever clarity these manage to get is drawn from a prior understanding rather than adding to it. Mostly they just obscure, or nearly destroy the prior intuitive clarity they feed on.

Nowhere is this more true than in the area we want to look at, that of necessity in nature, *de re* necessities, the bearing of laws on individuals, or, if you like, the relation of universal to particular. And this poses big methodological problems. Where can we start? With what ideas can we begin to work in any process of clarification?

Well, I want to start from the notion of the individual and the concrete individual, and that choice may look like needing some defence in the first instance. (In the end, of course, it will have to defend itself.) Despite the amount of philosophic puzzlement there may be about the nature of the individual and the concrete individual, in an ordinary, working, everyday sense we understand these notions quite well. We have no ordinary puzzlement about them, and that is good enough. The philosophic account can come later.

One way of putting it is to say that I want to take the notion as a *starting-point*, but not as a *foundation* for the discussion that follows. That is to say, it is relatively clear, but not absolutely clear. Or, perhaps better: it is clear in one way but not in another.

The contrast I have in mind can perhaps be brought out by noticing the way in which the older empiricist tradition took the notion of *experience* as not only clear enough for ordinary everyday purposes but as philosophically unproblematic as well, capable, that is, of bearing the weight of a whole philosophic system. Of course it can't, and we have these days come to see that.[1]

Now, in one way it is as clear as anything can be that we live and work in a world of concrete individuals, objects that move and change and act on one another. Our whole way of talking and thinking is built round that point. Of course we may be tempted by Hume into his study, and, thinking abstractly in that artificial context, be persuaded to look at our world as composed of, or created out of, experiences sewn together somehow. But when we come out into the light of day and actually engage with the world and with others, make a cup of coffee or play a game of darts in the pub, we can't sustain that viewpoint for a minute (as Hume himself admits).

But to take the notion of the individual or the concrete individual as a starting point is not at all to say that that notion is in every way clear and can serve as some sort of foundation for the explication for everything else. Specifically, it may be that the notion of the concrete individual needs to be philosophically clarified and determined precisely through a discussion of its relations to our modal concepts of necessity and possibility. And it may also happen that these notions are themselves clarified in that same discussion. This may sound a bit like two blokes agreeing to lift each other off the ground at the same time, but it's not really, and it is the way that philosophic clarification often works.

I shall leave it at that so as not to turn this into an essay on philosophic methodology.

Very roughly, my strategy will be to argue for an identity between the world of nature and the collection of concrete individuals and then raise the question of the anchorage of the modalities of necessity and possibility in nature as a question about the relation of those modalities to concrete individuals. No doubt this identification of the world of nature with the collection of concrete individuals can do with more examination than I am going to give it, but perhaps the use I want to make of it will help make clear just what further examination of strengthening it may need, or whether it can be accepted at all.

---

[1] Even Popper, (who comes the closest to carrying on the empiricist tradition) gives an ambiguous role and status to experience. For him, what he calls 'basic statements' carry the real logical load, and he describes the relation of experience to them (in successive sentences of the *Logic of Scientific Discovery*, p. 105) as 'causing' and as 'motivating' the acceptance of basic statements. What experience does *not* do, for him, is to *justify* the acceptance of basic statements, nor, presumably, the whole scientific edifice constructed with their help.

Having said a fair amount about the methodology, I had better start talking about the problem itself. Though I should perhaps add that the chief aim of the paper is to define and clarify and re-site the problem rather than propose a solution of any dramatic or definitive kind. Defining it will need a number of goes. (Maybe a lot more than will be made here.) I'll begin by trying to see how it has appeared at various times and to various people, and then try to identify its sources, and criticise some of the discussions and existing conceptual tool-stock to see if something helpful may emerge from all that.

One way we can start is from a remark in Aristotle's *Posterior Analytics* (87^{b}38): 'Sense *(aethesis)* is necessarily of the particular *(hekaston)* whereas science *(episteme)* is of the universal.' A great deal can be got from exploring the inherent paradox there. And all the problems of model and interpretation, theory and practice, are already embedded in those two facts remarked on. In what way can we know, (or can we know?) which way the individual thing will jump? We can't know it by *aesthesis* (something like Russell's *acquaintance*) as that doesn't put us in touch with the thing's past or with its future or with any connection between them. (A Humean point.) It doesn't put us in touch with causes or reasons. Aristotle's example is an eclipse. Sense tells us *that* the moon is darkening, not *why*. And it is the *why* that is transferable and puts us ahead of the event.

Science, on the other hand, doesn't tell us about *this* individual, only about things of this *sort*. So the problem comes up, what kind of knowledge do we have connecting this particular individual to some particular sort? If we have what can be called 'knowledge' here, it seems it can't be got through either *aesthesis* or *episteme* for obvious reasons: it has to span the relation between the objects of the one kind of knowledge and the objects of the other.

Well, that's the problem in its epistemological clothing, and though there may be faults in the way it is posed, it seems at first sight a good puzzle. But I'll leave the unravelling of it to others, for I want to take up the same problem in a metaphysical form and discuss it in a metaphysical setting.

Oddly enough, a way through to that is via Hume, even though in the end I hardly want to talk about the problem from his perspective or in his terms. Apart from anything else, for historical reasons, he seems to have a right to be consulted in any discussion of necessity in nature.

When Hume asks: 'Are there necessities in nature?', he seems at first to have made the question into what could roughly be called a semantic one: 'has our idea of necessity an internal, or has it an external, anchorage and reference?' But for Hume the *origin* and the *reference* of an idea are necessarily coincident, so that the semantic question can hardly be distinguished from an epistemological one. That is the result of his assimilation of the reference relation to the relation of copying. An idea is an idea *of* an experience and unless the experience is of something external, the idea will have no external reference either. This is a key stage in reaching his conclusion that 'the necessity of any action . . . is not a quality in the agent, but in any thinking or intelligent being that may consider the action.'[1]

Hume's motives for trying to base the referring relation on the copying relation are the individualistic ones common to empiricism. Men are thought of as essentially and at the outset isolated from one another, and it is only through the common focus of experience, ideas, and ultimately, language that they can be brought together in communication and community. The relation of copying is thought by Hume to be an 'objective' one, one that is capable of projecting and preserving an assumed common focus of experience into the realm of ideas and thereby language. It is supposed to guarantee that we are talking of the same things when we talk, and thinking of the same things when we think.

This underlying individualistic conception of men as at first isolated and then only later joined to others through experience, language, or social contract has been attacked in different ways by both Marx and by Wittgenstein. For them, men are first of all social beings, and, one might say, it is only later that they succeed in *detaching* themselves and seeing themselves as individuals. For those of us who have taken this message, language and the community of ideas are the expression of, or the embodiment of, the common life of human groups and not its cause or pre-condition.

But (though I am not going to pursue the point) one should remark here that Wittgenstein, like Hume, refuses to separate off questions about the reference of expressions from questions about the way we come to grasp the sense or use of those expressions. Of course, Wittgenstein's conception of this latter process is totally different from Hume's. It is a teaching–learning, social process and not something that can be carried out by an individual on his own in the privacy of his study, or his head. Kripke's account of naming moves in this direction too, and it seems likely that any successful attack on these problems will have to take place in this area. But first, we are trying simply to get the measure of the problems themselves.

For the moment, with the above criticisms in mind, let us go along with Hume, because his insistence on the question of the anchorage of the

---

[1] *Enquiry*, section VIII, pt 1. That conclusion is in itself a very dark saying. It is hard enough to understand what can be meant by calling necessity a quality of or in an agent, but to call it a quality of or in an onlooker seems beyond unravelling. One should note also Hume's bland substitution of the preposition 'in' for the 'of' that normally connects qualities and their subjects – a change that tends to blur, if not obliterate, the distinction between things and qualities.

modal notions of necessity and possibility is an important one even though, as I would like to say, its sense gets distorted by the assumption that an account of that anchorage must be given in terms of the origins of those ideas in the individual histories of the men who have them, histories spelled out in experiential terms.

It seems to Hume clear that necessity or possibility are not to be found in an individual experience. When we first meet a thing, stuff or situation, we can't tell how it may or must act or develop, what we can or cannot do with it. But if those ideas are not in the first experience by itself, they cannot be in the second, or the third, etc., since each of these, taken by itself, must be qualitatively identical to the first. And so, by a line of reasoning reminiscent of the paradox of the unexpected examination, if we take experiences to be individual and self-contained entities (as Hume does) it seems that the modal ideas cannot have their origin there. 'But', one is tempted to ask at this point, 'how is Hume to get the crucial notion of *habit* off the ground?' For, by parity of reasoning, if our first experience of A and B together has the power to create only a small degree of expectation, the second experience will have no greater, and ought only to *confirm* that minute expectancy rather than increase it. After all, our successive experiences of the blue of the sky hardly darken our idea of its colour.

However, picking holes of that size in Hume is a waste of time, and what I really want to do is to change the whole perspective of the discussion, though I have thought it helpful to see what the perspective is changed from.

Let's return to Hume's question of anchorage in a different way and ask: do the modalities of necessity and possibility attach to individuals or only to our classifications of them? Can we make sense of saying that *this* concrete individual must be or must do something or other? (Notice that this is a different question from asking whether we can have a sound basis for *claiming* such a thing. Though the questions are obviously connected, the nature of that connection is in no way obvious, and hasn't been made so, even by Wittgenstein's notion of criteria, which I think no one would claim as perspicuous).

To define the question a little more sharply, let's make use of the distinction between *de re* and *de dicto* modalities as it is drawn by Hintikka. The distinction itself has had a varied history, but Hintikka marks it[1] in a clear way that is useful here. For him a *de re* modality is one that applies or is attached to a definite individual, (in its own right, so to speak) whereas a *de dicto* modality is one that applies to whatever fulfills some condition, or 'whoever meets some description', simply on the ground of its meeting that description. In an older idiom one would have

---

[1] In 'Semantics for Propositional Attitudes', *Models for Modalities*

said that the *de dicto* applies to a thing *qua* member of some class or *in virtue of* having some property or other, whereas the *de re* applies to it in its own right. Our question then becomes 'are there *de re* modalities or only *de dicto*?' If the latter is the case, determinism seems to lose its grip. Necessities become conditional, not categorical, and unless the conditions are themselves fulfilled with categorical necessity, the whole thing gets no send-off.

Look at the problem another way that connects it up more clearly with our original question about necessities in nature. If we take the world of nature to be the world of things that act and move and change, then it seems clear that this is, as I have said, primarily the world of concrete individual things. Roughly, what I mean by that is that it is only embodied particulars that have strong enough criteria of identity for the concept of change to get a grip in any central and unproblematic sense. (Of course it is possible to – and we do – talk about change and development in non-concrete things – the sonata form, the institution of marriage, the conception of romantic love, the techniques of transplant surgery. But these are cases that are puzzling and difficult and require some understanding, not clear, paradigmatic and capable of giving it. It would be as silly and wrongheaded to base a discussion and found a conception on such examples as it would be to take the identification of gods and goddesses from Greek to Egyptian mythology as a central example for the discussion of the concept of identity. What we can in any case say is that the conception of change among *those* things is dependent on, and derivative from, what happens on the concrete individual level, perhaps at several removes, so that if there were no change at that level there is going to be no change, or conception of change at the other levels either.)

If the primary arena of change and action is the world of concrete individuals, it would seem that necessity will have to catch hold there if it is to have a toe-hold in the world of nature. (I'm only partly convinced by this argument, but let's start from there and see where it gets us.) Firstly it puts the weight severely on the notion of *de re* necessity. Must this concrete individual thing necessarily act or react in some particular way or does the necessity that seems to attach to it lie really in the ways we classify, identify or describe it? And what about possibilities or potentialities? Do they attach only to the type or can they attach to the thing *sans phrase*?

Making out the sense of that question is one of the chief objects of this paper, but *prima facie* at least it seems that almost all philosophers would line up against such an idea. Kneale, for example, says: 'If what I have just said is right, it is clear that there can be no ordinary properties which it is proper to say that they belong with absolute necessity regardless of the way in which those individuals are selected for attention. But there may be, and obviously are, some extraordinary properties, such as being a natural number, and a number of truistic properties, such as being prime-or-not-prime'.[1] Of the two exceptions Kneale allows here, the first doesn't apply to our case since Kneale is talking about the wider class of *individuals,* in which he includes numbers, and we are concerned only with *concrete* individuals. (Though perhaps some 'extraordinary' properties can be found even for them. Maybe the medieval 'transcendentals' would do.) And the notion of a 'truistic' property seems an empty one, internally contradicting the notion of *property.* To belong to all is to belong to none. The notion of belonging has evaporated.

In 'Naming and Necessity' where Kripke gives these topics an extended and important treatment, he seems to lay it even more clearly on the line at one point: 'whether a particular necessarily or contingently has a certain property depends on the way it is described' (p. 264). Now, Kripke and Kneale are here only talking about the necessary attachment of properties to individuals, and not explicitly about the necessity of an individual acting or developing in some way or of responding in some definite way to something done to it. However it seems fair to assume that under the heading of 'properties' they would include dispositional properties and others like *magnetic* or *heavy* or *hot* with definite implications for action and reaction, and so would be taking a stand on our problem. At the same time some of the things that Kripke says later in 'Naming and Necessity' seem to reopen the possibility of the direct attachment of modalities to individuals unmediated by a particular description or means of identification. For example at first sight it looks as though his concept of a 'rigid designator' might be put to such a use, and it will be helpful to look more closely at that notion.

When one looks in history for supporters of *de re* necessities, they turn out to be difficult to find, though there has been some press-ganging. Popper, with his passion for organising philosophers into parties, has planted a standard with the word 'essentialism' on it and has tried to frog-march Aristotle, among others, into its shadow. Essentialism is supposed to be characterised by the view 'that in every *single thing* there is an essence, an inherent nature or principle which necessarily causes it to be what it is and thus to act as it does.' Now that is a clear statement of a *de re* view together with a supporting metaphysic, and it will be helpful up to a point to look at Aristotle's views to see whether they correspond to it.

What Popper seems to have in mind here is the aristotelian concept of *'physis',* usually described as 'an internal principle of movement and change' and usually translated as 'nature'. Now what we have to look at is the relation between the *physis* and the thing that has it. Is it causal or constitutive? Popper describes the essence as 'causing' the thing to be what

[1] 'Modality de Dicto and de Re', in Nagel, Suppes and Tarski (eds), *Logic Methodology and Philosophy of Science,* p. 630.

it is and to act as it does. But of course Aristotle doesn't operate with Popper's concept of causation. And if he were asked which of his own four types of 'cause' to range *physis* under, there is no doubt whatever that it would have to come under his heading of 'formal cause'. *Physis* is in fact a kind of temporally articulated formal cause and therefore constitutive, not causal, in character. One cannot separate the formal cause from the thing. It isn't a case of something acting and something being acted on; there just isn't a separate something to be acted on. If one said 'being bounded by three straight lines causes the thing to be a triangle' (a paradigm of formal causation), the obvious question would be: 'causes *what* thing to be a triangle?' And one couldn't even answer 'the plane figure'. One would then need to know what the plane figure was doing before it was a triangle, or what it was apart from being a triangle.

The usual paradigm of *physis* is the acorn growing up into an oak. And the *physis* is the internal principle of that particular development. What Aristotle means by that is that there isn't something outside of the thing that is forcing it to follow that path and no other. Nor, of course, is there anything *inside* either, a sort of seed within the seed, with the obvious opportunities for regress that that would offer. No, 'internal principle' does not mean 'something inside'. 'Internal' has to be taken as in 'internal relations', a conceptual relationship. The fact that it is or could be growing up into an oak is just what constitutes the thing an acorn. If it were to leave off that activity or lose that potential and adopt some other principle of development, it would stop being an acorn by that very fact. Its specific identity and its trajectory are one.

It is precisely here that one sees the beginnings of the Leibnizian conception of the 'individual notion' or 'notion of an individual substance'. Leibniz is extending to particulars and concrete individuals the conception of *physis,* which Aristotle had reserved to species. One of the consequences of this is a determinism against which Leibniz is always fighting a desperate rearguard action. Aristotle's *physis* involves only the general direction of the thing's development, a direction which identifies it merely as a member of a particular species. His way of identifying individuals is different, and both types of identification leave open the possibility of different lines of development whether as an acorn or as *this* individual. Leibniz cuts out the second and makes his individual stick strictly to the scenario, which for Leibniz constitutes it *this* individual. If anyone is an essentialist, it looks as if it has got to be Leibniz.

David Lewis has tried to ease the deterministic situation within a general Leibnizian perspective by introducing his notion of 'counterparts', which look like bringing back a certain amount of slack into the system and opening up some possibilities to the individual. And it could be argued that the roots of this are already in Leibniz himself in so far as he allows himself to talk of 'an infinity of possible Adams' of which God has chosen only one. This seems to force a distinction between traits which are essential, defining or identifying and those which are accidental (which Mates has wanted to deny Leibniz had, in his paper, *Leibniz on Possible Worlds*). This and the notion of counterpart seem to make Adam into a class of creatures of which God *might* have chosen several, either successively or simultaneously (putting them on different planets if necessary). For Leibniz the individual is saved from expanding into a class only by agreeing to stick strictly to the script God has given him. Possibility gets detached from individuals and applied only to worlds as wholes on this sort of account.

I have my doubts about both the Leibnizian perspective that creates the problem for possibility and its solution by means of conceptions like the Lewis *counterpart*, which seems to me unclear and, in the end, unworkable. However, we are getting ahead of ourselves here. Let's return briefly to Aristotle in order to re-emphasise one important point before going on to look at the source of some of the attractiveness and difficulties of the possible worlds analysis of modals and the possibility that it seems to offer of a direct attachment of modal relations to individuals, particularly the modality of necessity.

We tried to show that neither the aristotelian concept of essence nor its diachronic extension in the concept of *physis,* committed Aristotle to Popper's essentialism or to *de re* necessity. The reason for this was that neither essence nor *physis* are connected to, or attributable to, or had by, anything. There is nothing, no separate something, to which they could be connected, or attributed, or which could *have* them. The subject is constituted by, and not connected to, those things. The word he uses to designate that relation, [which he calls an atomic (*atomos*) or *per se* (*kath auto*) relation] is *hyparchein,* which gets translated misleadingly as 'belongs to'. This is probably as good a translation as one can get, but it does give the mistaken impression that he is talking about a relation between separates or separables. He is not. This point is enough to seize on here, even though any adequate treatment of these matters would have to come to terms with Aristotle in some detail and be backed up with a thorough treatment on the scale and with the care shown by Hintikka's very useful book *Time and Necessity.* Aristotle's was the first, and, with Leibniz', the most powerful and impressive attack on the problems of change, time and necessity, but in an analysis as rough and schematic as this, he is going to get pretty crude treatment, being used only to lay down some bracketing fire on the problem I'm chasing, the problem of the attachment of the modality of necessity to the concrete individuals that make up the world of change and development within which we operate.

Let's turn now to the attractiveness and the limitations of the Leibnizian possible worlds analysis of modals. To see the attractiveness let's start with the classical Diodorian reduction of modals to temporal notions according to the neat schema: 'X is necessarily Y' reduces to 'X was & is & will be Y'; while 'X is possibly Y' comes out as 'X was or is or will be Y'. The odd and at first sight paradoxical thing about this reduction of modals to temporals is that it works all right for atemporal and abstract entities like classes, or universals, or numbers (or, perhaps, propositions) but when we try to apply it to time-bound particulars, to situations, events, or to concrete particulars that come to be and cease to be, we get straight into trouble. Necessity will apply to none, and possibility rather vacuously and artificially in most cases.

But this is not at all surprising when we reflect that the equation read in the other direction would equally allow the inference to temporally unrestricted modal assertions about changing individuals from incidents in their history. From the fact that I did once run a mile in a certain time it does not follow that that possibility can simply be attributed to me. I'm afraid that possibility was itself already all too time-bound and to that extent not available for further translation into temporal terms. (And here we see a limitation that has to be put on the scholastic tag *ab esse ad posse valet consequentia*. The inference is not valid for the concrete and time-bound individual or situation.)

No doubt with a good deal of ingenuity and fancy footwork, these difficulties can be staved off, but I'm afraid the cost will be great and the difficulties will only reappear somewhere else. Hence the attractiveness of the 'possible worlds' analysis if one is attempting to apply modalities to concrete individuals. What is interesting to see, and important to keep an eye on, is just what happens to the notion of an individual, or a concrete individual, under that analysis of modals.

If we are to try to apply modal notions directly to individuals we are going to have to modify slightly the classic definition of necessity and possibility in terms of truth in *all* and truth in *some* possible worlds. If we want to talk about some individual necessarily being, having, or doing something, we will have to say that it is, has or does that thing in all possible worlds; and with possibility we would have to say that it is, has or does it in some possible world. And here we come right up against the classic problem of 'transworld identification'. As usual, classes and universals are no problem; their whole point is to be transferable. But the concrete individual lands us right in it. How are we to talk about the 'same' concrete individual appearing in several different possible worlds without making him, her, or it sound like a member of a touring repertory company?

But one enters this Leibnizian 'enchanted world' at one's peril. Bearings and even one's ear for the English language are soon lost. Plantinga, for example, in his curious book, *The Nature of Necessity,* seems almost determined to confuse himself and his readers by indulging himself with expressions like 'existing in a proposition' and describing Quine as 'existing in the proposition' 'Quine is America's foremost rock-climber'. If Plantinga means the chap who once taught me logic, I wonder how he likes it in there? Perhaps we should send him a food parcel or alert Amnesty International. What else can one say?

If Quine the man is described as 'existing in a proposition' then clearly he will be able to 'exist' in an infinite number of them, and will, I guess, have to be described as 'existing' timelessly. He will have stopped being a locatable, datable chap and become a universal 'existing' no particular when and no particular where. It is hard to see the point of that sort of coinage or even what it is meant to achieve. What it does achieve is an obliteration of the distinction between the concrete particular and the universal, the individual and the general. Nothing could compensate us for that loss, and Plantinga's usage seems unlikely to catch on, even among philosophers, who have fallen for some pretty queer ways of talking before now.

Once he has confused himself to that extent, it is not surprising to find that Plantinga can't understand what problem there may be about 'transworld identification' (p. 98) and, more importantly, one realises that when he claims to have defended the notion of *de re* modality, it can't be the notion of *de re* modality we have been exploring, because he cannot be talking about the concrete time-bound, locatable individuals we are interested in.

Another would-be defender of *de re* modality, David Lewis, has similar enchantments for anyone who is enticed into his world of possible worlds, only his aim seems to be to undermine if not destroy the distinction between actual and possible. He does this in two ways. On the one hand he tries to drive a distinction between *being* and *existing,* saying 'there are more things than actually exist' (*Counterfactuals,* p. 86). But I'm afraid I just don't understand what that means. If I say that there *is* some sort of thing, what I say is true if and only if that thing actually *exists.* The terms are convertible. Of course, what I am claiming exists (or is) may itself be a possibility, but again, for my claim to be correct, there must actually *be* such a possibility. Ordinary English idiom would allow us to say just as well that the possibility 'actually exists'. But when I say that there is a possibility of snow, I mean only that the clouds and temperature are right, not that there is some unactualised snow waiting in the wings, lacking only the quality of existence to perfect it. The possibility of snow isn't a special sort of snow, 'possible snow' in a waiting-room full of hopefuls and rejects from the world of existence; it's just a set of meteorological conditions.

(Here, one can have all sympathy and support for Quine balking possible fat men in the doorway, while feeling both that he has misidentified what is objectionable about them, and that his own solutions are just as objectionable, and for similar reasons. The trouble comes with the move from talking about the possibility of a fat man in that doorway

— meaning just that the door is wide enough and the sill strong enough — to talking about a queer entity, not really known to the English tongue, 'a possible fat man'. Once we have one of *these* on our hands we don't know how to deal with him, or even how to apply the phrase. [I suppose for example that I could describe a friend as a 'possible fat man', meaning that he is saved from seventeen stone only by his wife's execrable cooking.])

We don't know how to answer the question: 'how many possible fat men can dance on the point of a pin?' even though we can easily handle the question: 'how many fat men can possibly dance on the point of a pin?' Now it may be that this is a possibility which has never been actualised, and no fat man has ever tried to dance on the point of a pin. But one feels no conceptual or metaphysical difficulty is created by that failure of the world's fat men to take up the challenge. No, it is the 'possible fat men' in themselves who create the difficulty, together with the would-be process of their 'actualisation'. One wants to say that there can be no such process, conceived (as it is here) as an absolute coming to be, because there is nothing to take part in it or nothing for it to happen to. When Aristotle talks about the actualisation of the potential (as he does in his definition of movement or change) he is talking about the actualisation of the potentiality in, or of, something that is already actual under another description. The man becomes fat, or the egg becomes a man or a fat man. If there is a potential fat man it is in the man or the egg that the possibility lies, not in thin air, or the imagination. Otherwise we can be talking about what an actual fat man could or could not do, e.g. stand in this doorway or dance on this pin.

But Quine's own solution to some of the difficulties in this area suffers from exactly the same faults.

Quine's complaint that allowing talk about unactualised possibles fills the world with untidy and inelegant elements shows an attitude to the relation between linguistic forms and conceptual schema that needs to be applied to his own suggested canonical language in which, among other things, he proposes to reparse names as general terms, or rather to split a proper name into two parts, a referential and a descriptive. But when 'Quine exists' becomes 'There is something that Quines', what is it that is supposed to engage in that supposedly idiosyncratic activity of 'Quining' or 'being Quine' or 'being identical with Quine'? We can't break Quine up into a bare reference point or a bare existent which is somehow fleshed out by the activity of 'Quining' any more than we could find a thing called 'a possible fat man' that could be brought into existence by being the subject of some process of actualisation.

(It is no wonder that the Ontological Argument is becoming popular again. Quantificational logic seems an absolute set-up for it.)

David Lewis's second move subversive to the actual/possible distinction is to maintain what he calls an 'indexical theory of actuality'. This theory involves, and may be equivalent to, the thesis that the word 'actual' behaves like 'I', 'here' and 'now' in that 'it depends for its reference on the circumstances of utterance, to wit the world where the utterance is located' (p. 86). One could spend quite a time on that single proposition, for one thing it is not at all clear that the word 'actual' has a referring function like the words 'I', 'here' and 'now', any more than the word 'dagger' has in Macbeth's 'Is this a dagger I see before me?' The referring function is there carried by the 'this' and the '(that) I see before me', and what Macbeth is wondering about is how to describe what has already been referred to: is it real or actual? Can he grab it? Can he kill with it?

(Also, one cannot help opening one's eyes rather wide when Lewis goes on to describe as 'less controversial' the analogous thesis that 'Our present time is only one time among others', and called 'present' because 'it is the time we inhabit'. One would be tempted to send him a copy of the *Critique of Pure Reason* but for the presumption that he must have one already. Except as a misleading description of some parts of Special Relativity Theory, that doctrine is not so much controversial as unintelligible and therefore not a very useful measure of problematicality.)

However that may be, Lewis's 'indexical theory' is meant to licence him to say: 'The inhabitants of other worlds may truly call their own worlds actual'. But that claim, if allowed, would not only relativise the actual/possible distinction, but would subvert and immobilise it. I could write a novel (that is, after all, a kind of possible world) which happens to be about a novelist who is himself writing a novel. The curious thing about this novel in my novel is it is about me writing *my* novel. In *my* novel my character will say of me and my story that they are possible worlds and of himself and his life and activities that they are actual. Now on Lewis's account, what my novelist says about himself and me will be true within the possible world which he inhabits, and relative to that world just as true as what I say within my world is of him. Lewis's theory seems to allow for no hierarchy and no ultimate choice between us. That is what the 'indexical theory' is all about. No matter that he is my creature or that his possible world has its origins in my imagination or my writing. It is a possible world, nevertheless, and his word, suitably relativised, is taken to be as good as mine by Lewis's theory.

This problem does not arise for Leibniz, the father of all this talk. His system has a monotheistic theological setting (a fact that is usually overlooked by logicians who think they can loot it for useful devices), and this enables him to maintain an absolute distinction between actual and possible. Leibniz can say that, for reasons best known to himself, God has chosen *me* to do the writing in reality and my novelist is not actually writing but only writing *in my novel*.

One could say a lot more about the Lewis theory, but it would take us out of our way. Though it may be just worth pointing out that by making

HUNT LIBRARY
CARNEGIE-MELLON UNIVERSITY
PITTSBURGH, PENNSYLVANIA 15213

actuality indexical, Lewis will be making truth indexical as well, since the two are correlatives, so that he will be in the end unable even to *talk* about his possible worlds and to say anything about them that is either true or false. Of course he might try the obvious dodge of talking about what one of the other-worlders could or could not truly say about his own world. But even that trick won't get Lewis past the gates. For Lewis's propositions to be true, there must be something actually the case in his own world which his proposition refers to. And what is that? Neither the other-worlder's utterance nor the actuality that makes it true in *his* own world are facts or actualities of Lewis's world; so there is nothing for Lewis to talk about and nothing to make his pronouncements true or false.

This is the inevitable result of cutting away the theological base on which Leibniz built his fantastic edifice of possible worlds. The notion of possibility has its origin in the capacities of types of things – to nourish, to be broken, to bear weight, to hold water – and has to be attributed to those things. By extension, possibilities can be attributed to situations or complexes of things. But still, the (dangerous, volatile, auspicious) possibilities inherent in those situations derived ultimately from the potentialities of those things which were the elements of the situation.

The seventeenth century philosophers and scientists sought to go behind the aristotelian individual substances to find deeper explanations of why those individual things or types of things had the potentialities they did. Because the philosophers were then looking for ultimate foundations, those who were not materialists could find no stopping point short of God. But for Leibniz, God was not just the ultimate cause or source of those potentialities or capacities, he was in a way their ultimate subject as well. The possibility of a possible world lay in God's power, God's actual power. But those who these days try to operate the Leibnizian scheme without God don't seem to notice that there is no subject for the possibility of their possible worlds actually to inhere in. A possible world is like a possible fat man and the objections to them are much the same. One might as well ask 'how many possible worlds can rotate on the point of a pin?' Unless they can be given some kind of anchorage in the actual, there is no way of discussing them or settling any arguments about them.

That is perhaps why Kripke, whose important work in modal logic was centered on possible worlds, has, in his recent move into philosophy proper, at the same time retreated rapidly from them to something more like an aristotelian position based on concrete individuals rather than stories or scenarios, (which is what possible worlds are.) In *Naming and Necessity* he even apologises for his past misconduct. Though he does give an explicit definition of his concept of a *rigid designator* that seems to appeal to them; a rigid designator is one that 'designates the same object in any possible world'. At the same time he makes it clear that his own view is that the problem of transworld identity is pretty well a pseudo-problem and that our whole talk about possible worlds is parasitic on our talk about concrete individuals (his favoured example is Nixon), and on our ability to talk about what Nixon might or might not do in different circumstances. Since he wants to claim that this ability is not based on the association of any set of descriptive terms with the rigid designator, in this case the proper name 'Nixon', it looks at first sight as though we might have here a means of designating an individual that would allow us to attribute necessary features to it, in its own right, features that in this case could not be found wrapped up already in our means of designation.

Might Nixon have been a frog, or might he become one? Or can we say that he must *necessarily* be a human being? Is there at least this necessity attached to the individual, Nixon? To answer this question, to make sense of it even, I think we have to go right back to the aristotelian insights into the difference between change and development, on the one hand, and destruction and replacement on the other. By and large, we would say that Nixon couldn't be a frog. If one moment we had Nixon in front of us and then suddenly a frog, knowing the sorts of things that happen on stages, we might suspect that he had been spirited away in some extremely clever way and rightly refuse to make the identification. Even if we witnessed a continuous deformation from man into frog, we might still not know what to say and would probably want to withold judgement until biologists and physiologists had a chance to study the case. And there would be a great many things we would want to know. For example, unless he turned into a very large frog, we would want to discover what had happened to the excess material. Without answers to these questions, we might still suspect some very clever trick or illusion and would withold judgement or identification. On the other hand, if as in Ionesco's play *Rhinocerous*, people started doing that sort of thing all over the place, we might think again. We might then recognise it as a stage in human development, like senility, or like metamorphosis in insects, and be happy to say: 'yes, it is Nixon, all right'.

What's the lesson of all this? Well, without having room to argue it out or to bring out all the points that very much need making here, I can only come to the platitudinous conclusion that our ways of making identifications have to do with regularities we find in development and therefore follow, rather than preceed, experience. The illusion we sometimes have of *a priori* necessities in this area comes from the fact that our classifications sum up past experience and can, for a time, and within limits, blinker future experience.

14

EMPIRICISM IN ETHICS

Stephan Körner

The purpose of this essay[1] is to exhibit certain crucial shortcomings of some representative empiricist and anti-empiricist ethical theories and to sketch an empiricist ethics which is not exposed to these objections and adequate to our cognitive and practical position in the world. The discussion falls into two parts. Part I, which is mainly critical, begins with a general distinction between empiricist and anti-empiricist ethical theories and surveys the assumptions which are permissible to the former in the sphere of factual beliefs, practical attitudes and logical inference (section 1). It then examines the central theses of three kinds of empiricist ethical theory, namely utilitarian, contractual and emotivist theories (section 2) and of three corresponding kinds of anti-empiricist theory which can be viewed as attempts at correcting the faults of their empiricist counterparts (section 3). Part II, which is mainly constructive, contains a sketch of a new empiricist ethics (section 4) and in its light a brief discussion of various types of moral system (section 5) of the limits of moral pluralism and the nature of moral argument (section 6).

I

1. A distinction between empiricist and anti-empiricist theories

The historically and philosophically important opposition between empiricist and anti-empiricist ethical theories can be sharpened in a number of ways which depend on the sense given to the notion of an empirical attribute. Here an ethical theory will be regarded as empiricist if, and only if, it implies that the moral attribute of an action – in particular, its being morally good, bad, indifferent, obligatory, forbidden or permitted – is an

---

[1] The H. B. Acton lecture was founded during Professor Acton's lifetime in gratitude for his work as editor of *Philosophy*. Since his death last year it has become a memorial lecture and I can only hope that this essay will not be an unworthy tribute to Acton the philosopher and the man.

empirical attribute in the following senses of the term: (i) The moral attribute is subjective or subject-dependent; (ii) it is a contingent attribute of the action; and (iii) it is a natural attribute of it.

A moral attribute of an action is subject-dependent in being an attribute which the action possesses, not independently of any person's system of practical attitudes of which the action is an object, but as an attribute which the action possesses as an object of such a system. It is thus a relational attribute of the action, more precisely an attribute containing an implicit reference to a system of practical attitudes or a class of such systems, which may include that of the agent or of his judge. The dependence of moral attributes on a person's system of practical attitudes — the preferences and indifferences between options which he believes to be realisable — is analogous to the dependence of perceptual attributes on his system of perception and cognitive organisation. In neither case does the subject-dependence imply or exclude inter-subjective agreement in the systems to which the relational attributes implicitly refer and, hence, in the application of these attributes.

A moral attribute of an action is a contingent attribute of it in that its possession by the action is not a logical consequence of the possession by the action of its non-moral attributes. The contingency of an action's moral attributes is particularly important if its individuation does not involve such attributes. In that case one may characterise the contingency of moral attributes as allowing the logical possibility that one and the same action, for example a bigamous marriage, be immoral with respect to one person's system of practical attitudes and not immoral with respect to that of another person. The usual manner of individuating actions — for example for the purposes of the law — by the agent's bodily conduct, beliefs and practical attitudes does not rely on whether the agent or the person judging his action applies one of the moral attributes to it and, if so, which of them. This does not mean that the agent's considering his action moral or immoral may not be relevant to the moral judgement of his judge.

What makes, or would make, moral attributes natural attributes of actions is more problematic than what makes them subject-dependent or contingent. Yet since the distinction between naturalistic and non-naturalistic ethical theories has been considered central to ethics, one must make an attempt at capturing its meaning. It presupposes the acknowledged distinction between moral attributes and purely self-regarding or egocentric attributes of actions — *i.e.* the attributes of being from a purely selfish point of view a good, bad, indifferent, obligatory, forbidden or permitted action. On the basis of this distinction one may regard a moral attribute of an action as natural if, and only if, its analysis does not refer to any beliefs, feelings, attitudes or other items of awareness which differ substantively from those to which the analysis of the corresponding egocentric attributes refers. This distinction still needs some explanation of what one means in speaking of a non-substantive difference between items of awareness. In what follows only one non-substantive difference between two items of our awareness will be needed, namely the difference between two practical attitudes which consists in their being located in two structually different systems of practical attitudes. In other words, just as two bricks made out of the same clay may differ non-substantively in that one forms part of a dwelling house and the other part of a factory, so two practical attitudes favouring bigamous marriage may differ non-substantively in that one forms part of a devout Muslim's system of practical attitudes and the other forms part of that of a devout Catholic.

The kinds of belief which are implicit in the meaning of moral and of egocentric attributes include in particular beliefs about the course of events, about the causal, probabilistic or other determination of a sequence of events by a preceding sequence of events, about the possibility of interfering in the course of events by chosen bodily conduct and, hence, about the possibility of effectively choosing between various practicabilities or options. The kinds of practical attitude which are implicit in the meaning of moral and of egocentric attributes are a preference for one option over another or indifference between two options or a pro- anti- or indifferent attitude towards one or more options from a set of options believed to be mutually exclusive and exhaustive. Among the kinds of practical attitude which — though they may enter the meaning of both moral and egocentric attributes — are particularly important for the analysis of moral attributes are two which are often neglected. One comprises practical attitudes towards practical attitudes as in the case of a person who has a practical pro-attitude towards eating ice-cream (which he realises by frequently eating it) and a practical anti-attitude towards this pro-attitude (which he realises by undergoing aversion therapy). The other comprises practical attitudes which are directed not only to the realisation of certain options but also towards requiring their realisation — either *simpliciter* or in accordance with a code of conduct. Paying attention to practical attitudes of the first kind is necessary in exhibiting the structure common to all moral systems, while paying attention to practical attitudes of the second kind is necessary in exhibiting some structural features which are peculiar to an important species of moral systems.

2. *On three kinds of empiricist ethical theory*

A kind of ethical theory which is empiricist in all three senses of the term is utilitarianism, according to which an action is morally good if, and only if, it is conducive to at least as much happiness or conscious well-being as any of its alternatives. Thus, one or more persons' happiness is subject-dependent since conscious well-being — whether conceived as crudely physical or as mental well-being — is a state of being which is *ipso facto* the object of a person's practical pro-attitude. It is impossible that somebody consciously regards a realisable state as a state of well-being and yet has no practical pro-attitude towards it. It is, for example, impossible that somebody regards being drunk or drugged as a kind of happiness without having a practical pro-attitude towards it — even though he may at the same time have an anti-attitude against this very pro-attitude. The subject-dependence of conscious well being, happiness or *eudaemonia* is emphasised by Bentham as well as by those of his successors who disagree with Bentham's simple identification of it with states characterised by the presence of pleasure and the absence of pain.

Next, 'being conducive to the greatest possible happiness', as conceived by the utilitarian, is a a contingent attribute of an action in the sense that its possession by an action is not logically implied by the action's possessing any conjunction of attributes which it possesses independently of being an object of a person's system of practical attitudes. Lastly, 'being conducive to the greatest possible happiness' is a natural attribute since the practical attitudes involved in the notion of happiness, as conceived by the utilitarians, do not substantively differ from the practical attitudes involved in the analysis of the various egocentric notions of happiness. Indeed the moral attribute of being good in the sense of utilitarian ethics coincides with at least one species of egocentric goodness, namely in the case of hedonistic utilitarianism with the "lower" pleasures, in the case of more subtle versions of utilitarianism with the "higher" pleasures.

A classical utilitarian holds that a person who asks himself what morality is and what his morality is, is asking himself essentially the same question to which the simple answer is: utilitarianism. Yet, unless there is only one morality, he is just as wrong as a physicist would be who confused his analysis of physics with a description of the physics which he happens to accept at the moment. The utilitarian's mistake of identifying a description of his own morality with an analysis of morality is not peculiar to him but fairly common among moral philosophers. It engenders the further mistake of inferring that whoever disagrees with them in accepting a different morality is *ipso facto* mistaken in his analysis of morality and that, conversely, whoever disagrees with them in the analysis of morality is mistaken in accepting the morality which he in fact accepts.

Another type of empiricist ethical theory, which is compatible with some forms of utilitarianism, defines an action as morally good if, and only if, it conforms to the regulations of a well-regulated system of social institutions; and defines a system of social institutions as well-regulated if, and only if, it would coincide with the system which a group of people satisfying certain (Lockean, Hobbesian *etc.*) conditions would agree to create for the regulation of their life and that of future generations. That the moral characteristics of actions according to such a theory are subject-dependent and contingent is obvious. That they are natural holds for all those contractual theories which are meant to serve as the foundation of a morality and not to be partly founded on it. (Whether or not Locke's doctrine of natural rights puts his theory into the former or the latter category is an exegetic question which is here of little importance.) Contractual and utilitarian ethical theories are alike in that they describe particular moralities rather than analyse morality in general. Yet their comparison advances the analysis in at least three ways. It underlines the possibility — and the historical fact — of different moralities. It draws attention to different types of morality, namely purely regulative or deontic moralities in which the moral characteristics of actions are determined by their conforming or not conforming to regulations; purely evaluative (axiological, non-regulative) moralities; and mixed moralities in which the moral characteristics of actions are determined partly by reference to regulations and partly independently of regulations. Lastly, it raises the problem of the relation between moral evaluations and moral regulations in all or, at least, some moralities.

While utilitarian and contractual theories define morality by the nature of the options which are the objects of practical attitudes — a personal or social life of maximal well-being or one that is lived under well-regulated institutions — the emotivists define morality by the attitudes themselves without in any way limiting the options towards which they are directed. For some emotivists the morality of actions consists simply in pro-attitudes towards them, for others in pro-attitudes combined with attempts at evoking similar attitudes in others. The main shortcoming of these theories is that they fail to distinguish clearly enough between moral, prudential and egocentric attitudes and hence to do justice to the complex structure of systems of practical attitudes which include all of them. According to the emotivist theories the moral characteristics of an action are clearly subject-dependent, since they consist in a person's attitude towards it; contingent since an action's being an object of an attitude is not logically implied by its other attributes; and natural since being the object of an attitude is a natural attribute of an action. Indeed, because emotivist theories are so manifestly empiricist, their failure to distinguish moral from other attitudes is often taken as typical of all empiricist theories with the consequence that the potentialities of an empiricist ethics for yielding an adequate analysis of morality is often overlooked.

3. On three kinds of anti-empiricist ethical theory

A strong motive for rejecting empiricist ethical theories is their alleged inability to distinguish between moral and non-moral, especially prudential, evaluations and regulations. Yet, though this defect may be peculiar to the three types of empiricist ethical theory so far mentioned, it is not characteristic of every such theory. Before expounding an empiricist ethical theory in which the required distinction arises quite naturally, it will be useful to examine some anti-empiricist theories, based on the assumption that the crucial difference between moral and non-moral evaluation and regulations lies in the absolute or objective validity of the moral and the merely relative or subjective validity of the non-moral ones. Each of these anti-empiricist ethical theories corresponds to one of the empiricist ethical theories discussed earlier and can be regarded as an attempt to cure its empiricist counterpart of the relativism or subjectivism which allegedly renders it inadequate.

One kind of anti-empiricist ethical theory can be regarded as an attempt at overcoming the subject-dependence of moral evaluations (and indirectly of moral regulations) by construing the correct moral evaluation of an action as the mere apprehension of the fact that the action has a certain moral attribute. Since this fact is assumed not only to exist independently of the moral evaluation by which it is apprehended, but also to be incapable of being apprehended in any other way, both the apprehended fact and its apprehension are quite different from any other facts and their apprehension. The fact is considered a specifically moral fact and its apprehension a specifically moral perception or intuition. An example of such an intuitionist moral theory is ideal utilitarianism in which the rôle of conduciveness to subject-dependent well-being is replaced by conduciveness to a subject-independent ideal state of affairs.

Since in accordance with ethical intuitionism a moral attribute of an action is not subject-dependent, it must depend on the action's non-moral attributes. This dependence is conceived by some ethical intuitionists as a specifically moral, necessary implication. Thus Ross declares it as analogous to, but different from, logical deducibility, while Moore who is equally sure about its not being contingent confesses his inability to explain its meaning.[1] Their kind of anti-empiricist ethics thus offers to explain the difference between moral and non-moral attributes at the price of countenancing special, and specially obscure, kinds of facts, perceptions and entailments.

Another kind of anti-empiricist ethics can be regarded as an attempt at overcoming the subject-dependence of accepted moral regulations (and indirectly of moral evaluations) by construing the correct moral regulations as issuing from a special authority, in particular the will of God or *the* rational will. Such a will is conceived as the source of universal imperatives which are characteristic of moral conduct and differ essentially from those practical preferences which are involved in merely prudent or egocentric conduct. Theories which analyse the moral attributes of actions in terms of regulations issuing from the rational will, assume not only the subject-independence of these regulations but also the possibility of

[1] See W. D. Ross, *The Right and the Good* (Oxford, 1930) pp.121ff., and G. E. Moore 'The Conception of Intrinsic Value' in *Philosophical Studies* (London, 1922)

determining the moral validity or otherwise of any regulation by a quasi-logical inference, *e.g.* the application of the categorical imperative. The method fails in determining which, if any, of two persons' incompatible convictions, is moral, if each of them is internally consistent, sincerely held and universally applicable. And this failure adds to the difficulties of understanding the nature of regulations whose moral validity is independent of any person's system of practical attitudes.

Unlike intuitionism and rational will theories, which explain the difference between moral and non-moral attributes independently of any person's system of practical attitudes by assuming special moral facts, perceptions, entailments or regulations, a third type of anti-empiricist ethics does so by assuming a special kind of moral attitude. This type of theory which goes back to Descartes, and has been most clearly elaborated by Brentano, characterises a practical attitude such as a loving, hating or preferring as moral if, and only if, it is self-evidently correct. In other words, just as Descartes explains the truth of a proposition in terms of self-evident cognition so he and, more explicitly, Brentano explains the moral attribute of an action in terms of the self-evidence of a practical attitude.[1] According to Brentano's theory moral attributes are subject-independent since they are defined by self-evidently correct practical attitudes which any being capable of practical attitudes would have if it existed. The main objection to this theory is that the feeling of self-evidence is at least as unreliable in the practical as it is in the cognitive sphere, and that the test of self-evidence is no more effective than the quasi-inferences determining the regulations of the rational will.

In summing up the critical part of the discussion the following points are worth emphasising: (i) Utilitarianism, contractual theories and emotivism cannot explain the difference between the moral and the non-moral attributes of an action. Their anti-empiricist counterparts — intuitionism, theories of the rational will and the theory of morality as a kind of self-evidence — which seem to explain the difference employ notions which though in need of clarification, are left obscure. (ii) Both kinds of theory fail to distinguish between the analysis of morality and the analysis of a particular morality — the empiricist because they regard moral monism as an obvious empirical fact, the anti-empiricist because they regard it as an obvious philosophical truth. (iii) Both kinds of theory try with varying success to satisfy certain other requirements which any ethical theory has to fulfil, in particular to explain the claim of moral convictions to universality and superiority over other practical considerations, as well as the possibility and nature of moral disagreement and moral argument.

---

[1] See in particular *Vom Ursprung sittlicher Erkenntnis* (Leipzig, 1889, etc.)

II

4. *A sketch of a new empiricist ethical theory*

If one acknowledges the fundamental difference between moral and non-moral attributes and refuses to account for it by identifying moral with non-empirical attributes of a special kind, one is faced with a dilemma which none of the theories so far mentioned is able to overcome. One way of escaping it is to develop an empiricist ethics which explains the moral or non-moral character of a person's practical attitudes, not by considering them in isolation, but by considering the relation which they bear to the other practical attitudes in his practical system. Such an empiricist ethics can be developed if one takes note of a feature which, though familiar in one's practical experience, has been strangely neglected by moral philosophers, namely the possibility of a person's having practical attitudes towards his practical attitudes. It is this stratification of practical systems which enables one to account for, and to analyse, the distinguishing features of moral attitudes, attributes, judgements and inferences.

As has been pointed out earlier, it is a perfectly feasible empirical fact that somebody should have a practical pro-attitude towards eating ice-cream and at the same time have a practical anti-attitude towards (his having) this pro-attitude. It is no less empirically feasible that somebody should have a practical pro-attitude towards enjoying certain privileges, while not only having an anti-attitude towards their existence, but also towards his pro-attitude towards his enjoying them. These examples, to which a host of similar ones can easily be added, allow us to introduce the crucial technical concepts of the level of a practical attitude, of its being positively, negatively or indifferently dominated or of its being un-dominated, as well as of the notion of practical inconsistency. They further allow us, partly in terms of these notions, to define other moral concepts which are needed in any ethical theory.

A practical attitude is of first level if, and only if, it is directed towards an option which does not involve the change or preservation of any practical attitude. It is of second (third, *etc.*) level if, and only if, it is directed towards an option which involves the change or preservation of a practical attitude of first (second, *etc.*) level. A practical attitude which in this fashion is the object of a practical attitude of the next higher level will be said to be dominated by it — positively dominated if the higher attitude is a pro-attitude, negatively dominated if it is an anti-attitude and indifferently dominated if it is an attitude of indifference. It is important to distinguish between an attitude which is dominated by an attitude of indifference on the one hand and an undominated attitude on the other. For our present purpose it is sufficient to consider practical systems of at most three levels since no important new questions arise for systems with practical attitudes of higher level.

Practical systems are thus structurally much more complex than was supposed by the older empiricist theories. This complexity manifests itself, for example, in the different kinds of conflict or practical inconsistency which may arise between different practical attitudes. Giving each of these kinds a different name, we may briefly and sketchily define them as follows: Two practical attitudes are *opposed* if, and only if, they are of the same level and if their joint implementation is impossible. According to the kind of impossibility different species of opposition may be distinguished. (For example, a pro-attitude and an anti-attitude towards the same option are logically opposed.) Two practical attitudes are *discordant* if, and only if, they are of different level and one of them is negatively dominated by the other. Two practical attitudes are *incongruent* if, and only if, they are of the same, but not of first, level and if they together either constitute a pro-attitude towards two practical attitudes whose joint realisation is impossible; or an anti-attitude towards two practical attitudes, the non-realisation of at least one of which is impossible. (For example a pro-attitude towards a pro-attitude towards smoking and a pro-attitude towards an anti-attitude towards smoking; or an anti-attitude towards a pro-attitude towards smoking and an anti-attitude towards a pro-attitude towards not smoking.)[1]

It seems best to approach the definitions of a moral attitude and of a moral principle in a number of steps and to represent each of them schematically. We start by assuming that a person, say S, has a practical attitude of first level towards an option described by f, such as smoking, telling a lie, joining a certain political party, *etc.* According to whether $S's$ attitude is a pro-attitude an anti-attitude or an attitude of indifference one might express it respectively by $S+f$, $S-f$ and $S\pm f$. If the nature of his attitude does not matter, it may be represented by $S*f$. From the point of view of empiricist ethics it is important to remember that the same attitude $S*f$ may or may not be (positively, negatively or indifferently) dominated. Writing $[S*f]$ to indicate that the attitude is undominated, $*[S*f]$ that it is dominated and $\ldots [S*f]$ that the question of being or not being dominated is open, we may express our assumption that S has a practical attitude of first level towards f by

(i) $\ldots [S*f]$

which is far from expressing a moral attitude or principle.

The second step which introduces the most elementary way of having practical attitudes towards one's own practical attitudes can be expressed by

(ii) $\ldots [S*[S*f]]$

[1] For a more detailed discussion of these distinctions and the other topics of section 4, see 'Rational Choice', *Proc. Arist. Soc.*, *XLVII* (1973)

for example a dominated or undominated pro-attitude of S towards his own pro-attitude to telling the truth about his income.

The third step introduces the element of supremacy over other attitudes which is a necessary characteristic of moral, as opposed to all other practical attitudes, by assuming that the practical attitude of second level is undominated. Schematically,

(iii) $[S * [S * f]]$

The fourth step introduces the element of personal universality into S's undominated practical attitude of second level. More precisely, it assumes that S's second level attitude is directed not merely towards possession of the first level attitude by himself, but towards possession of the first level attitude by every human being and thus *eo ipso* by himself. Writing U for the universal class of human beings, the result of the fourth step may be schematically expressed by

(iv) $[S * [U * f]]$

It is one of the theses of the present empiricist ethical theory that a moral attitude is an undominated, personally universal practical attitude. While a full defence of this thesis transcends the scope of a short essay, it is obvious that this definition is sufficient to distinguish moral from non-moral attitudes by their place in systems of practical attitudes.

In order to arrive at the definition of a moral principle further steps must be taken. The most important of these is to assume that S's second level attitude is "circumstantially" general, *i.e.* that the first level attitude which is its object is directed towards a kind of situation or class of situations X exemplified by f rather than towards f as such. Schematically,

(v) $[S * [U * X]]$

By analogy to mathematical and other cognitive principles a moral principle must not be inconsistent with, or implied by, any other such principle. The inconsistency and the implication in question are, of course, practical inconsistency, whose nature has been briefly explained and practical implication which is − in the usual fashion − definable in terms of practical inconsistency. For our present purpose there is no need to elaborate these points.[1]

5. *On some types of morality*

Since the moral or non-moral character of a person's practical attitude depends on its place in the person's practical system, his morality is an aspect of this system. Bearing this in mind, one can clarify and justify the usual distinctions between different types of morality. One such distinction is that between a concrete- or "situational"- morality and a

---

[1] For some further details see 'On Some Relations between Logic and Metaphysics', in *The Logical Enterprise, Essays in honour of F. B. Fitch* (Yale University Press, 1975).

morality of principles. A person's morality is concrete if, and only if, none of his moral attitudes, as represented by (iv), can be generalised to, or regarded as a substitution instance of, a moral principle, as represented by (v). (In such cases the propositional description of the option which is the object of the concrete moral attitude must be regarded as necessarily incomplete.) Whether a person's morality is concrete, whether all his moral attitudes are generalisable into moral principles or whether some are and some are not, is an empirical and — if asked for groups of people or the whole of mankind — an anthropological question.

The difference between concrete moral attitudes and moral attitudes which are, or are generalisable into, moral principles is reflected in the important difference between two kinds of moral attributes of options and, indirectly, of other entities. A moral attribute of the first kind, which might be called "primary moral attributes", is simply a relational attribute of the person's option, namely its being the object of a person's moral attitude. A moral attribute of the second kind, which might be called "secondary moral attributes" (e.g. 'leading to a maximisation of the gross national product' or 'leading to an equal distribution of wealth') must fulfil two conditions: (a) It must characterise the person's option independently of the moral attitudes of which it is the object (and, hence, of any change in the person's moral attitudes); and it (b) must be the object of one of the person's general moral attitudes or moral principles (that is to say of a moral attitude which is directed towards the option not merely as a particular option but as an instance of the attribute mentioned in the principle).

An important type of morality consisting of general practical attitudes or principles is deontic morality. A person's morality is deontic if, and only if, his practical system contains one supreme moral principle (by which all his moral attitudes are practically implied), namely the general, moral pro-attitude towards the continued observance of a specific code of conduct. Schematically such a principle might be represented as: $[S + [U + \text{Observing } M]]$. By a code of conduct, whether or not its observance is the object of a supreme moral principle, is meant a set of regulations — of form "If so-and-so is the case, then such and such is to be done by the following persons . . . ' — which fulfils certain conditions of consistency and adequacy and which in a precise sense of the term "deontically implies" obligations, permissions and other "code-dependent" characteristics of actions[1] A code of conduct which is the object of a person's supreme moral principle is his moral code.

Codes, regulations and code-dependent obligations thus are moral not because they issue from a civil or supernatural authority, but because their acceptance and continued observance is the object of a moral principle or

---

[1] For details see 'On the Structure of Codes of Conduct', in *Mind*, *LXXXIII* (Jan 1974)

general moral attitude in the sense of the new empiricist ethics. Although compared with asserting this thesis of the primacy of moral attitudes over moral regulations a detailed classification of deontic moralities is here of little importance, one may briefly note the distinction between those which are substantive and those which are formal. A person's moral code is substantive if (like the decalogue) it is specified by the enumeration of its regulations. It is formal if its regulations are determined as satisfying a general necessary and sufficient condition (such as Kant's categorical imperative).

The opposite of a deontic morality is a purely axiological morality, in which no moral principle is directed towards the continued observation of a code of conduct covering some aspect of life. Although a purely axiological morality contains no code-dependent moral obligation, it may contain code-independent moral obligations — an action being in this sense morally obligatory if not only its performance, but also requiring its performance, is morally obligatory. In such a morality it may be morally obligatory to fulfil one's promises because doing this and requiring that it be done are both the object of a moral pro-attitude, while a certain type of saintly conduct may be morally good, because it is the object of a moral pro-attitude, but not also morally obligatory, because requiring such conduct is not the object of a moral pro-attitude. A mixed morality contains no supreme moral principle directed to the continued observance of an all embracing code of conduct, but at least one moral pro-attitude directed towards the continued observance of a code of conduct covering some aspect of life. Such a morality contains both code-dependent and code-independent moral obligations.

The distinction between them is not sharp. But it is obvious in cases where a person who has a moral pro-attitude towards a certain code of conduct is clear in his mind that, while he regards a certain action as morally obligatory because it follows from the code of conduct, he would not so regard it if the code were changed. A Catholic who regards it as a moral obligation not to commit suicide might do so only because it follows from the code prescribed by his religion and yet be clear in his mind that he would cease to regard suicide in this way if the code were to be changed. The situation is similar when a person has a moral pro-attitude towards observing a professional code which he himself is trying to change. Indeed one may well have a code-dependent moral obligation to observe all regulations of one's professional code of conduct and also the code-independent obligation to change them all.

The moral function of codes of conduct is not exhausted by giving rise to code-dependent obligations and other moral characteristics of actions. A fuller inquiry would have to consider the various ways in which the adoption of a code of conduct may be qualified. Thus, it is possible to have a moral pro-attitude towards adopting a code of conduct only under conditions in which a quick decision is needed or only under conditions where conforming to a simple regulation which approximates to a complex moral principle is morally preferable to an attempt at conforming to the principle itself *etc.* There is no need to elaborate these subtleties. What has been said about them should, however, help to protect our empiricist ethical theory against some accusations of crudity which have been levelled against its predecessors.

6. On the limits of moral pluralism and the nature of moral arguments

The preceding account of the general structure of morality is proposed as exhibiting an aspect of the systems of practical attitudes which as a matter of empirical fact are discovered by introspection and the observation of others. It leaves room for moralities which differ from each other in structure, as does a deontic from a purely axiological morality, and in substance as does the morality of an orthodox Catholic from that of an orthodox Communist. The extent to which the moralities of different persons and groups differ within the restrictions of their common structure, is a matter for detailed empirical inquiry. In undertaking it – or in conjecturing its results without undertaking it – it is well to guard against some misunderstandings of the influence which the structure of a morality has on its content.

Thus, it is tempting to overrate the influence of structural differences, as is often done when the apparent rigidity of a deontic morality is opposed to the flexibility of a purely axiological or minimal morality. Yet a morality of complex regulations containing qualifications and exceptions may admit more morally relevant distinctions than the concrete morality of many a self-confident, self-important and self-appointed moral educator of his society who judges every case strictly on its merits. Indeed, that so many philosophers are denying that there are moralities of different structure – for example holding every morality to be ultimately axiological and all codes of conducts to be merely convenient simplifications – is some evidence that people whose moralities differ in structure may yet largely agree in judging that certain actions are morally good and certain others are morally bad.

Again, one must not overlook that the general structure of a moral attitude or principle (See (iv) and (v) of section 4) presupposes considerable cognitive and practical agreement between different people. Because any moral attitude is directed towards everybody's having a certain practical attitude towards some option, it involves certain assumptions about what is common to all human beings. Moreover, because these assumptions arise, and are tested, in people's social interactions it is reasonable to conjecture that the assumptions which members of the same society make about their common physical, cognitive and practical nature will resemble each other and that their moral attitudes will, consequently, also be similar. As to determining the precise extent of the similarity — whether for example incest is immoral in all practical systems — the philosopher of morals is as dependent on the work of the anthropologist as is the philosopher of mathematics on the work of the mathematician or the philosopher of physics on the work of the physicist.

The complex structure of morality and moralities admits, and calls for, a variety of arguments by which moral principles are shown to "imply" certain conclusions — conclusions which, moreover, if they turn out "impossible" or "not to agree with experience" discredit the principles from which they are deduced. Of the older empiricist and anti-empiricist theories even those which acknowledge the possibility of rational moral arguments throw little light on them. As against this our new empiricist ethical theory leads to an analysis of rational moral argument by drawing attention to the employment in it of practical implication (defined in terms of practical inconsistency, as mentioned in section 4 above), of ordinary logical implication and of deontic implication. For our present purpose it will be sufficient to explain the use of these implications by simple examples.

Let us in order to exemplify the employment of practical implication consider a crude utilitarian who has an unqualified moral pro-attitude towards maximising the gross national product of the nation to which he belongs (schematically, [S + [U + G.N.P.]]). His moral attitude will practically imply the immorality of a second level anti-attitude towards everybody's having an anti-attitude towards not maximising the gross national product and the morality of a first-level pro-attitude towards such maximisation. In order to exemplify how this first level attitude may "not agree with experience" we may assume that our utilitarian is actually confronted with a nation in which the maximisation of the gross national product is achieved at the sacrifice of great misery for some citizens. If he finds his misery so unbearable that he no longer can accept his utilitarian principle, he will be in a position which is analogous to that of a scientist who ceases to believe a scientific hypothesis because a logically implied consequence of it is not borne out by observations.

In order to exemplify the employment in morals of logical implication we note that 'being the maximisation of the gross natural product' is a secondary moral attribute with, as it were, a separable empirical content. Hence, to argue that the maximisation of the gross national product together with the laws of economics implies certain measures is to use ordinary logical implication in showing that the implementation of these measures is moral. It is obvious that if a morality is deontic or involves the auxiliary use of a code of conduct deontic implications will be involved in moral reasoning.

Of these types of implication practical implication is the most fundamental because it alone is applicable in every morality — whether or not it comprises moral principles rather than concrete moral attitudes and whether or not its moral attitudes are directed towards the continued observation of some code of conduct. The reason why it has nevertheless been ignored by moral philosophers is that its definition involves the equally neglected notions of dominated practical attitudes and stratified practical systems. One of its possible uses, which has just been exemplified, is the deduction from a moral principle of a conclusion which by not agreeing with actual experience discredits the principle and enforces its replacement. By exhibiting this function of practical implication our empiricist ethical theory not only allows for moral change, but goes some way towards explaining it.

INDEX